To: Ron Karle

I really [appreciate?] your friendship over the years. You have contributed much to Michigan State University and the people of the Greater Lansing area. I wish you the very best in all you do.

Clarence Underwood
3/7/06

Greener Pastures

Clarence Underwood
Greener Pastures

*A pioneer athletics administrator
climbs from
spartan beginnings to the top at
Michigan State*

With Larry Paladino

First Edition

Copyright © 2005 by Clarence Underwood
Second Printing December 2005

Library of Congress Control Number: 2005933136

I.S.B.N. 0-8187-0361-X

Dedication

This book is dedicated to my wife, Noreese, our children, Jacqueline, Alvin, and David; my deceased parents, Clarence and Iola Underwood. Also to my sisters and brothers, Eva Calloway, Laura Nelms, Loveless, Bessie Brooks, Willie, Lorene Harrell, Ralph, Ernest, Jimmy, and Nathaniel. To David's wife, Cheryl, and grandchildren, Morgan, Parker, and Blake. To all of the male and female student-athletes I taught and counseled at the East Lansing Public Schools, Michigan State University, and every place else I ever worked. And to Carver High School and Trinity AME Church and the young athletes who have aspirations of competing at the collegiate level.

Co-author dedication

To my parents, Irene Sabo Paladino and Joseph Paladino, who, despite an array of challenges, were able to instill strong values and a vital sense of justice in my sisters, Janie and Claudia, and I. And to my wife, Marilyn, our daughters Sheri and Lisa, and grandchildren Anthony, Dominic, Natalee Rizzo and Christian Olejniczak.

About the Authors

Clarence Underwood Jr., Ph.D., former college athletics administrator, is the author of three books, including *The Student Athlete – Eligibility and Academic Integrity, and How to Go Undefeated in Your College Career.* He spent 30 dedicated years providing leadership to improve intercollegiate athletics at Michigan State University and the Big Ten Conference. He retired as MSU athletics director  in 2002 but continues to work in youth programs and live in East Lansing, Mich., with his wife, Noreese.

Larry Paladino has been a journalist since 1967, including 12 years at the *Associated Press* in Detroit where he was the Michigan sports editor. He is retired from the *AP* and the *Birmingham Eccentric* newspaper, where he was the editor. He has co-authored four books, including *From the Inside* with late University of Michigan Athletics Director Don Canham, and *Charlie Sanders' Tales of the Lions.*

6

Acknowledgements

To Noreese, thanks for your supreme patience, sacrifice, and understanding to permit me to use what should have been our precious evenings and weekends together to communicate and socialize. Instead, I worked late into the evenings on the book. I confess that I owe you big time.

I am grateful for the tremendous and unselfish assistance I received from the following good people: Keith Williams, whose inquisitive review and keen critiques were sources of encouragement for me; Dr. James Potchen, whose wisdom, solid advice and passion for the book kept me going in the right direction; attorney Kathy Lindahl, whose friendship and probing mind made a valuable contribution to the book.

Joe Farrell provided important insights in so many ways and shared his thoughts that enriched my thinking; Dr. William Lazer, a friend and advisor who kept me focused on the principles and goals; Dr Eugene Pernell, whose friendship and sustained urging helped prod me to write the book and now he needs to start on his own book.

Cullen Dubose, a dear friend, whose nagging inspired me to work harder; attorney George Brookover, for your commentary, friendship and support; Becky Scott, thanks for your editing and professionalism. To Judy Vanhorn, a great person and excellent compliance administrator; Teresa Ryan, I appreciate the many days you met me after work to get materials to type over night and on the weekends; John Lewandowski, Paulette, Becky, and other capable members in the Sports Information Office who assisted with photos and materials.

Finally, to my grandchildren, Morgan, age 9; Parker, 6; and Blake, 3, who experienced their first reality of work by shredding voluminous amounts of paper on the weekends. Naturally, I had to pay them more than the minimum hourly wage.

My personal thanks to Karen Langeland; Shelley Appelbaum; Greg Ianni; my son, David Underwood; Gary Spicer, a rare individual with a winning personality who knows how to get the very best out of people while smiling at them; and Larry Paladino, whose energy, compassion, and editing skills are outstanding.

Noreese and I with Gary Spicer

Table of contents

Addressing the crowd at the 2000 Citrus Bowl football game
pep rally

Preface:

A CLASS ACT
CHRONICLES A FULL LIFE

A Half-century Climb to the Top

ALL OF US WOULD LIKE TO TELL OUR STORY IN a book. Few get the chance. But who'd care, anyway, other than our friends and relatives?

From time to time, though, someone who isn't necessarily a household name will chronicle a lifetime of struggles and triumphs and make it appealing to most of us simply because of its poignancy or its ability to relate to others who have struggled and triumphed.

Some tales can touch us in such a way as to stir a pallet of emotions and paint word pictures to form a mosaic eliciting love, anger, joy, empathy, and more.

Whether or not we have risen to the top in our field, the challenges we faced and overcame along the way aren't dissimilar to those who have made it to the crest. Clarence Underwood is one of those who made it to the top of the mountain and whose story is worthy of national attention — although his quiet efficiency and easy-going demeanor has mostly kept him away from any headline grabbing. There were a couple times, though, when reporters misrepresented some facts and that made for several misguided headlines, something that sticks in his craw.

Underwood didn't make the climb by accident. He didn't claw his way past others, grease palms, take advantage of someone else's misfortune — or compromise his principles. That is, perhaps, the most important part of his legacy.

Success for the retired Michigan State University athletics director, however, wasn't a given. There were plenty of obstacles along the way, not the least of which was the difficulty inherent with being born during the Great Depression. He was one of 13 children of a black Alabama sharecropper's family living in the segregated South. When he played football, the stadium was segregated. He and his teammates couldn't even use the locker rooms of the city-owned facility and there were no toilets — unless you were white.

Shortly after Clarence was born, his father moved from Marion, Ala., to Gadsden, Ala., to get a job at a lumberyard, working double shifts as a boiler fireman. Clarence also got a job there when he was 16, earning 85 cents an hour — but having to endure taunts of, "Pick up the lumber, nigger." He learned then how to fight back the hate that could easily surface (including in the North, that often was more racist than the South). His restraint through it all would serve him well the rest of his career.

"Hatred, like love, consumes the best part of a person's mind and soul," he says. "It stays with you all the time. One is good and the other is bad. Love will make you happy and hatred will twist your mind negatively and cause problems."

However poor the Underwoods might have been, they were rich enough in love and family values that Clarence was able to absorb the ingredients needed to climb tenaciously from poverty. It was a long way from the three-room house in Gadsden to the office of athletics director at one of the more prominent NCAA Division I programs in the land — a position, by the way, that probably should have been given to him about a decade sooner.

"The best part of a large family is the love,

camaraderie and unity demonstrated toward each other," he says, as he chronicles his boyhood years in Chapter 1. Other chapters cover Underwood's early days at Michigan State; fallout over an NCAA investigation of the university's football program; a controversial memo; erosion of ethics and accountability; the brief Saban era; dealings with news media; Title IX and the women's program; molding the character of young people who will eventually become today's student-athletes; health problems and advice; great football and basketball moments and other memorable athletes; the difficulty for blacks to get head football coaching jobs in college; plus the road to the athletics director job and some of the pitfalls along the way.

Underwood, who served as a paratrooper in the 82nd Airborne Division, married his high school sweetheart, Noreese Lindsey, and ignored a small track scholarship to Tuskegee Institute to go to Michigan State in the mid-'50s.

The Clarence Underwood Award for Character is presented to the Michigan State football player who best exemplifies the trait.

He had seen all the black players on Coach Duffy Daugherty's 1954 Spartans Rose Bowl team that got national TV attention during its game against UCLA. When Clarence did enroll at Michigan State — with the help of the G.I. Bill — he wound up going out for football as a walk-on, one of 175 players on the freshman team.

From those early days until July 1, 2002, when he turned over the athletics director position to hockey coach Ron Mason, Underwood would see many detours. Among them was a stint in the Big

Ten office in Chicago as an assistant commissioner. Others included teaching and other education-oriented jobs in East Lansing, Mich., the Michigan Department of Education, Northern Michigan University, the Southern Christian Leadership Conference, and the University of Wisconsin extension in Milwaukee.

He even had a business partnership for a while, booking big-name entertainers, including the likes of Ike and Tina Turner, Ben E. King, Etta James, Jerry Butler, Motown stars, and more, into Lansing-area venues. To this day, Underwood still enjoys song writing among his hobbies

Instead of knocking him off his path to success, the diversions became a way in which he could hone his managerial and people skills. Often he had to bite his lip and play the good soldier role, becoming a confidant and advisor, while others less qualified served in the positions of power.

Underwood probably should have been MSU's athletic director for the final 10 years of his long and distinguished educational and athletics career. He was a strong candidate for the post in 1991 and 1995, being passed over both times. It would have saved the university a lot of turmoil, not to mention money, if it hadn't made a number of poor hiring decisions in the '90s (and before). But even the three-plus years he spent as A.D. was enough to put Michigan State back on the right track and send him into retirement with the respect and admiration he richly deserves — and after also having beaten prostate cancer and diabetes.

What does he have to say in his book? Plenty. There are a number of touchy issues he has faced over the years, but the subjects need to be broached and Underwood has done that. Sometimes the truth isn't comfortable to some. Although a few sensibilities may be tweaked, Underwood gives his critical analyses of various people and events in the same manner in which he handled his career — with integrity and class.

— *Larry Paladino*

CHAPTER 1:

EARLY YEARS

Sharecropper's son rises from poverty

AMERICA WAS FOUR YEARS INTO THE GREAT Depression when I was born in Marion, Ala., Oct. 10, 1933, the fifth of 13 children of Clarence and Iola Underwood.

Alabama, like all of the southern states, was racially segregated. My father was a sharecropper in Marion, but when I was 3 weeks old we moved to Gadsden, Ala., an industrial town, so my father could search for more steady and profitable employment. He found it in an adjacent city, getting a job as a laborer at Etowah Lumber Company, located in Alabama City, which was contiguous to Gadsden. He often would work double shifts as a boiler fireman, building a fire with coal and sawdust in the boiler to steam dry green or wet lumber stored in the kiln.

We lived in a three-room rented house with my four siblings: Eva, Laura, Loveless and Bessie, and had to sleep three to a bed. Each of us was born two years apart and the two-year trend continued with the later births of Willie, Arthur Lee (who died a few weeks after birth),

Lorene, Jeannette (who was still-born), Ralph, Earnest, Jimmy and Nathaniel. (Eva, Ralph, Willie, and Bessie have since passed away.)

The best part of a large family is the love, camaraderie, and unity demonstrated toward each other, feelings that seemed to peak mostly during the winter nights while we sat around the fireplace. My father had a piano, guitar and a harmonica. Each night he attempted to play one or two of those while listening to the Grand Ole Opry on the radio.

My mother would go to bed as soon as it became dark outside because she would arise early in the morning to fix breakfast and my father's job started at 6:30 a.m. All the children would sit on the wooden floor, covered with linoleum, around the fireplace to keep warm, do homework and chat. It was located in my parents' combination bedroom-living room. During the spring and summer months the front porch was the spot until bedtime.

On weekends the children would bake sweet potatoes in the ashes of the fire and roast peanuts in a pan over the flames. Those were happy times. Our father always brought some humor with his musical instruments because he could not carry a tune on any of them. He tried incessantly and we would constantly tease him by trying to guess the songs he was attempting to play. He enjoyed teasing as much as we did and, in fact, he seemed to get energized over the playful exchange.

Another way our dad would tease us was by telling ghost stories during winter nights. He then would purposely send one of us–usually me–to the corner grocery store just before it closed at 9 p.m. to buy a loaf of bread or something. It was dark outside, with no street lights and the wind blowing. I was so scared. I would run to the store and back with my eyes closed because I was afraid I might see one of those frightening ghosts my dad had described.

That was the kind of home environment we had. There was love, fun, and discipline and, while in elementary school, I thought that atmosphere would never end. My parents were good people and they tried to teach us right from wrong. Whenever we made dumb mistakes or did not obey their instructions according to their expectations, we received whippings with a belt or with a long twig from a tree.

The saddest day of my life was when my oldest sister, Eva, married a neighbor, Earnest Calloway, and they moved to Buffalo, N.Y. I must have been 11 or 12 years of age when they got married. I really was fond of her. She was the leader among us siblings and she was pretty and smart. She used to help me with my homework. She would talk to me a lot and explain different things to me. She was kind to me. She was a member of the high school choir and I used to accompany her to the choir concerts. She was the treasurer of Sunday School and fun to be around. The fireplace chats never were the same for me after she left. I missed her so much and she seemed so far away in Buffalo.

Her husband Earnest wanted me to go to Buffalo in the summer months to compete in amateur boxing. My dad bought two pair of boxing gloves when I was 12. I was the most courageous and best boxer among guys my age in my neighborhood. Earnest wanted me to fight competitively in Buffalo and I wanted to go, but my parents didn't think it was a good idea. Besides, we didn't have money for transportation. My other brothers and sisters were fun to be around, kind, talkative, and I loved them, but I felt like a hole had penetrated my heart when Eva left Gadsden.

I recall experiencing similar feelings earlier in my young life when my mother was admitted to Holy Name of Jesus Hospital for exploratory breast surgery. The tumor was diagnosed as benign. I must have been 8 or 9 years old. I could see the top of the hospital building from our back porch and each night while daddy was visiting her I would sit on the back porch alone and think about my mother. She meant the world to me and I missed her so much.

I learned at that early age that there is no one like mother. She was hospitalized for about a week and each night I would sing the song, "It's a highway to heaven and none can walk up there but the pure in heart." Somehow that song stayed on my mind. It is still one of my favorite songs. Being close to my family always has been important to me.

One of the family requirements was Sunday school each week at the Sixteenth Street Baptist Church, which was about a mile and a half from our home. We would always walk to church. After services we would go home for dinner and return to church around 6 p.m. for the Baptist Training Union. That is Bible study.

We would always stay for the gospel concerts. Those singing groups, which came mostly from Birmingham, Ala., were incredible. They would make appearances at several local churches beginning in the early afternoon and they would nearly always visit our church last, many times after 9 p.m. They would sing a few songs to put everyone in the spirit and then pass the hat for a donation. They wouldn't continue their singing until the donations reached their monetary expectations. One of those groups was the nationally famous Five Blind Boys. Man could they sing. Sometimes we would not get home until 11 p.m. Sunday was a fun and spirit-filled day, which helped to strengthen my faith.

Helping father at work

Some of us had to help the family in different ways. When my brother, Loveless, was about 12 he had to carry my father's lunch to him by walking two miles to the lumber company during the summer. He stayed to assist him with his work until quitting time. He would help daddy by taking turns putting sawdust or coal into the furnace. The pattern continued until Loveless was old enough to get a summer job on his own.

When I was 12 or 13 I was required to follow the same pattern of carrying lunch to my father and helping him at work. The hours were long and the work was hard. Often he had to work two consecutive eight-hour shifts, particularly on weekends when one of the night shift workers did not show up for whatever reason. When I entered high school I often assisted the lumberyard midnight shift person, who was paid 85 cents an hour, to fire the boilers. He paid me $3 each night for helping him with the eight-hour shift on Friday, Saturday, and Sunday nights. There were Monday mornings during the school year when I would finish the shift at 6:30 a.m., walk home and then walk to school for an 8 a.m. class. It was tough, but the options to earn money for school lunches and other necessities were limited.

When I turned 16, I worked during the summer at the company full time for 85 cents an hour, doing a variety of jobs, but my primary one was to pull certain grades of wet lumber from the pulley belt, load them onto a mule wagon, and take them to stack up near the kiln. Other employees would load the lumber onto a wagon on the kiln dock so it could be pushed into the kiln for drying. What struck me about the lumber company was that it was white owned and all of the employees, about 20 to 25, were black, with the exception of two white supervisors and one white night watchman who worked one of the shifts. There was no white person working all day in the hot sun as many of us were, doing the hard work.

I worked there three summers full time and other times part-time to assist my father and another employee. Looking back, the company did me a great favor. It clearly taught me the advantages of staying in school because I surely did not want to spend all of my life doing such hard physical labor for such meager wages and subjected to less than pleasant treatment from the owner.

The white boss had a practice of calling the black workers by nicknames instead of their formal names. He would frequently use the word nigger. I would become so upset with him whenever I heard him use that word to address one of us black workers. In my neighborhood, it was such a derogatory and hurtful word to call someone that it would often trigger a fight. But the black workers seemed to suck it up and move about their business on the job. Few of us had other alternatives.

Hatred, like love, can be all-consuming

I learned many years ago that you can't grow without being a whole person. And you can't be a whole person if you carry within you feelings of hatred, vengeance, and disrespect toward another human being. It doesn't matter what the person may have done to you or how adversarial the behavior, you have to forgive the person and move on with your life without the negative baggage.

If you instead hold the awful feelings of retaliation and retribution in your heart, only you will suffer and it may destroy you like a cancer. You can't remain healthy and grow with such a twisted attitude. That philosophy first occurred to me when I was working at that lumber company. The company owner was mean-spirited toward me.

Sometimes, while handling four or more pieces of wet lumber, one would drop on the ground. It seemed like every time that would happen to me, the owner would be standing nearby and would yell at me, "Pick up the lumber, nigger." He would carry out the charade several times during the summer. At first I would get so mad at him I wanted to retaliate in some vicious manner. Every time he would call me nigger I wanted to hurt him. I really hated to see him walk in my direction. So one night I was thinking that if I harmed him it would hurt me, too, because surely I would have at least gone to jail or

20

have been killed. So my options weren't very good, but I knew I had to work for the money and keep focusing on my goal of enrolling in college when I finished high school.

I concluded that words could not hurt me. His epithets inspired me to show him what I already knew, that I was not a "nigger." He never changed, but I did. So every time he would call me a nigger, I would say to myself that even though he is the owner, has money, drives a new Cadillac every year, he is ignorant. In his estimation I may have been a nigger, simply because my skin color was black. But in my value system I had integrity and wisdom, while he was ignorant, which I thought was much worse. I said then that I would rather be someone intelligent and black than to be an ignorant fool. But we needed each other. I needed his work to make money and he needed my skills to earn him money. Since that day I made a concerted effort not to hate anyone. I try to understand the other person's views and positions in all situations.

Hatred, like love, consumes the best part of a person's mind and soul. It stays with you all of the time. One is good and the other is bad. Love will make you happy and hatred will twist your mind negatively and cause immediate and long-term problems, including death. One of the lifetime principles I learned from dealing with the owner that has stayed with me is working relationships don't require friendship, but simply alliance.

My grandfather, John Henry, worked at the lumber company also, as a shoe man for the mules. And my father's three brothers worked there for many years, with my brother, Loveless, and me. Eventually they all left for better and more profitable employment. I left for the Army after graduation from high school at age 19. (In Alabama, you could not start school then until you were 6 years old. I missed a whole year because my sixth birthday didn't come until October, a month after school had started.)

My grandfather, John Henry Underwood, also worked at the sawmill where my father and others in my family worked.

In fact, I was the first in my family to finish high school and first to enroll in and finish college. Each of my older siblings left high school. It was a shame because they were good students. My sister, Bessie, won an oratorical contest in the 10th grade but dropped out in the 11th to get a job. My brother, Loveless, was an A student but dropped out in the 11th grade to seek employment. Eva and Laura did the same, dropping out to obtain domestic employment. Later, though, Bessie, Eva, and Laura earned their diplomas.

There were hard times with five children in the house at any given time and another child being born every two years. With my father earning just 85 cents an hour, it was tough just to pay the rent and keep enough food on the table for growing children. Clothes were difficult to get and often were hand-me-downs. My sisters made some of their skirts out of cotton flour sacks. I would sometimes wear my brother's jackets and shirts. He was

6-foot-2 and I was 5-8. I wore patched denim pants as a result of the holes in them from wrestling or falling while playing football or baseball in the gravel streets. We burned wood and coal in the fireplace and whenever we were out of them I remember walking the nearby railroad tracks in wintry weather to pick up loose coal that had fallen from railroad boxcars so we could stay warm until the next load was delivered to our house. Sometimes we waited several days for the delivery.

Our family wasn't the only one experiencing poverty. There were many children in the elementary and high schools who were economically disadvantaged, although there were some who did not demonstrate that problem. I recall a good athlete who dropped out of elementary school in the sixth grade to get a job to help support the family when his father died. That's the way life was in the black community: poor people, hard work, meager wages, and large families locked into a depressed environment that was very hard to get out of, an environment with segregated neighborhoods, schools, and water fountains, ones for the whites and ones for the blacks.

Blacks couldn't attend the public library and in order to vote for public officials you had to pass a literacy test. There was a special $3 poll tax for blacks to vote in the elections. Furthermore, the tax was exacted retroactively for each year a black was eligible to vote and failed to do so. I don't know of any blacks who voted for those officials who didn't represent them or treat them with any respect and who contrived the test.

Blacks were made to sit in the back of the bus so that whites could sit up front. There were also segregated movie houses. Blacks lived in the section of the city with dirt roads and minimum and unreliable public services. The lily-white police force had no respect for the black community or for a black person as a human being. That was the South in which I grew up, where even blatant racial discrimination was not discussed openly by black teachers in the black schools I attended.

It was too political and much too risky for them to criticize a system that paid them only modest salaries and provided them with no protection. The teachers did what they were expected to do, teach their academic subjects well. The teachers understood the system and were fully aware that education was the black child's only escape to a better life. They cared about their students and established high academic expectations for us.

There were great athletes in my neighborhood who dropped out of high school to search for work. I tried compassionately to get them to return to school to join me on the football, track, and baseball teams but they had greater economic needs. They couldn't see the long-term advantages of a high school education for a black person in a negative and grossly unequal environment.

Athleticism comes to the fore

Without question, athletics helped to develop my passion for an education. As far back as I can remember I was good in sports. We played street ball year-round and every day in the summer. I was almost always selected first to a team when the older kids in the neighborhood chose sides. I was short, muscular, fast and very physical. I loved to challenge my friends to wrestle me or to run a race. Those successes bolstered my self-esteem and helped me to experience the thrill of victory. Winning always was fun and the few times I lost I asked for a rematch so I could win.

Sometimes I would not be given a rematch. I recall one day in the third grade, I asked my classmate, Eugene Robinson, who later became my best friend in high school, to wrestle me outside on the playground during the recess period and he refused. I grabbed him anyway and encouraged him to challenge me and when he did I wrestled him to the ground and sat on him for the remainder of the recess period. I kept encouraging him to try to get up but he could not. He was my age and size, and was an athlete. It was my way of having fun, testing my strength and confidence and, I suppose, venting my anger.

Anyhow, Eugene lived near the elementary school and had several older brothers in high school. One afternoon as I was walking home from school, Herbert Robinson, one of his brothers, was walking home from the high school and we met face to face. Herbert went to a willow tree and pulled a long twig from it and began whipping me. He told me to leave his brother alone. I regretted that Eugene and Herbert had misinterpreted my motives. I wasn't trying to hurt Eugene on the playground, but apparently they thought I was. I was just having fun and needed a challenge to test my growing strength.

When I entered the fourth grade at West Gadsden Elementary School in Alabama City, a city adjacent to Gadsden, I was eligible to participate in the after-school recreation program for boys in the fourth through sixth grades. I really loved the program. We played mostly touch football in the fall and softball in the spring. We didn't have hoops to play basketball.

I used to love May 1, May Day, Many school-planned activities would culminate in a softball game between West Gadsden and South Gadsden elementary schools. About 15 boys from South Gadsden would walk four miles to our school for the afternoon game. Unfortunately, South Gadsden had a good team and always would beat us and that is where I experienced the agony of defeat. It didn't feel good. I walked home after those games with a heavy heart. The feelings motivated me to practice my skills. I wanted to hit, throw, catch, run the bases, and have fun winning just like the guys on the South Gadsden team did.

My first game was when I was in the fourth grade and had a chance to pinch hit late in a lopsided game, hitting the ball to the shortstop. I was so disappointed I didn't run to first base. The shortstop kept challenging me to run and I did not. I took it for granted that I had made an automatic out and didn't see the need to be further embarrassed by running to first base. The principal and recreation director, J.T. Williams, talked to me later about the importance of running out all balls. Over the years, I distinctly remembered that game and the advice given by the principal. I learned that nothing in life is assured; never take anything for granted and don't give up on anything worthwhile. I was a much-improved player in the fifth grade and learned to play harder and compete until the end and that quitters never win.

In the sixth grade I was a star and could hit the ball all over the park. I played right field and recall throwing strikes to the plate to nail guys who tried to score from third on fly balls. I always had a strong right arm and could throw a ball accurately. In touch football, I was the quarterback, fast, and could elude one-hand touches.

Carver High School in Gadsden was an all-black school with grades 1-12. I entered the seventh grade in the fall of 1947 and went out for the varsity football team. Two seventh-graders were on the squad that year, fullback James Hall and me. I played the left halfback position in the single-wing formation, which is critical in that type of offense and similar to the tailback position in the current day "I" formation. I played briefly as a substitute in two games at left halfback. Our team had an 8-1 record, the loss being 6-0 to Parker High School from Birmingham, in our stadium. My passion for football really developed with that game.

Parker was the largest black high school in America, with grades 9-12 and 5,000 students. It was a powerhouse in football. Its school colors were purple and white and the team would come onto the field wearing purple capes over their uniforms. They were the biggest guys at every position I had ever seen. Carver's school colors were maroon and gold. And it was the only black high school in the entire county for years. Carver had a monopoly on black talent. We could play against any opponent and do well.

In 1951, Etowah County built a black high school in Attalla, which was about five miles from Carver. The students in that area started going to Norris High. Carver never played Norris while I was in high school (I graduated in 1953). But the new school affected Carver's talent pool. We played Parker every year on a home-and-home basis. Carver's head coach, Mr. L.V. Johnson, and Parker's coach, Major Brown, had gone to college together and promised to compete against each other when they became head coaches.

Carver never had beaten Parker and each year the score was either 6-0 or 7-0. We never had scored on Parker. The 1947 game stayed with me because we had a very good team, dominated by seniors. We felt we could beat Parker at home and when we lost I saw seniors crying and angry. They had played their hearts out against a big physical team and they wanted another chance. But there were no high school playoffs or post-season games then for black schools, as there were for white schools. So we had to wait until the next season to have another opportunity to beat them.

The seniors, Eugene Weatherly, Howard Green, and Al Sims, to name a few, taught me how to compete. They were outstanding athletes and proved their abilities when they later played for one of the traditional black colleges, Alabama State University in Montgomery. Those guys loved to win and would play just as hard in practice as they did in competition. They were leaders. If they saw a teammate doing something half-heartedly, they would talk to him and show him how it should be done. They led by example and football was a serious game with them. They accepted me as a seventh-grader and taught me how to improve my skills. They were my role models. They taught me about helping other young athletes.

When I returned to the team in the eighth grade I

got the shock of my life. I was looking forward to having more playing time and was highly motivated to compete for the starting tailback position. I felt I had learned a lot in the seventh grade. I ran races and played street touch football every chance I got in the summer to get ready for the fall. Plus, I was strong from having worked in the lumber company with my father. But when the head coach put together the six teams in the fall, I was left off. I was one of the extra players on the sideline because there weren't enough guys left to make up another team.

I was deeply hurt but was too modest to talk to the coach about the issue. I surely thought he would remember me from playing in two games in the 7th grade and was one of only two seventh-graders who stayed out for the team all year. Guys trying out for the first time were ahead of me. Although I felt crushed, I wasn't about to give up. I already had learned that lesson from the softball game in the fourth grade. I believed I eventually would get the chance to help the coach to remember me because I was much better than many of the guys on the six teams.

My big break came after three weeks of practice. And, boy, did I make good out of it. Our first game was on the road against Tuscaloosa. We traveled with 35 guys. On Wednesday before the Friday night away game, near the end of practice, the coach told the first and second teams to go in and take a shower. He was going to select the remaining 13 guys from among the players left on the field.

A chance to get noticed

At one point the coach called for a pass play and for some reason the quarterbacks in the scrimmage couldn't execute the play. Out of frustration, the coach looked to the sidelines and yelled, "Give me a passer." I ran into the scrimmage and became the left halfback who also was the passer in the single wing formation. I went back to pass and was rushed by the entire defensive line. Those guys were hungry and were trying to make the traveling squad and I was just trying to get the coach to notice me. But I stood in their way.

Realizing that I didn't have time to pass, I took off running and ran for a touchdown. The coach blew his whistle and told the squad to go take a shower. He called me over and asked where I had been all fall. I said, "Coach, I have been here every day on the sidelines."

I made the traveling squad and alternated between third and fourth team at left halfback for the rest of the season. So, in the eighth grade at age 14, I became a highly valuable and publicly recognized football player on the varsity. I played in every game. I learned that even when others don't recognize your abilities and talents, don't give up, believe in yourself, stay prepared, and when your chance comes, seize it aggressively.

In the ninth grade I was second team left halfback and a defensive back. I did most of the team's passing. A senior, T. Ellis Phillips, was the starting left halfback and another senior, Herbert Dupree, was the quarterback and punter. In the single-wing, the quarterback was mostly a blocking back. At times I would substitute for the quarterback. I got a lot of playing time as a freshman.

Carver's record was 5-4 in 1949. We lost to Parker in Gadsden, 26-12. It was a memorable game because it was the first time our Wildcats ever had scored against Parker. I threw the two touchdown passes late in the fourth quarter. What appeared to be a third one went awry when the receiver, who was all alone, great running back Eugene Robinson, turned to his left when the ball was thrown to his right.

We tried unsuccessfully to run our single-wing offense against Parker. With about four minutes left the coach told me to go into the game at left halfback and start passing. Parker had most of its starters out of the game and had just scored and kicked off to us. On the very first play after the kickoff, I went back to pass and it seemed the entire defensive line of Parker came after me. I ran toward the sideline, leaped up and threw a long strike to one of my receivers in the end zone for Carver's first ever TD against Parker. On the ensuing kickoff, we recovered a Parker fumble. I threw the second touchdown on the first play from scrimmage, to a different receiver. He was crossing right to left into the end zone. The Carver crowd went crazy.

A young Clarence Underwood Jr. on a sweep right during a Carver High School football game

Parker put its first team back into the game and once again we kicked off. Parker fumbled and we recovered and, on the first play, I threw the pass down the middle to Robinson, who turned the wrong way, so we didn't get another TD then. The game was featured in the local newspaper. I was told I was also featured in the *Birmingham World* newspaper, but I never saw the article.

What made that rivalry so special was that we played the game in Gadsden every other year. It was considered a special event for the entire black community. There would be a parade down Broadstreet, which was in the heart of the city. Even white merchants would recognize the event by closing their stores during the parade, which featured bands from Carver and Parker, cheerleaders, plus a few decorated cars. Parker had a big band and Carver's band had about 60 members. The sidewalks would be lined with both white and black fans, but they stood separated by race. It was an exciting event that usually started at noon and our team was allowed to leave school then and go home to rest for the game.

Segregated stadium

All of the Wildcats games were played in the city-owned Murphee Stadium at 7:30 on Tuesday nights. The city's two white high schools, Gadsden and Emma Sampson, played their home games on Friday and Saturday nights, respectively. There were as many white fans at Carver home games as there were black fans, again separated by race. The whites would sit on the opposite side in permanent concrete seats on the press box side and the black fans from both teams would sit on the bleachers on the other side.

Neither of the black teams was permitted to use the locker rooms in the stadium and would dress for the games at Carver and ride buses to the stadium. At Carver, opponents were given a classroom in which to change from street clothing to game uniforms. After the game, some teams would come to our locker room to shower and dress. At other times, some teams would simply change back to their street clothes and leave without showering.

Blacks weren't allowed to use the press box. At halftime, each team sat at the two ends of the field to hear from their coaches. I recall one time our team wasn't playing well and was losing at halftime. Coach Johnson was angry and decided it would be best to speak with us in the tunnel of the locker rooms during halftime, rather than at the end of the field. It was the first time he had done that, though he never discussed his reasons for doing that. I initially thought he was upset with the segregated system, as well as frustrated with his poor performing team. I believe we still lost the game.

Along with not being allowed to use the locker rooms, there were no toilet facilities for the teams. The last thing every player did before leaving the locker room at Carver to get on the buses was to use the toilets. I don't know whether such facilities were available for the black fans in the stands because I never sat there. Blacks were permitted, however, to use the concession stands to sell hot dogs, pop, candy, etc., for the PTA.

Blacks and whites usually behaved well at the games and there were many white policemen in attendance. While whites could attend our games and had access to the best seating, we couldn't go to their games at Murphee Stadium. That situation bothered me. I would listen to Gadsden and Emma Samson games on the radio. I often wished I could attend just to see and compare their abilities to those of the Carver Wildcats. I often wished we could have played annually against each of those schools.

When I was a junior, our coach arranged to take our team to one of the games at Etowah County High School, which was white. The school was located in Attalla and had its own stadium. We would travel by bus, sit together near the end zone, and leave as a group when the game was over. Why as a team we could go to the white county high school for one game a year and not attend the city schools' games was never explained to us. I used to wonder what harm would be done if blacks were permitted to sit in a section of the stadium for games of the two white city schools.

High school football games were a social event and the white merchants had no problem selling merchandise to blacks, even though the blacks may have arrived in the store first and served last. Nor was there a problem with most restaurant owners who would sell food to blacks from their back doors on a takeout basis. But sitting in a corner of the end zone at a white football game for blacks was taboo. Yet the city reserved a section of the stands along the third base line for blacks at its Class B baseball stadium.

All of those restrictions and injustices made me angry and I didn't trust white folks. From my perspective, I saw nothing good then for a black person living in the South. Even at our season-ending football banquet the white superintendent and his deputies would be in attendance to speak and give out awards to members of the team. There was no way that coach Johnson or Mr. Williams could get close to the banquets sponsored by Gadsden and Emma Samson high schools.

I had a saving grace in my mother, who was ethical, practical, loved her family, and communicated much wisdom to her children. Her mother died when she was a baby and her father died shortly thereafter. She grew up with a younger sister and an older brother, all raised by relatives. She entered the 12th grade but didn't graduate from high school. My mother spoke directly and clearly. She had the courage to speak her convictions. She didn't like lying and cheating, nor did she like racism and segregation. But she had enough sagacity and humility to advise her children and help keep them out of major trouble in a vicious environment.

She taught us not to hate anybody, irrespective of how we were treated. She said folks who hate do not have peace of mind and don't live long lives. She said be civil, but stay away from those who are untrustworthy and dishonest. She advised us if we were walking on the sidewalk and a group of whites were walking toward us to give in and walk around them.

If a policeman stopped us for any reason, even when he had no reason to do so, she said, speak humbly and truthful. She asked us to be big enough in spirit to walk away from an argument, but if someone outside of the family deliberately tried to physically hurt us, hit them harder. Those and other instructions from my mother were successful in teaching us how to survive in an oppressive environment. None of my family members encountered any real physical harm from others. I remember being involved in only three brief fistfights as a youth with other black children in my neighborhood and no one got hurt.

The neighborhood – Black Creek

My neighborhood was officially named Black Creek. I don't know why it was so named except that the citizens were black and there was a creek running along side the area. The creek was muddy and the boys would go to a certain spot during the summer mornings to swim. There would be 10 to 15 of us swimming each weekday morning, safeguarded by the older boys in the neighborhood.

Sometimes the white boys from the area would arrive there first and we would leave. We had fun swimming and did so for years until one of our younger guys drowned one afternoon. It was a strange incident. None of us ever went swimming in the afternoon. We would go as a group between 9 and 10 a.m.. But on that particular afternoon, that young guy, around 12 years of age, who had gone swimming with us often, that particular afternoon went with a few other friends by themselves and the boy drowned. It was a sad day for folks in the neighborhood and I don't believe any of us ever went swimming in the creek again.

There were rows of three-room "shotgun" houses, which were rented by the families. They were called "shotgun" because the front door was lined up with the back door. You could stand at the front door and see straight through the back door, if it was opened, much the way one could look through the front sight of a shotgun clear through to the one at the end of the barrel. Most of the men worked either in the steel mill, the foundries, construction, the lumber company, the bakery, or other itinerant jobs. The women either stayed home to raise their children or did domestic work for the white folks. Some of the men and women sold bootlegged liquor for a living. It was against the law because Etowah County was dry, which meant no alcoholic beverages could be sold or consumed at any time. Every now and then police, who often raided the neighborhood looking for homebrew and moonshine liquor, would catch one of the sellers.

Payday usually was on Friday and a regular group of men would assemble in one of the backyards and shoot craps, which was a form of illegal gambling. They would sometimes gamble all night and lost most, if not all, of their paycheck. Sometimes when those crap games were in progress, the police would drive by and the men would run in different directions to get away. A few would get caught and were taken to jail. But each week the gambling continued.

Almost every weekend there would be a big fight between some of the gamblers, probably over allegations of cheating. Invariably, the fighters would retreat to the front yards. Men would get cut badly with a knife or razor and required hospitalization. I saw a man being stabbed in the temple area and the knife blade broke off and the doctors wouldn't remove it out of fear that he would bleed to death. He recovered and lived with the knife blade lodged in his temple.

I witnessed two brothers chase a man and catch him on his front porch. They cut him unmercifully many times and then escaped. When police arrived (there were no ambulances) they wouldn't take the injured man to the hospital in the squad car because he was too bloody.

The policemen first had to get blankets and sheets from neighbors to wrap the man before they would put him in the squad car.

Another time I saw two women fighting and they stripped each other naked. All the children who were outside had to go inside.

One Friday night when I was in high school, I was assisting a man who worked the midnight shift in the furnace room at the lumber company, helping him put sawdust in the furnace. He and another employee were shooting craps. An argument ensued between the two. The other employee wrestled the man I was helping and straddled him, taking out a knife and holding it to his throat and said, "I ought to kill you and the only thing stopping me is I do not want to go back to prison."

Naturally, I was very scared and felt most uncomfortable because I didn't want to see anybody hurt. And for sure I didn't want to witness a murder. That incident, gross as it was, left an indelible impression upon me. I thought to myself, here is one of the most notorious men I know, who had a reputation for wounding other men with a knife. He had done so several times in my neighborhood. Yet he had enough memory of the Alabama prison system to restrain himself that night.

I surmised then that prison must be awful and dehumanizing, a place I never wanted to go to. I have since made many speeches in several of the prisons in Michigan. I have used those cumulative experiences to help in the counseling of young folks who were headed down the wrong path.

One person who was subsequently significant in helping me to counsel student-athletes who demonstrated inappropriate behavior was Capt. Ferman Badgley of the MSU Department of Public Safety. He was a former basketball player at Central Michigan University. He volunteered his services to talk with student-athletes upon my request. He would explain the difference between right and wrong behavior and what the consequences of unlawful acts would be. We would meet with each athlete in my office.

Badgley was a genuine person and among the qualities I like about him was his straightforward manner in speaking to the athletes. He never was remiss in directly pointing out to them about the mistakes they had made, and he offered sound advice for good future behavior. I considered him an excellent role model and the kind of policeman who should be hired anywhere to help counsel young folks about values and ethical conduct.

Weekend cookouts

Friday and Saturday also were big fish fry and barbeque nights in my neighborhood. Some neighbors would fry fish and sell sandwiches. Others would barbeque baby back ribs and sell slabs or sandwiches. All of that would be going on in the front yards, with the blues being played loudly from a record player. It was a lively night. Although my family had as many hotdogs as we could eat for dinner on Fridays, which were paydays, or as much fried fish as we wanted, after playing ball in the street the fish and barbeque sure did smell good in the evening. Occasionally, my parents would buy a couple sandwiches and share them with us. I always liked to eat the bread that was saturated with hot sauce. I continue to use hot sauce today on meats, fish, and poultry.

There were two small grocery stores in the neighborhood, plus a fruit stand. Whites owned them all. Steve Woods, a black man, previously owned one of the grocery stores, but a white man ended up with it. White peddlers would drive by trying to sell their merchandise. They would peddle fresh fruit, vegetables, nuts, and ice for iceboxes. Other peddlers would bring around quilts, blankets, and novelty items.

My mother didn't want her children to go too far

from home. So each morning the girls and boys would come to our house. We would play Old Maid cards, jacks, shoot marbles, jump rope, and clown around with each other. In the evening we played ball games in the street.

Growing up, my long-time best friend from the neighborhood was Howard Lewis. He was a year younger and a solid buddy. We paled around and would do almost anything for each other. Howard wasn't an athlete. He was just a good person and our personalities were compatible. We went through elementary and high school together. He still lives in Gadsden with his family. Howard had a brother named Pete, who was my age, and we were in the Army together.

Other neighborhood friends were Sherman and Dock Calloway and their brother, Ernest, who married my sister, Eva. Robert Glasper was one of the best all-around athletes I've ever seen. Willie and George Smooth were two great athletes. June Moore was a very good baseball pitcher. Leotha Woods was a football player who stood more than 7-feet tall. His feet were so big he made his shoes out of inner tubes and car tires. His sisters were Sweetie and Savannah.

Earl and Julie Bell Lee were two other friends, as were football players Willie and Early Burroughs and their sister, Hazel. Others who played street ball with us were Ossie Mae Williams, Bertha Ousley, Mattie Williams, Fannie Mae Jackson, Wanda June, Catherine Jones, Ruby and Georgiana Williams, and my sister, Bessie. There was Elmo Harp, who married young; Charlie Nelms, who married my sister, Laura; Jimmy Townsend; and George Terrell.

It was a rough neighborhood to grow up in but so was every other black neighborhood in Gadsden. Black folks were segregated, powerless, frustrated, angry, and insecure. They were confined to areas that didn't provide for constructive social outlets and they had no legal protection in their own neighborhoods. In the words of Langston Hughes, "What happens to a dream deferred?

Does it, like a raisin in the sun, dry up? Does it rot and go away? Or does it explode?" Many of the behaviors I saw and experienced in Gadsden were simply manifestations of human explosions out of deep-seated frustrations and hopeless dreams.

School speaker becomes role model

Role models and mentors come into your life with different experiences and you never know how one may affect your life. My high school occasionally would invite accomplished black men and women to speak at assemblies where students in grades seven through 12 had to attend. I'll never forget one speaker who appeared when I was in the ninth grade, Dr. Mary McCloud Bethune, founder and president of Bethune-Cookman College in Daytona Beach, Fla. Things she said that day helped to transform my young life.

At that time, I was not highly motivated academically, making C grades without working hard. But I was really turned on to sports. Bethune said as a girl she lived in a small two-room house that had no electricity. She would walk five miles each way to school and back. She had one pair of shoes and when the soles wore down she'd put cardboard and paper in the bottom to help keep her feet dry. When it rained, her feet got wet. She had one dress, which she washed every night and hung by the fireplace to dry. She would use the light from the fire to read and do her homework. Through it all, she never missed a day of school and was an A student.

I must have been 15 when I heard her speak. I sat there using my imagination and my own experiences to relate to her story. Our stories were strikingly similar. There had been days when I had to put cardboard in my shoes. There were many days when I went to school with no lunch, without lunch money, and wearing patches on my pants. I told myself that if she could accomplish what she did with such limited resources and yet become so successful, I could do better in school and be a better person. She inspired me and gave me a mission and a goal of which to aspire. I wanted to be somebody and it was Bethune who turned the light on in my head.

For the time being, though, sports were my forte. I had a great year as a freshman, with 14 TD passes. I could throw both short and long with accuracy. Though only 5-foot-8 and weighing 155 pounds, I had a powerful throwing arm. Even though we had Korean War veterans on the football team, I was voted co-captain as a sophomore, junior and senior. (My future bride, Noreese Lindsey, meanwhile was chosen Homecoming Queen for the 1952-53 school year.) In each of those years I played the quarterback position and shifted to left halfback whenever we would pass. The shift was obvious to the defense, so the coach gave me the option to run or pass. The decision depended on how well we were progressing and how aggressive the defense was.

We played some of the best black high schools in Alabama, Georgia and Tennessee. Some of them besides Parker that frequently appeared on our schedule were: Alabama schools Cobb High of Anniston; Calhoun County Training School; Booker T. Washington and Carver high schools of Montgomery; Alexander City; Fairfield, Druid and Winona of Birmingham; Tuscaloosa; and Demopolis; plus Howard High of Chattanooga, Tenn.; and Booker T. Washington of Atlanta.

Sad night for the Wildcats

One of the most memorable but sad football games I ever played was in the fall of my senior year against Parker in 1953. It was on a Monday night at Legion Field in Birmingham, site of all Parker home games. About 5,000 people were in the stands. It was very late in the fourth quarter in a 0-0 game and Parker had the ball at midfield and called a time out with two seconds left. We all knew the last play would be a pass.

When time resumed, the quarterback faded back and threw as the horn sounded signaling time had expired. The short pass went to the left end, who made the catch directly in front of our right defensive back, senior Charles Elders. Elders wrapped his arms around the receiver's legs but didn't tackle him. Figuring the game was over after hearing the horn, he turned him loose. The receiver ran for the winning touchdown.

It was a sad night for our team. Most of us began to cry and vented emotions at Elders. It was a long and silent bus trip back to Gadsden, about 60 miles away. It reminded me of my first game against Parker in 1947 when our seniors cried because we lost 6-0. To this day there are folks in Gadsden who have not forgotten that game. Whenever I return home to visit relatives and friends, that game is mentioned.

As I reflect back on it, however, I don't blame Elders. He didn't lose the game, the team did. All of Carver's defenders on the field during that play, including me, stood in our places and watched the fiasco. None of us tried to assist Charles make the tackle or go after the receiver. We were not into gang tackling as a team. The coach had taught us one-on-one tackling. It was our trademark. I said that if ever I became a high school coach, which was one of my lifelong goals, my players would do gang tackling. It was a tough lesson to learn in a big game that team sports is about we and us and not I or me. Charles Elders didn't lose that game — we did. As someone said, there is no "I" in team. Everyone on a team is a contributor and must share the pain during a loss, as well as the glory during victory.

Another tough game that we lost but should have won was against a little country school named Collingsville High, located about 18 miles from Gadsden. It was an all black school in the heart of farming land. I believe the school had an enrollment of fewer than 500 students because it was in a small town. Carver was a Class A school and I believe Collingsville either was B, C or D.

Percy Weatherly, a cousin of my former teammate Eugene Weatherly, was instrumental in arranging the game with coach Johnson. He had played at Carver under Johnson. He was a great quarterback at both Carver High School in Gadsden and Alabama State College in Montgomery. In 1950, he was the head football coach at Collingsville. At least three days a week he would visit Carver's practice sessions after conducting his team's practices earlier in the day so that the students could help their families with farming chores.

Percy would ask Johnson for a playing date each time he attended Carver's practice sessions. I heard Johnson telling Weatherly many times that he didn't want to embarrass him with a lopsided defeat of his team. The discussions would continue each time Weatherly came to practice. Finally, for the 1951 season, Johnson consented and scheduled Carver to play a Saturday night game at Collingsville.

The wooden stands were overflowing with fans. The white farmers tried to dress like city folks. Some of the men wore a tie and shirt with overalls and boots. As always, the stands were segregated, with whites on one side and blacks on the other. After both teams warmed up and, just before kickoff, Carver's starters were stunned by a decision by Johnson that the third team would start. Some of us complained to the coach, but his word was final.

Collingsville, which had two great runners in the Carnegie brothers, scored first. Some of us starters begged Johnson to put us in as a unit, but he refused. Instead, after the first quarter, with Collingsville leading 6-0, he began to substitute individual third-string players with second-string players. Collingsville scored again just before the half against a combination of second- and third-string Carver players, making the score 12-0.

After halftime, Johnson started the second team. In the third quarter, we scored to make it 12-6. In the fourth quarter, Johnson started substituting individual second-team players with first-team players. With about five minutes left he put the entire first team into the game hoping for a miracle. It didn't happen. It was too late and Carver lost 12-6.

That loss hurt deeply. Mighty Carver had no business losing to small Collingsville. It happened because the coach underestimated his opponent and overrated his own talent at the second- and third-team levels. The coach also disrupted the order and team unity for competition. If he were going to start the third team he should have told the entire squad upfront during the practice sessions leading up to the game. Telling us just before kickoff broke the team focus, created disharmony and lowered the expectations of our team.

On the other hand, besides having two great runners in the Carnegie brothers, who later starred at Alabama State, Collingsville's team became overwhelmingly encouraged and motivated because it had scored twice against our second- and third-stringers. Motivation is a big part of the psyche of an athlete. It can help overcome deficiencies, but if you lose it in competition you are dead, whipped.

What did I learn from that game?

- In competition, never underestimate your opponent. Go for the jugular from the outset.
- Don't spring negative surprises on your team, family or the folks you work with. Communicate and share communication with others.
- To become dominant as a team there needs to be a clear plan, strategies and goals that everyone understands and must adhere to throughout the season, including the coach, supervisor, or leader.
- Leave the pain on the field of play, which means you must out-prepare and out-compete your opponents to be successful. Don't experiment with success or what's working by trying something new on the spur of the moment in competition.

I never have been one to brag, boast, or put my

chest out over my abilities, skills, or accomplishments, but I was aware that I was an outstanding high school player. My teammates and coaches confirmed that by naming me co-captain three consecutive years. In addition, former Carver players, my teachers, college students, the media, and others told me so. The son of my boss from the lumber company would attend our games and he gave me a dollar for every touchdown I either tossed or ran. Often, he paid me three dollars after a Tuesday night game.

I made many great friends in high school. Oscar Meadows, an outstanding basketball player, was one of them. He and his wife, Ernestine, remained close friends with Noreese and me. Ernestine died in March 2005.

There were some great football players at my school, all of them devoted Wildcats: Eugene Robinson, Johnny Gaston, William Gary, James Cole, Charles Thornton, Chick Foster, Danny Littlefield, James Hall, Thomas Hill, Charles Steel, Ronald White, Julius Myers, Jasper Harrell, George Sears, George Valentine, Hershell Thornton, T. Ellis Phillips, Herbert Dupree, Pete Taylor, Charles Elders, and Charles Lipscomb, to name a few.

Love of baseball

As good as I was as a football player, I believe I was much better as a baseball player. I learned baseball from my street ball days playing with older guys in my neighborhood. Occasionally we'd find a hilly lot for our games. There also was an open, well-maintained baseball field in Alabama City adjacent to the United Steel mill. I never was sure who owned it. My father, who loved baseball, would take me and my younger brother, Willie, there on Sunday afternoons to watch the Gadsden black baseball team play another local or regional black team. Those were exciting games to me. I always enjoyed watching skilled athletes. Some players on those teams were very good hitters, strong fielders and fast runners.

They made the game exciting. Whenever I practiced or played street ball I tried to act just like them.

When I was 14, I played shortstop for the Black Creek men's baseball team, which consisted of adults and three other players around my age. We usually played an opponent on a Sunday afternoon. Later, the Brown Derby baseball team from the south side asked me and the other three guys my age to join their team. Brown Derby was trying to put together a stronger Gadsden team, rather than having several such teams competing against each other. I also played with the Attalla team whenever it played a good out of town team. Although shortstop was my regular spot, I could play any position, including catcher, a position that I played frequently.

One Sunday we were playing a team in Gadsden City Park, home of the Class B professional baseball team, and our pitcher didn't show up, so I volunteered to pitch. I had the confidence because, as a catcher, I had worked with pitchers over the years, plus I had a strong arm. I remember completing the game, which I believe we lost, 4-3. It would later prove beneficial to me as I entered military service.

I graduated from Carver High in May 1953. It was a class of about 50 seniors. I received a $50 scholarship from an alumni fraternity, which was available to me after I enrolled at the college of my choice. But I never did request payment. Somehow it slipped my memory after I entered military service and changed my choice of colleges. I also had been awarded a partial athletics scholarship to Tuskegee Institute by the track coach, Mr. Owens, who wanted me to run track and play football. One of my teachers, Ms. Griffins, who taught economics and physical education, had graduated from Tuskegee and recommended me to Owens.

I had visited Tuskegee during my junior and senior years with the Carver track team. We participated there in a black high school state track meet. It was a combined high school and college meet during each of those two years. I wasn't able to compete either year in the 220- and 440-yard dashes because of leg injuries, but the coach took me as a morale booster and to assist the team in other ways.

I saw some of the greatest athletes in those meets. At the time, Florida A&M University was known for having the most successful black collegiate football team in the nation under Coach Jake Gaither. I talked to him at the track meet in my senior year and asked him whether I could play football at his institution. He looked at me carefully, put his hand on my shoulder and told me that I was too small. I was then 5-feet-8 inches tall and weighed 155 pounds. I thanked him for his assessment, but he didn't shake my confidence. I knew I was a very good athlete and would enroll in college.

During the meets at Tuskegee I was impressed with the attractiveness of the campus and aware the football team had been successful at times under Cleaves Abbott. So when coach Owens later offered me the partial scholarship and a part-time job, I was very pleased and excited. I looked forward to entering Tuskegee in the fall of 1953.

In the summer of that year I worked at the Etowah Lumber Company, saving as much of my earnings as I could. But it wasn't adding up to much that would defray upcoming college expenses. My weekly take-home pay was $28. I gave my dad $10 to help pay for groceries. I kept $8 and put $10 away for college.

One Saturday in July, as I was walking downtown, I met a former school friend, Walter Bond. He was formerly a student aide to the football team and had graduated a year ahead of me. He was a very good student and a great guy. He asked me which college I planned to attend in the fall and I told him it was Tuskegee Institute. He told me he was dropping out of Alabama State after a year because he had run out of money. He said he had volunteered for the military draft and would be entering the U.S. Army for two years in September and would thus qualify for the G.I. Bill of Rights upon discharge. He suggested I could consider doing the same.

After evaluating my financial situation, I concluded that I, too, should volunteer for the draft. I didn't have enough money to pay for my portion of projected educational expenses at Tuskegee and was also concerned about working part time, playing football, running track and having to study. It seemed like a lot to do as a freshman, so I went to the Selective Services Board at the post office and volunteered for two years in the U.S. Army. The Korean War was ongoing at the time.

Army life at Basic Training

I left Gadsden by bus on Sept. 8, 1953, en route to Fort Jackson, S.C., Army base. Eight friends and former schoolmates were on that bus that left the post office at 8 a.m. I had no idea what I was getting myself into. It didn't take long to realize Fort Jackson was a different place and the toughest place I ever had lived. The loss of privacy made it difficult, as did the lack of flexibility in the daily schedule. My time was not my own. As the first sergeant told all of us one day in formation, "Your ass belongs to me." And he meant every word of it. In 1953, there was no segregation in the Army or overt acts of racism. There were blacks in leadership positions.

I lived in an open barracks where there were 10 double-decked beds on each side of the aisle. Each soldier had a footlocker where he could store his personal belongings. The Army required footlockers, which were at the head and foot of each lower deck bed, to be neat and clean. They were subject to formal inspection anytime. There was a small closet to hang our Army issued and civilian clothes. The two soldiers occupying the double-decked beds slept in opposite directions. There was a common bathroom (latrine) with several showers, stools, and wash sinks. We all took turns in a group basis cleaning it completely.

We usually would be awakened by reveille, blown on a bugle, at 5:30 a.m. We had an hour to shave, shower, dress, make our bed, and clean the barracks for daily inspection. That was important because there were four barracks in a company. The one that finished first in an inspection was first in line for lunch. The soldiers from the barracks that finished last ate last. Sometimes we only had 40 minutes for 256 guys to eat lunch or dinner. All the meals were served in a line with servers giving small portions.

Private Underwood in his early days in the Army

Breakfast was at 6:30 and we had formation for all soldiers at 7 a.m. There was no such thing as being late for formation without some sanctions, which ranged from pushups to extra after-hour duties. One of the worst things that a soldier can do is to get on the bad side of the first sergeant. He has the authority to make life miserable for anyone who got on his bad side. The first sergeant calls it his "shit list". It has the names of soldiers who have misbehaved or transgressed against company policy, but not egregious enough to warrant a court-martial. Believe me, I have seen guys on that list and what they had to do after work wasn't pretty. By 7:30 a.m. we would march as a company to classes and return to headquarters around noon for a one-hour lunch period.

Soldiers from each barracks ate lunch by the order in which they passed inspection. Sometimes we arrived back from training or classes quite late, but the lunch hour wasn't extended. If you were the last unit to enter the mess hall you might only have 10 minutes or less to eat. It was a rush-rush deal and time often ran out.

I recall once when our barracks finished last in the inspection and each of the 50-plus men in my group, in addition to eating last, had to do 10 pull-ups before we could enter the mess hall. There was an overweight soldier just ahead of me who could only do one pull-up. Consequently, I, along with many others, never entered the mess hall because time ran out. Each soldier was required to stay in the same order as we lined up. No one was allowed to cut in front of another person.

There were some angry and hungry soldiers who never ate lunch and had to return to the field hungry. But we never were last again and the soldier who failed to do the pull-ups was severely criticized and harassed about his weight. He worked hard to lose 50 pounds.

When we arrived back at headquarters we would line up in formation, find out about inspection, hear announcements about the day's activities up to that point, and receive mail. I looked forward to the letters I received from Noreese Lindsey, my high school sweetheart and future wife. They lifted my spirits each day and reassured me she was the person for me. Sometimes she would send a cake that she baked. It arrived crumbled, but it didn't go to waste, especially with my buddies from my hometown anxious to help consume it.

Afterwards we returned in the afternoon or early evening, usually ate dinner, then returned to our barracks for more detail work, including cleaning our rifles, the latrine, scrubbing floors, doing kitchen patrol (KP), shining our boots, cleaning our footlockers and showers, etc.

We usually got to bed between 11 and 11:30 p.m., with 5:30 a.m. reveille each Monday through Saturday. We were off at noon Saturday and had that afternoon and Sunday to ourselves, unless you were scheduled for KP or guard duty (watching over equipment). Soldiers who lived close to the post usually would leave for home Saturday afternoon and return late Sunday night. The rest of us who lived farther away would spend Saturday at the Post Exchange (PX) drinking beer, or go to a local movie or the post library. I spent most of my free time doing basically three things: going to the PX or library, reading in my barracks, and writing letters to friends back home.

One never could claim to have lived at Fort Jackson without mentioning Tank Hill, the area where the infantry was trained. As late as midnight you could hear training sessions going on, with marching and singing in cadence as the soldiers marched. It was an intimidating sound for those of us who weren't housed in that area. It gave the impression that Tank Hill soldiers never slept and were being trained and harassed more than other groups of soldiers.

I spent four months of training at Fort Jackson then was sent to Fort Lee in Virginia for ordinance training school, where I found an environment that was a little more relaxing. Just like at Fort Jackson, there was no segregation by race and there were several black leaders. The daily schedule was similar except that the weekend, starting Friday night, was completely your own. I was tempted several times to travel to nearby Washington, D.C., to visit some former high school friends, but I never did. I continued to spend my weekends just as I had done at Fort Jackson: the PX, writing letters, resting, visiting the library and reading books. I rather enjoyed that pattern because I was preparing myself to enter Tuskegee Institute upon my discharge.

Airborne all the way

Fort Lee was my home for three months and when training ended I volunteered for the 82nd Airborne Division, located at Fort Bragg, N.C., because I wanted to be among the best-trained soldiers in the Army. I reported there in March 1954. The day I arrived, at least three airborne troopers were killed during their jumps, an introduction that was rather frightening. But once I commit myself to something, I usually go through with it and I was willing to give paratrooper training my very best.

"Jump School" was by far the most challenging training I ever had encountered. It appeared to be remnants of Tank Hill in South Carolina — but 20 times more difficult. I was assigned to an airborne ordinance company and was transported by truck each morning at 5:30 a.m. to the airborne training site. There must have been 400-500 soldiers going through training, which consisted of heavy physical training, including calisthenics, in an atmosphere of harassment and verbal abuse. We ran at least five miles a day, did 100 or more pushups a day, plus jump squats. Hour after hour we also received instruction and practice in how to jump.

The first of the procedures involved jumping (with the aid of safety harnesses) from a 4-foot platform and landing in soft dirt or sawdust. Next came the 34-foot tower, with troopers actually simulating jumping from the door of an airplane. From 34 feet up you would jump out the door of the tower and, hanging from a harness, you would slide down an angled pulley to the ground, with non-commissioned officers at the other end for safety purposes, ready to slow you down.

The tower was scary. You weren't supposed to look down, but look straight ahead. There was a sergeant sitting downstairs on a high chair grading each jump. After landing, the aspiring trooper would stand in front of the sergeant for an evaluation. He always found things wrong. He'd start off by saying, "Number 322" (or whatever number was on your helmet), "Your eyes were closed, your fingers were not spread on your reserve chute, your feet were apart, and your knees were not bent. Jump down for 10 pushups and get back at the end of the line."

A trooper may need to jump from the tower 200 times before making the five successfully-graded jumps that would qualify him to move on to the next level, the actual airplane jumps. The tower gave us a sense of a real jump, but to earn our wings we had to make five jumps from an airplane. I soon realized that the pushups and other physical training had a purpose. Paratroopers needed strong upper arms to control the parachutes on the way down, plus strong legs, and overall conditioning definitely was necessary for the rigors of the job.

Our uniforms consisted of fatigues, a steel helmet (over a helmet liner), jump boots (higher than ordinary boots), backpack, rifle, parachute, and reserve chute. The equipment must have weighed 40 pounds.

It seemed as though half of the men who started out on the first day had dropped out by the day of graduation. It was a proud feeling to have the general pin the jump wings on you that Friday morning of graduation. I felt like I had accomplished something worthwhile. I felt the same level of pride I had experienced when I was a young high school star athlete. I had used my abilities, talents, perseverance, self-discipline, and self-esteem to compete and be successful at the top level. Just like with my high school football team, many aspiring young men tried out, but only the committed ones endured to become paratroopers.

I learned the importance of discipline in airborne school. Each new paratrooper was given the weekend off and was told to go beat up five "straight legs" (non-airborne troopers). Some of our guys literally carried out that tongue-in-cheek suggestion. I spent my time, though, in the PX and with Noreese, who had become my wife.

Photo 1D: I was really loaded down for a jump, with a parachute strapped to my back, a pack and reserve chute in front, and a rifle case on my side.

I didn't experience any racial segregation in the Army. Assignments and duties were given without regard to the color of a person's skin. My bunkmate at Fort Jackson was white and was from my hometown of Gadsden. In fact, I learned a valuable lesson about white folks' attitudes toward blacks at Fort Bragg. Contrary to what I believed in Alabama, I found out all white folks weren't mean-spirited toward blacks.

One morning our company was preparing to go on bivouac, camping out in the woods for 10 days. We were in formation listening to instructions from the first sergeant. Each of the four barracks in my company was headed by a master sergeant. In formation, he stood in front of the men living in his barracks. I heard one of the white master sergeants from South Carolina suggesting to the white master sergeant from Georgia that was over my barracks that, "When we get to our bivouac destination, let them niggers dig the holes for trash and for other usages." I observed that my master sergeant didn't even acknowledge the other master sergeant's comments. He simply walked away from him.

Having overheard the racial remark I had the opportunity to observe how first sergeants would make the detail assignments from my barracks when we arrived one evening at the bivouac destination area. My first sergeant selected soldiers who had a history of getting into trouble. They were both black and white soldiers. I don't believe anybody would have argued about his selection process. It was very fair and made sense. He could have easily complied with the suggestions without any reprisals, but he chose to be fair and do the right thing without regard to a person's skin color. I gained a tremendous amount of respect for my first sergeant and felt like he would treat me fairly in all situations. I tried my best to be the best soldier in the barracks. I would have done anything for him because I believed in him.

High school sweetheart

I met Noreese when she was in the ninth grade and I was in the 10th. As with most popular young male athletes, it wasn't a problem getting girlfriends. I had been casually dating one girl on Friday and Sunday nights at her home, but one Friday night she used a barrage of unprovoked profanity that really turned me off. I said then and there that I could do better.

The next week I was in the school hallway as the ninth-grade girls were going to lunch and I checked them out to see who might appeal to me. It was Noreese, who was pretty and handled herself with class. She impressed me as being a nice, decent person. Eventually I approached her during one of the lunch hours. I asked whether I could visit her sometime. She never had a date. She had some friends, both boys and girls with whom she socialized at church and school, but no boyfriend-type dates.

She told me I had to ask her mother, who would then decide whether I could come to their house to see her. Well, it so happened that Noreese's mother, Mildred Lindsey, knew who I was because she was active in the Carver PTA and worked concessions at each of our home football games.

The Lindsey family lived about eight blocks from the high school. So one day at noon, I walked to their house where Mrs. Lindsey greeted me and invited me in for something to eat. I politely declined the food and told her I wanted to visit Noreese at her house. Mrs. Lindsey responded that she knew me from the football games and many other folks had spoken highly of me.

She wanted to know where I lived and I told her on Norris Avenue in the Black Creek area. She said she heard it was a rough area, to which I responded that there were many rough areas in the city and all the people who lived in them weren't bad. She agreed and asked me where my father worked and I said he had been working for the Etowah Lumber Company for a long time. I guess I passed the test because she said I could visit Noreese two days a week, preferably on weekends. I thanked her.

I enjoyed going to their house because it was like a family affair. In the spring and summer we would sit on the front porch and talk. Mostly, Mrs. Lindsey and I would be engaged in conversation about various subjects. Noreese had a married sister who lived in another part of the city, and a younger sister and two younger brothers who lived at home with her and their parents.

Mrs. Lindsey often would have something good for me to eat. She was an excellent cook. Noreese and I fell in love with each other and she went to summer school so that we could graduate at the same time. We continued to date until I went into the Army and we continued to be committed to each other. She wrote daily and we decided to get married on April 5, 1954, at a Justice of the Peace in Fayetteville. We thought about several other options, but mainly due to my airborne training schedule, with little flexibility for days off, we decided to take that quick route. (I hadn't made Noreese aware of my airborne training because I didn't want her to worry about me.)

Mrs. Lindsey arrived in Fayetteville on April 6 because, as she described it, she didn't want any "mess". We all lived in the guesthouse on the Army post for about a week. Satisfied that everything was above board and there was no "mess", Mrs. Lindsey and her daughter, my wife, returned to Gadsden. Noreese came back to Fort Bragg in June and we stayed in the guesthouse for a short time.

Somehow Noreese found a three-bedroom apartment for rent on post. A young, black sergeant and his wife, who didn't have children, decided to rent both vacant rooms to two couples. Shortly after we moved in the sergeant qualified for officer's candidate school (OCS) and left the area for formal training, while his wife, Freddie, remained at home.

I still had not told my wife I was involved in paratrooper school because I simply didn't want her to worry about it. It was after I completed training and received my wings in July that I finally told her about it. Just as I thought, she reacted by questioning my motives for doing such a risky thing and she became very concerned about my welfare. So I never shared with her when I was scheduled to jump and didn't tell her after I had jumped.

We decided that Noreese should enroll at Alabama State in the fall semester of 1954. She did it, reluctantly, because we were still on our honeymoon and deeply in love and needed so much to be with each other. We concluded that both of us would be further ahead if we made the sacrifice and she began her college education a year ahead of me.

Leaps of faith

We were required to jump at least once every three months to earn "jump pay" of $50 a month, which supplemented our regular monthly pay. Sometimes we'd jump more often, from C-119 aircraft, which held 40 paratroopers, 20 on each side of the aisle facing each other (a "stick"). Some guys had more than 200 jumps to their credit and others had as few as five.

It didn't make any difference how much experience a person had jumping or what age he might have been — everyone was intimidated about jumping out of an airplane. All of us were aware that it took just one miscue for disaster to happen. We were given small garbage bags to use in case of an upset stomach and we could not keep food down. I saw old and young guys use the bags. I, too, was nervous but never resorted to using a bag or anything else. I always prayed and had faith that my chute would open.

We had two or three night jumps. They could have been trouble, particularly if a person became disoriented and could not recall how to get to the assembly point. But the most dangerous part of jumping is being unable to recover from the drag when the wind fills the canopy after you land. If you can't collapse it, you could be dragged unmercifully, sometimes to death. Techniques are taught to every airborne trooper about how to land and recover from the drag. During my 17 months at Fort Bragg, I must have had about 10 actual jumps, not counting training school.

The most humorous thing I ever observed about jumping was when a transfer from Fort Campbell, Ky., reported to Fort Bragg about a week after we had finished our jump training. He walked around our company bragging about how he could jump from an airplane and do somersaults and other tricks before he landed. None of us could figure out what he was saying. We all said what he purported to do was impossible, unless you did free-fall jumping, which we didn't practice.

On our next scheduled jump that guy was on the plane and I was on one of the 20 seats on a side of the plane. As we approached the drop zone (DZ) the red light changed to green, signaling that we were over the target and ready to jump. The jumpmaster asked the young man to come to the front of the stick so he would be the first jumper from his side of the plane. The young man went to the front and hooked up. All of us were standing facing the front of the plane so as to move up as the person ahead of us jumped.

The jumpmaster, who was a first sergeant in rank, opened the door and told the young man to go, meaning jump, but he wouldn't do it and kept backing away from the door. After several unsuccessful attempts to get him to jump, the red light reappeared, which meant the plane had passed over the drop zone. As the plane circled back for another pass over the DZ, the first sergeant asked the young man to unhook and go sit in the back of the plane. When we returned to the barracks, he was shifted out that day to Fort Benning, Ga., and we never heard from him again, or ever encountered anyone with such a wild imagination.

Baseball at Fort Bragg

In April 1955, I decided to try out for the baseball team that was being formed by a lieutenant in our airborne division. He would become the manager. There must have been 40 to 50 guys who tried out. Lt. Shoppel and I were the only two guys from my company to try out. When the manager asked me what position I was trying out for, I told him catcher, but he said he already had a Class B professional catcher so I wouldn't make it there.

Then I said I'd try out for shortstop and he said there was no need for that since *HE* would be the shortstop. Now I really became bold. I had a strong throwing arm and I could throw accurately. I remembered the time I volunteered to pitch for my Gadsden team when the regular pitcher didn't show up, so I told the manager I would pitch. He looked at me in disbelief, but said, "OK."

Soon we had scrimmage games among ourselves to trim down the squad. I had only two pitches, a fastball and curve. I was just as effective and accurate throwing both pitches overhand or sidearm, which I often did to right-handed batters. I was the most effective pitcher during the scrimmages and gave up very few solid hits. Most players would hit groundouts or soft fly balls against me.

One day when the manager had me pitch against his projected starting lineup, I got out of each inning with ease. Lt. Shoppel, my company officer who gave me a ride to practice and competition in his car each day, was a projected starter. He batted left-handed and was a good hitter. I kept breaking off overhand curve balls to him that went in on his fist. He became frustrated, finally hitting a soft roller to the first baseman. I thought he might get upset with me and stop giving me rides.

But after practice en route back to our company, he complimented me for my good pitches.

When we opened the regular season one night against a Fort Bragg infantry regiment team, I was the starting pitcher for our team. The other team had been around for a number of years and had won the division title the previous year. Two brothers led that team. One was a left-handed pitcher and the other a first baseman. Both were very good and both were great hitters, batting third and fourth in the lineup.

We lost 3-2. It was exciting and my teammates played great defense. Twice the brothers hit long fly balls that were caught up against the wall by our center fielder Larry Headen. Another time with the bases loaded and two outs, with a 3-2 count on the pitcher, I threw him a sidearm fastball and struck him out. Although I never would let it show on my face, I loved striking out good hitters.

We played that team twice and lost both times by one run, but overall we had a successful season. I never kept track of how many games I pitched. I know there were a lot. Often I started a game and pitched six or seven innings and would be called upon two days later to pitch in relief. My arm would be so sore, but I never complained. Any pitcher who ever has thrown hard for 12 to 15 innings within a four-day period knows what I'm talking about. I tried to do what was best for the team.

Unlike pulling guard duty at night when we still had to report for work early the next morning, baseball had its benefits. Whenever we would play a night game we were given the next day off from work, but we still had baseball practice later that day. We were never given a day off for working nighttime guard duty.

After the regular baseball season ended our manager arranged for our team to play an exhibition against a Class B professional team from Pembrook, N.C. It was comprised mostly of former major leaguers who had been sent down to the minors for various reasons. I remember the names of Rocky Bridges and Aaron Robinson, both former Detroit Tigers, but there were other ex-major leaguers on that team. Bridges played for the Tigers in 1959-60 and Robinson in 1949-51.

I was our starting pitcher in the exhibition. We batted first and went out 1-2-3. Next, Pembrook went up and it was three-and-out. I remember walking back to the dugout and my manager said to me, "Little Newt" (a reference to Don Newcomb, famous black pitcher for the Los Angeles Dodgers), "This will be a game tonight." Well, it was a short-lived game because after our team went out again, three up and three down in the top of the second, I could not retire a batter in the bottom of the inning.

Everything I threw was hit either for a single or double. I watched those pros not swinging, but gauging the speed of my first thrown pitch, then teeing off on the next hittable ball. I threw overhand and I threw sidearm but it didn't matter, they got a hit. It was late August and I was counting my days until I would be discharged from the Army.

Chapter 2:

MICHIGAN STATE BECKONS

Injustices spurred determination to succeed

It was while on guard duty on New Year's Day 1954 that I had made a decision to change my college preference from Tuskegee to Michigan State University. I was in the dayroom, a place to rest for two hours after walking and protecting property for four hours. During that respite I saw Michigan State on television in the Rose Bowl game against UCLA.

Having been raised in Alabama where segregation laws prevented socializing among blacks and whites, the game really caught my attention. It was the first time I had seen blacks and whites play together on the same collegiate team. Michigan State appeared to have played 10 or 12 different black players. UCLA had fewer, but it was obvious that all of the blacks were impact players. I was so interested and amazed by those integrated teams that I decided that night I would research MSU in the Army library and apply for admission. I was later accepted.

My discharge date was Sept. 8, 1955. I was scheduled to report to Michigan State to begin orientation on Sept. 19. As I was being processed out of Fort Bragg, I was required to take a medical examination and was delayed from being honorably discharged by one day. After further medical tests, x-rays, and diagnoses I was released without explanation. I didn't find out the reason for the delay until I enrolled at MSU.

Noreese, our three-week old baby Jackie, and I left Fayetteville by train Sept. 17 en route to Lansing, Mich., arriving at the depot in the early afternoon of Sept. 18. We didn't know anyone in the area. Everything we owned was either in our pockets or in the one footlocker we brought with us.

I had applied too late for on-campus married housing. Noreese and Jackie remained at the train depot while I searched for a room or an apartment for us to rent. I bought a *Lansing State Journal* and called numbers from each of the ads that had rooms/apartments for rent in East Lansing. Being unfamiliar with the area I didn't know the distance between Lansing and the campus, plus I didn't have a car. I figured that living in East Lansing near the campus would be convenient for us.

Each person I called in East Lansing wanted to know whether I was Negro. When I responded in the affirmative I was told that either the room/apartment had already been rented or simply that they do not rent to Negroes. That raw prejudice shocked me. I thought I had left that kind of attitude in Alabama and North Carolina. I had deceived myself by believing that the numerous black athletes I observed on Michigan State's football team in the 1954 Rose Bowl game represented openness and acceptance in a university setting based on the character of the person rather than skin color.

I became discouraged, angry, and wondered if I had made a mistake by coming to Michigan State. It occurred to me after making numerous telephone calls without success that maybe I should have gone to Tuskegee

Institute where I was welcome and had a partial athletics scholarship waiting for me. The thought came to mind that I never had known or heard of any Carver High graduate who had gone to a collegiate undergraduate institution outside of the traditional black southern colleges and maybe they understood that racism is pervasive.

I started to feel the same insecurity I had experienced in the South — feelings of discrimination, restrictions and no protection. I couldn't help but wonder how the black football players were coping in the East Lansing community. I hadn't even seen the city or the university but had gotten very unpleasant vibes from the results of my telephone calls. It is an intimidating feeling to be thinking about moving your family to a community where you aren't welcome.

I continued looking for a place to rent by walking the pavement and finding where the majority of blacks lived in Lansing. It was approaching 6 p.m., almost four hours since our arrival, and I was getting concerned about my wife and baby. Noreese was bottle-feeding Jackie and I didn't know how much milk she had left or whether she was able to handle everything and get some food herself from the concession stand. Safety wasn't as much of a concern then as it is today. People left their residences and cars unlocked, something we would be crazy to do today, although even now there are a few foolish people who aren't safety cautious.

I met a black man named Bob (I can't remember his last name) on Butler Street in Lansing. I identified myself and asked him if he knew where I could rent a room or an apartment for my family. He told me he had a room for rent in his house and I could have equal access to the living room, kitchen and bath. I think he charged about $15 a week. His wife was named Bessie. She was a thin woman weighing about 100 pounds or less, while he was about 5-feet-11 and about 240 pounds. They fought a lot but were nice to us.

We later found an upstairs apartment at 211½ Main Street in a house owned by the Bookers, who lived on the first floor. They charged $22 a week and they, too, were nice to us. We subsequently were called for a married housing apartment on campus on West Maple Street. It was a barracks-type structure with two bedrooms, a living room and kitchen. The university supplied cots for the bedrooms and a refrigerator. I think it cost $40 a month.

It was a modest apartment but was convenient for walking to class and becoming acquainted with other married students living in the barracks. We found that most families were struggling financially the same as us. The couples in our housing unit would get together occasionally in one of the units, preferably at the end of the academic term, and we would chip in to buy a couple cases of beer and eat popcorn. We would sit around and talk and play charades.

Our next move on campus was to 1405 Spartan Village, a brand new two-bedroom that rented for about $115 a month. The university had begun to demolish the barracks-type apartments.

Health checkup raises a flag

Orientation for new students consisted of placement testing in math, reading, composition and English. We met with academic advisors, selected academic courses, and went to the stadium to meet the football team and coaches, plus learn the Spartan fight song. It was great to meet the football coach, Duffy Daugherty, and players like Clarence Peaks, Earl Morrall, Gerald Planutis, John "Thunder" Lewis, Buck Nystrom, Jim Hinesly, and others. I was awestruck by those football players.

We also underwent a physical exam at Olin Health Center, getting our eyes, ears, and throats checked. Our blood was tested and we had chest x-rays taken. That

This 1955 Spartans football team was loaded with talent. Included here were quarterback Earl Morrall (21), Gerald Planutis (45), Clarence Peaks (26), and John Lewis (front row far right).

took place on a Thursday and Friday. On Sunday I got a call at night from a nurse asking me to report to Olin at 8 a.m. Monday. The doctor told me the x-ray showed I had a shadow in my chest and advised that since I was a veteran he would refer me to the Veterans Administration Hospital in Ann Arbor for additional testing and was admitted there for five days.

I took a Greyhound bus to Ann Arbor and walked several miles to the hospital. The day I was discharged, the doctor there told me I had a condition called sarcoidosis, a little-known disease that he said was like putting a torn-to-pieces letter in the trashcan. Nobody knows what it's about or how to treat it. He put me under medical observation. My family doctor later told me that sarcoidosis is a lymph nodes disease of unknown cause.

I visited the Veterans' Hospital every six months for a day or two over the next three years and eventually the shadow disappeared without treatment. I believe the Army was aware of my condition when I was discharged but never felt the need to tell me about it.

Learning early to have a second option

When I enrolled at Michigan State it was with two academic goals in mind. I had learned as a child to always have two plans for everything because in most cases, Plan A, or the first goal, may not be successful. You need to carry on with the alternative plan, Plan B, in case the other one fails. I learned the strategy from incidents in the segregated South. For example, if you are waiting at the bus stop to catch a bus for work and the white driver seemingly deliberately passes you by when the bus is half-full of whites, you'd better have an alternate plan to get to work on time or get fired. In most cases that means arriving at the bus stop early enough so that you can walk to work if you get passed up.

My first goal was to major in pre-law. I wanted to become a lawyer so I could be the first black lawyer to represent blacks in Gadsden. My second goal was to become a high school football coach. There were three significant occurrences that drove my desire to be a lawyer deep within my mind. First, it was the general environment. Blacks had no authority; we were helpless, segregated, and there were no black policemen. We had separate schools and we were subjected to unprovoked brutality and humiliation at will.

Second, I have seen decent and law-abiding black men after they had been beaten simply because they did not respond expeditiously to white policemen. Some of the victims stuttered or had other speech impediments, or they would be walking home from work at night and be stopped without cause and harassed. They would be asked a question and would be beaten with a black jack (a piece of metal enclosed in leather, with a leather handle), if the response was too slow in coming. There were several guys in my neighborhood who were beaten in this manner.

Third, when I was 17, I had a painful tooth extracted by a white dentist in the summer of 1951. The gum continued to bleed profusely over several days and I went back twice. The first time he stuffed the gum with cotton and I continued to bleed and was getting weak, plus I was working at the lumber company doing hard work in the hot sun.

On my second visit the dentist said he couldn't help me anymore. I believed he had a professional responsibility to further advise about the bleeding gum. I sought the counsel of a white lawyer and told him what happened. He said he thought I had a good case, but when he asked me whether the dentist was white or Negro, I told him he was white and the lawyer abruptly said, "Boy, I can't help you." I was further convinced that an ethical black lawyer was desperately needed in Gadsden. But I soon discovered that my meager funds were insufficient for me to remain in school seven consecutive years to pursue a law degree. So I resorted to Plan B, which was to earn a bachelor's degree in physical education and become a high school teacher and head football coach somewhere in the United States.

I found that Michigan State wasn't a very accommodating institution for blacks. In 1955 there were about 100 black students on campus out of a total student population of about 18,000. Many of the blacks were student-athletes. The campus was virtually segregated. The only thing different from the conservative South was that blacks and whites could attend classes together, live in the same on-campus residence halls, live in on-campus married housing apartments, and play some sports together. It wasn't popular for blacks and whites to socialize together. And there weren't many black female students there. Several black football players told me they got in some of the assistant coaches' doghouses after being seen walking across campus with white female students.

There was only one black player on the baseball team. He was a pitcher, but he couldn't accompany the team when it made the annual southern tour. That situation deterred my interest in trying out for the team.

Men's basketball had two black players, Julius McCoy and Johnny Green, after Rickey Ayala had integrated the sport in 1952. I don't believe there were blacks in another sport besides football and track. Willie Atterberry was in track. John Horn was an All-American boxer, but the sport was being phased out.

There were no black athletics, physical education, or recreation employees and I never had one black teacher in any of my classes and never heard of any. I remember associating with or having phys ed classes with some black athletes: football players Peaks, Hinesly, Lewis, John Young, Jerry McFarland, Willie Boykins, Henry Young, Carl Perryman, Howard Neely, Blanche Martin, Harold Dukes, Ellison Kelly, Joel Jones, Herb Adderley, and Art Johnson, plus basketball players McCoy and Green.

Frequently I was the only black student in my academic classes, the exception being physical education classes. Black students usually would assemble between classes at the grill in the Union Building. They had to travel to Lansing to have their hair done, attend parties, and for other entertainment. Since I was a married man I never attended private parties except with married housing students. And I once attended a veterans' club social for new military veteran students, held off-campus in a cow barn. I was the only black in attendance.

Some of the black athletes and students would occasionally come to my campus apartment on Friday nights to socialize. I was off from work on Friday and Saturday nights. We would drink a little beer, eat popcorn, tell jokes, and dance to songs played on the radio. The few black students who lived in East Lansing rented rooms over the Smoke Shop on Grand River across from the Union Building. Several students roomed together in the unkempt housing unit with a communal bathroom.

When I initially moved to the married housing barracks on campus in 1956 I was doing day work between classes to help meet expenses. The $160 I was receiving monthly from the G.I. Bill wasn't adequate to pay rent, buy food and clothes, pay medical expenses and transportation, plus defray tuition and fees costs for a young family.

I responded to an advertisement by Dr. Robert Overholt, a dentist who needed someone to clean his office on Grand River in East Lansing. It was a good fit. He also hired me to do work at his residence and that's when I met his family: his wife, Frances, sons Peter and David, and daughter, Nancy. I also worked for Frances' father, Mr. Lostutter, and his wife, Bertha, who lived nearby in East Lansing. Mr. Lostutter was a journalism professor at MSU.

Bob and Frances Overhold, seated center, and family

They were good and decent people who befriended me. They gave me as much work as they could. Often I would do odd jobs for them at dinnertime and they would insist that I eat dinner with them. I can honestly say that the Overholts, in particular, and the Lostutters, were the first white folks whom I felt comfortable with and trusted. They were genuinely fair and unpretentious

71

people. I later taught the Overholt children in elementary school physical education classes in the East Lansing School District.

Noreese's and my friendship with the Overholts remains strong and we frequently socialize. He has supported me, unsolicited, professionally on numerous occasions. Although I am most grateful for that support, there were times I wished he hadn't written a letter on my behalf because I didn't want anyone to think I was exploiting our friendship. But anyone who knows Bob and Frances knows they can't be tempted to do anything they don't want to do. They are highly moral and ethical people, and a great family.

Family grows, time shrinks

Alvin, our second child, was born Feb. 27, 1957, in Sparrow Hospital in Lansing. At the time, I was working a full-time night shift for the Michigan Secretary of State Driving Records Division, while carrying a full load of academic courses at the university. The job entailed sorting and filing traffic moving violations. I had taken a civil service examination in October 1956 for a records clerk position. I passed the exam and was hired Dec. 26 for the third shift, from 12:30-8 a.m. I was pleased to get that job because it would help our budget.

I would leave work at 8 a.m. and rush to classes that started at 8:10. I tried to cluster my classes between 8:10 a.m. and 1 p.m., then I'd be able to go home, get something to eat, play with our children for an hour or so and go to bed for about five hours. I would get up at 7:30 p.m. and study until it was time to go to work. It was tough leaving my young family at midnight to arrive at work at 12:30 a.m. Studying was a struggle and I stayed tired. I didn't perform as well academically as I was capable. It was tough becoming accustomed to working all night and then having to go to classes at least half of the morning.

The Secretary of State position was permanent and steady but the pay was low. I remember my net take-home pay was less than $100 every other week. I still was having difficulty paying tuition every quarter, so I decided to withdraw from the university beginning in the fall/winter semester 1957. I wanted to find a better paying job so I could save more money each payday to help resolve the tuition crunch. I tried unsuccessfully to find such a position. Noreese, Jackie, and Alvin returned to Alabama to live with my parents until I could get things resolved financially.

I continued to work at the Secretary of State's office. Then I got an unexpected break. James Riley moved to Lansing from Detroit and opened the city's first black funeral home. Robert Jones, an MSU black student and a friend, told me that Riley needed someone to assist him with his duties and I was hired. I lived rent-free in a small upstairs third-floor apartment over the funeral home. Riley and his wife, Doressa, lived on the second floor. They are very nice people. We continue to be friends.

The arrangement lasted about a year and enabled me the opportunity to pay off some small debts and save some money. Noreese and the children rejoined me in early 1959 and we were successful in moving into another new apartment, in Spartan Village. David, our third child, was born April 10, 1961, in Sparrow Hospital. He, just like Alvin and Jackie, was a healthy baby. Four months later, August 1961, I received my Bachelor of Science degree in physical education.

Student teaching sparks interests

In the fall of 1960, the semester before my graduation, I was assigned to do my student teaching in physical education at East Lansing's junior high school, where some 600 boys and girls were enrolled. James Oestriech, the boys' physical education teacher, was my supervising teacher. He was a graduate of MSU and had established a solid skills development program for the boys. Liz Flinchbaugh had a similar program for the girls. Overall, it was a good program and Liz and Jim worked very well together in their separate programs.

Oestriech was a very fair person and a great mentor who provided every opportunity for me, as the first black professional ever to work in the school system, to learn and grow. He made certain I was included in all social events. I learned from him how to organize and teach a class. We made a good pair because I brought some knowledge and skills that supplemented his training and methodology. He was a stickler for punctuality and details and I made sure I abided by those criteria.

We had fun arranging and participating in noontime touch football games with other men teachers. The games were competitive. Jim and I always were on opposite teams. Occasionally we'd attend a Tigers baseball game in Detroit. I couldn't have asked for a better mentor and friend.

Most of the other teachers accepted me as a colleague and the principal, Ray Budde, was an intellectual but down-to-earth man who often would play football and basketball with us at noon or in the evening. Other teachers who frequently participated in those games included Neil Weinbrenner, Tony Egnatuck, Steve Arnest, and Mr. Bond. Howard King was a great supporter. They were great guys and we had fun together.

There were some very talented and gifted male athletes in the seventh and eighth grades that year. Oestriech and I often talked about how many of the boys would be outstanding high school athletes. We followed their careers at East Lansing High School, where some became impact football and basketball players, while others excelled in track, baseball, and other sports.

As my student teaching assignment was ending I got a letter from Budde. Written at the top of the first page was a handwritten note from him saying, "I wish I had an opening for you." As I read on I discovered that the seventh and eighth grade boys and girls had signed a five-page petition requesting that I be employed in the East Lansing school system.

The principal acknowledged in his note that the petition was a real tribute to me. It felt good to know that I had won the confidence of the students, but I didn't put much faith in landing a job in that system. No other black was employed in the school system. East Lansing was a very insulated upper middle class community comprised of high-level professionals, corporate executives, university faculty members and administrators. Additionally, there were probably no black families who owned houses in East Lansing. Most blacks lived in Lansing.

I misinterpreted the significance of the petition. I was honored to receive it but I never thought it would help me get hired. About two weeks after my teaching assignment ended I received a phone call from Budde offering me a part-time job at the junior high school. He offered me a position that included teaching two phys ed classes for boys, one in the seventh and the other the eighth grade. I accepted and taught the classes back-to-back in the afternoon, while continuing to work in the evenings at the Secretary of State's office. Thus I became the first African-American teacher in the East Lansing School System beginning with the 1961-62 academic year.

I enrolled in graduate school, majoring in physical education and counseling, and took two master's level courses each term around my schedule. I really enjoyed teaching the boys. It was an exciting and challenging time. I wanted them to become physically and mentally tough while learning and improving their skills. I devoted extra time to the less skilled students to make sure they learned the basics to participate. This is where I developed my passion for teaching. I love children and teaching them was fun.

My philosophy on skill development was inclusive rather than exclusive. I made certain the boys were adequately prepared to compete in the after-school recreational programs and certain season-ending tournaments such as wrestling. Many boys from my two classes engaged in the activities and I was satisfied we had done a good job of teaching and improving their skills and interacting during my first year.

I signed a contract to return for the 1962-63 academic year on the same part-time basis. I would continue to pursue my master's degree program while working at the Secretary of State's office.

Job offer enticing — at first

In July I received a telephone call from Van Mueller, the superintendent of schools in Ashley, Mich. He told me he had reviewed my credentials at the MSU placement center and wanted to offer me a job as head coach for football, basketball, and baseball and to teach two classes a day. I felt at that moment my lifelong goal to be a head football coach had come true.

The job was offered and accepted over the phone. I drove that day to Ashley to meet with the superintendent in his office and signed a contract for, I believe, $4,400 a year. I was happy as a lark. That is, until I went home and told my wife. She asked me to take her to Ashley so she could see the area, a typical rural farming community. I believe most students were bussed to school. I drove Noreese and our three children around the downtown and the high school, which appeared to be a consolidated school.

As we left Ashley, Noreese told me she and the children weren't going to move there because she perceived a lack of racial diversity. I told her I was going to commute there because I really wanted those coaching positions and the opportunity to help develop the physical, social and intellectual qualities in the young men — and win some games, as well.

I called Superintendent Cecil McDonald in East Lansing and made him aware of the Ashley offer and asked to be released from my part-time teaching position for the 1962-63 school year. He recommended against my accepting the Ashley position, though he never specified the reason and I didn't ask him why. He told me he would offer me a full-time job in East Lansing and would call me back the next day. Sure enough, Budde, the East Lansing Junior High School principal, called the next day and offered me a full-time position that would allow me to continue to teach the two phys ed classes there, plus be a part-time physical education teacher who would work with the elementary schools. I accepted the job at a salary of $4,700.

I drove alone to Ashley to meet with the superintendent and told him about my wife's concerns and about the counter offer from East Lansing. Mueller was most understanding and said he didn't want me to withdraw from the contract for any other reason than something personal. He said he could understand my position. He had received some unfriendly phone calls from a few of the neighbors who had seen me leave his office. I also resigned from my job at the Secretary of State's office.

In my East Lansing schools position, in addition to the middle school assignment, I was assigned to Bailey, Central, Glencairn, Pinecrest, Donley, and Spartan Village elementary schools. I had an uneven daily schedule, with my time divided each day over three schools. On Mondays I would teach at the middle school and Central and Bailey elementary schools. On Tuesdays and Thursdays I would teach at East Lansing Junior High, Glencairn, and Donley elementary. On Friday I would divide the day between Pinecrest and Spartan Village schools.

I really did enjoy working with the children, who were honest, innocent, and eager to learn. I developed a comprehensive program in the elementary schools that taught motor skills such as hand, arm, foot, and eye coordination. Each of the games we played was designed for skill development and fun. We did many physical fitness activities, with emphasis on full participation. No student was too fat, too slow or unskilled to participate.

I taught the children to be helpful and demonstrate great patience with their classmates whose skills didn't equal theirs. That was particularly true in team sports such as softball, volleyball, soccer, basketball, touch football, kickball, and crab ball. I believe we made some progress in those areas. There were many other social and individual skill developments that were taught. I continued that individualized and team skill approach during my time with the East Lansing Public Schools.

It was quite an honor to me when the East Lansing MSU Chamber of Commerce selected me from a number of candidates to be the Young Outstanding Educator of the Year for 1962-63, based upon my teaching performance and an essay I wrote.

Finding a house in East Lansing

In the summer of 1962, there were five members in my family. We needed more space than the two-bedroom apartment we were renting in Spartan Village. I wanted to get situated before I started teaching full time in East Lansing that fall. I made some inquiries about vacant rental property in East Lansing and was turned down on the basis of my skin color.

We saw a small house for rent on the west side of Hagadorn Road, but the owner wouldn't rent to us. Steve Arnest, a science teacher who lived in a house off of East Grand River in East Lansing, tried unsuccessfully to help us move in a vacant house next to him, but the owner wouldn't do it.

Noreese and I had started to look at rental property in the Lansing black community when we received an unexpected telephone call from attorney John Brattin, who lived in East Lansing. He said, "I understand you are trying to find a place to rent in East Lansing." I responded that we had tried unsuccessfully to find rental property. He said, "I have a three-bedroom house for rent at 1403 Beech St. in East Lansing directly across from Edgewood United Church. He mentioned that my family should take a look at the house and if we were interested he would sell it to us on a land contract. We inspected the house and bought it from John for $14,500. We lived there until we moved to Marquette, Mich., in the summer of 1965.

(Dr. Robert L. Green, a black Ph.D. student at Michigan State, also experienced difficulty in 1963

Our house on Beech Street.

obtaining housing for his family in East Lansing. Eventually, he found a house for rent at 221 Durand St., two streets from Beech. An article on the problem of blacks finding housing in the city appeared in the East Lansing *Towne Courier*. Green and I were interviewed about the subject. On. Sept. 16, 1963, the East Lansing City Council appointed a human relations commission to review the issue of open housing in the city. Serving on the commission were Stephanie Barch, Robert L.

Green, Wallace Robertson, Dan Learned, Thomas Schepers, Mahlon Sharp, James Ehinger, H.S. Tien, and Robert Morgan.)

The Beech Street house was a good move for us. Besides being a nice and cozy house for our family, we met some great neighbors. The Schwartz family, Harvey, Kay and their children Tom, Amy, and Lori, were our next-door neighbors. They welcomed us with open arms. They lived at the corner of Hagadorn and Beech. Our children played together and I don't believe there were better neighbors than Harvey and Kay. We communicated and socialized a lot. Even though my family moved around to different cities, our families kept in contact with each other until Kay died in the middle 1980s. We still see Harvey occasionally, but that family will always have a place in our hearts.

In addition, Rev. Truman and Rev. Eleanor Morrison, ministers of Edgewood United Church, befriended us. They often would stop to chat and inquire about our welfare. We were members at University United Methodist Church in East Lansing, but occasionally attended Edgewood. Charles Rock and his family also were good neighbors. They lived on Beech Street and often invited us to their house and their trailer home up north.

Entertainment side career

While I worked at the Secretary of State's office I met John Taliferro, a fellow worker and student at Michigan State. He introduced me to Johnny Green, who was employed at the office as a courier. The three of us formed a business relationship to sponsor entertainment in the Lansing area, something that was missing and which we felt was needed.

We rented an American Legion hall in Mason, about 10 miles from Lansing, and brought in bands from the Detroit area. We charged an admission fee and sold food and soft drinks. We also sold setups (ice and soft drinks) for those who brought their own bottle of liquor. We hoped to earn enough money to defray expenses and reap a profit — but we never did. After four or five engagements we decided it was time to do something different, agreeing to bring in a nationally recognized entertainer. We wanted to see if that would make a difference in the revenue. Ike and Tina Turner was the act we brought to the hall on a Saturday night. The couple had a big hit at the time, "I Know It's Going to Work Out Fine."

What excitement and what a show! We had about 500 people who showed up to watch, but the bottom line was that we lost money. We brought in one more Detroit show, which also lost money, and terminated the business relationship.

Somehow, Ike and Tina Turner got me energized about the possibility of making money with that kind of high-energy entertainment. It turned me on and I became a part-time entrepreneur, forming temporary partnerships with various persons to promote such entertainment. Over a three-year period we brought some of the nation's outstanding entertainers to the state.

We promoted soul brother James Brown on three occasions, twice in Lansing and once in Muskegon. He was the very best entertainer and we never lost any money with him. We promoted Etta James, Solomon Burke, Jerry Butler, Bobby Blue Bland, Ruth Brown, Little Junior Parker, the Motown show featuring Marvin Gaye, The Four Tops, The Shirelles, The Contours, The Marvelettes, Kim Weston, and Willie Tyler and Lester. That is when I developed my passion for music. I used to listen to the blues and country music in Alabama and Randy Records out of Tennessee at night on the radio. I always have liked music, but seeing the entertainers in person really turned me on to music.

We also promoted The Four Seasons ("Big Girls Don't Cry"), Jimmy Gilmer ("Sugar Shack"), Ramsey

Lewis, Little Milton, Bill Doggett, Wilson Pickett, Ben E. King, Joe Tex, and others. I had fun with those promotions and some of the entertainers were quality people and some shows made a profit. I only encountered three problems with the promotions.

Solomon Burke appeared late at a scheduled performance at the Stairway to Stars hall in Flint, without a band. I refunded the customers their money and filed a claim against Burke with the New York Federation of Musicians and was subsequently reimbursed. Etta James, with her big hit, "Stop the Wedding," delayed taking the stage for a 9 p.m. performance at the Lansing Armory, finally appearing before a packed house about 90 minutes late. It was a tense situation that finally worked out all right. Joe Tex arrived two hours late at the Lansing Armory. He promised to give a makeup date in Flint, but never did. All the other entertainers were strictly business and fully complied with terms of their contract.

In the spring of 1965 I met a barber named Robert "Bobby" Husband of Lansing. He was aware of my promotional activities and invited me to his home to listen to some songs he had written. I liked one or two of them and felt with more work they had commercial appeal. Bobby also contacted an up and coming young entrepreneur, Joel Ferguson. The three of us consulted an attorney to form a musical entertainment corporation. The attorney advised us that we should engage the services of an accountant instead of an attorney, which we planned to do.

Northern Michigan U. comes calling

However, in May I was recruited by Northern Michigan University to work in its Women's Job Corps center on campus. Richard Lutzke, a former MSU student and a next-door neighbor in Spartan Village and an industrial arts major recommended me for the job. I

CABLE ADDRESS
UNICTRACT

MAKE ALL DEPOSITS PAYABLE TO:

UNIVERSAL ATTRACTIONS, INC.
200 WEST 57th STREET, NEW YORK, N. Y. 10019
JUdson 2-7575

Nº 9039

(DA)

AMERICAN FEDERATION OF MUSICIANS Local Number 252

THIS CONTRACT for the personal services of musicians, made this **9th** day of **JUNE** , 19 **65** ,

between the undersigned employer (hereinafter called the employer) and **TEN (10)** musicians (hereinafter called employees) represented by the undersigned representative. (Including Leader)

WITNESSETH, That the employer employs the personal services of the employees, as musicians severally, and the employees severally, through their representative, agree to render collectively to the employer services as musicians in the orchestra under the leadership of

Name and Place of Engagement **JAMES BROWN & FAMOUS FLAMES ORCH. & REVUE** , according to the following terms and conditions:

Name and Address of Place of Engagement **AUDITORIUM, MUSKEGON, MICH.** L C Walker Arena

Date(s) of employment **AUGUST 21, 1965**

Hours of employment **9pm-1am**

ATTACHED RIDER BINDING PART OF THIS CONTRACT

L.C. WALKER ARENA, MUSKEGON, MICH.

DEPOSIT RECEIVED

1125 00 7/9/6

Type of engagement (specify whether dance, stage show, banquet, etc.) **show & dance**

Employer agrees to furnish a public address system in perfect working condition and assume

all operating costs. **SIGNED CONTRACT MUST BE RETURNED TO THIS OFFICE IMMEDIATELY**
X
The employer is hereby given an option to extend this agreement for a period of weeks beyond the original term thereof.
Said option can be made effective only by written notice from the employer to the employees not later than days prior to the expiration of said original term that he claims and exercises said option.

PRICE AGREED UPON $ **3000.00 guarantee +50% privileges of net receipts over $6000**
(Terms and Amount)

This price includes expenses agreed to be reimbursed by the employer in accordance with the attached schedule, or a schedule to be furnished the employer on or before the date of engagement.

To be paid **deposit immediately, Bal. @intermission, @age @discretion of rd.**
$1125.00 (Specify When Payments Are to Be Made) **mgr.**

ADDITIONAL TERMS AND CONDITIONS

ATTACHED RIDER BINDING PART OF THIS CONTRACT:

MINIMUM ADVANCE TICKET $2.50
MINIMUM TICKET AT DOOR $3.00
IN THE EVENT PROMOTER CHARGES LESS THAN THESE PRICES, HE WILL BE
CHARGED THE DIFFERENCE BETWEEN HIS PRICE AND THE STIPULATED $2.50
ADVANCE TICKET AND $3.00 AT THE DOOR.

Name of Employer **CLARENCE UNDERWOOD** Accepted by Employer

Street Address **1403 Beech St.,** Accepted

City **E. Lansing** State **Mich.** Address
(Orchestra Leader)

Phone By
(Representatives of Employees)

If this contract is made by a licensed booking agent, there must be inserted on the reverse side of the contract the name, address and telephone number of the collecting agent of the local union in whose jurisdiction the engagement is to be performed.
FORM B-2 Printed in U.S.A.

This is a copy of the entertainment contract with James Brown, who we booked into the Walker Arena in Muskegon in June 1965.

was appointed as the recreational director for the center. I resigned from East Lansing Public Schools and moved my family to Marquette, Mich., in late June 1965. We rented a house at 135 Hewitt Street.

We had 300 young women between the ages of 16-

21. They were high school dropouts and some were socially maladjusted. My primary responsibilities were to get the women involved in social, cultural, and recreational activities to broaden their skill levels in those areas. The students were engaged in a comprehensive structured educational/skill development program during the daytime. My recreational program was in the evening and on the weekends.

We took bus trips to various parts of the Upper Peninsula, including Mackinac Island, Taquahmenon Falls, Iron Mountain, St. Ignace, all in Michigan, plus Canada. We sponsored monthly dances and would hire a band from Chicago and invite as our guests airmen from the K.I. Sawyer Air Force Base. All the dances were peaceful and fun, but someone at the university complained about the airmen being on campus, so the dances were terminated. The women didn't want to dance with each other and the regular students on campus didn't accept the Job Corps women as their equals.

Some Marquette citizens didn't accept the young women either. We frequently received calls from folks in the community alleging that a Job Corps woman had stepped on their flowers, broken a window, or something else. We would investigate and find that the alleged incident occurred when the women were enrolled in class. Half of the 300 women were black and Hispanic. Marquette was 99.9 percent white. As far as I know, only three black families lived in the community: Dr. Dave Dickson, an English professor at the university, and his family; a gentleman who shined shoes at a local bank; and the Underwoods.

Our son, Alvin, was a third-grader in the elementary school and would come home claiming that the white children were calling him derogatory names in school. He claimed he was being called nigger and a burnt hamburger. Noreese and I kept encouraging him to simply ignore the students and tell the teacher when he was called such names. He continued to complain about the incidents. We could see the intimidation was affecting him.

The elementary school children were permitted to go home for lunch. One day I left work to put myself in a surveillance position to watch Alvin as he left school and headed home for lunch. I observed six or seven children walking along beside him yelling at him. Alvin appeared to be intimidated and was trying to walk fast ahead of them with his fist clenched. He was very frightened and I couldn't take it anymore. I went to the principal and made a complaint. I don't believe it happened again. I don't recall any problem in school with Jackie, who was in the fifth grade, or with David, who was in kindergarten.

Marquette was by far the coldest place I ever lived. The first summer there was a July 4 parade. We had a Job Corps float and had to wear gloves and overcoats to keep warm. The summers usually end the middle of August. In the two years we lived there, it snowed every day beginning in October and running until April. The snow banks would be five to seven feet high.

Noreese used to buy the freshest whitefish from the fish market on Friday mornings. We had it for dinner and the fish was some good eating. The other food we liked was pasties. There were different type pasties but we normally ate the ones that were made out of potatoes and ground beef inside of a bread wrap. We would eat them with ketchup and they were delicious.

My immediate supervisor in the Job Corps center was Bill Green, the director of student services. The overall director was Dr. Bert Jones. Green often would ask me to accompany him to his cottage. With my evenings and weekends occupied by my recreational schedule, I never took the time to do so.

Racism at a rural tavern

On April 1, 1967, Green asked me again to go with him to his cottage. Since Noreese and I had made the decision to return to the East Lansing schools in the fall, it was probably my last chance to go. Bill, his father, and I drove to the cottage, which appeared to be 15 to 20 miles from Marquette. We left at 10:30 a.m. in two vehicles. Bill and I rode in his car and Bill's father followed in his own vehicle. We arrived at the cottage shortly after 11 a.m. and went inside. It was cold and Bill's father offered to make some coffee. Bill and his father had one cup each. I declined. We hung around for 20-30 minutes, then Bill and I left in his car and his father stayed there to lock up. As we drove away, Bill suggested we go have a beer.

We arrived at the Halfway Tavern close to noon. As we entered, I saw two college-aged men playing pool. Green and I sat at the bar and Bill asked the bartender to bring two Stroh's beers. The bartender faced us from behind the bar. He pointed to Bill and said, "I can serve you but I cannot serve him (pointing to me) because he is already drunk." Bill asked him to repeat what he had said and the bartender repeated his assertion. Green began cussing at the bartender and denied that I had been drinking.

I asked Bill to calm down and step outside, but he became belligerent and again I asked him to step outside. As we exited the tavern, Green scolded me and wanted to know why I wanted to go outside. I said, "You and I both know that neither of us has had anything to drink. Arguing with the bartender will do no good. Let's go to the city of Marquette State Police post and get a Breathalyzer test."

When we arrived at the state police post we told the officer what had happened and asked for the Breathalyzer. The state policeman said, "It is obvious you guys have not been drinking and I will not administer such a test to you." I then requested to file a formal complaint against the Halfway Tavern and the bartender. The complaint was registered and a jury trial was held in Marquette Township in the court of the magistrate on April 27, 1967.

The jury found the defendant and bar owner, Stanley Hudson, not guilty on the basis that I was never refused a beer because I had never asked for one. Hudson's attorney twisted things around claiming Green was refused because he had been drinking. This was a stunning and technical decision. On May 4, 1967, I mailed a letter to the Michigan Civil Rights Commission making it aware of the case. It was my understanding that the commission did investigate and accepted an agreement from Hudson that he would never again refuse services to a black person.

This is a copy of my letter to the commission:

135 W. Hewitt
Marquette, Michigan
May 4, 1967

Michigan Civil Rights Commission
1116 South Washington Avenue
Lansing, Michigan

Gentlemen:

This is written to inform you of a case of what I consider a gross violation of my civil rights here in Marquette. I am a Negro.

You should know that this case was recently tried in Marquette Justice Court. The defendant was charged with a civil rights violation and acquitted by a jury. Perhaps it is too late to bring this case to your attention but just for the record I wish to register an official complaint with your office for your consideration.

On Saturday, April 1, 1967, Mr. William Green, who is white, a co-worker, and lives in Marquette, just as I do, invited me to accompany him to his cabin. It was located on County Road 950 in Marquette. We arrived there around 11:05 a.m. and left around 11:40 a.m. While there, Mr. Green had a cup of coffee. I did not drink anything.

After we left, Mr. Green suggested that we go to a tavern and have one beer before returning to our homes. He drove to a tavern by the name of the "Halfway Tavern." It was located on County Road 550 approximately one mile from Mr. Green's cabin.

We entered the tavern around noon and sat at the far end of the bar away from the front door. The bartender, Mr. Hudson, approached us from behind the bar and asked if he could help us. Mr. Green ordered two Stroh's beers, one for each of us. Mr. Hudson, the bartender, told Mr. Green, "I can serve you," pointing to Mr. Green, "but I cannot serve him," pointing to me, "because he is already drunk." At this moment, Mr. Green told Mr. Hudson, "You must be kidding." Mr. Hudson replied, "No, I am not kidding. I can serve you but I can't serve him," pointing to me, "because he is already drunk."

Without making any fanfare, I suggested to Mr. Green that we leave the tavern. As we left, I suggested to Mr. Green that we go directly to the Marquette State Police Post to file a complaint against Mr. Hudson, and also request the breath test. After some discussion with the state policemen, we were told that it was obvious that neither Mr. Green nor I had been drinking and there was no need to administer a breath test to us.

The case was brought to court last Friday, a jury trial in the Marquette Township Justice Court with Justice George Fezzey presiding. The prosecuting witnesses presented the case to the jury just as I have stated herein. However, the testimonies of the defense witnesses were grossly inaccurate. Their entire defense was completely reversed from what actually happened in the tavern. The defense claimed that Mr. Green, and not myself, was refused service in the tavern. The defense claimed that Mr. Green had been drinking prior to entering the bar. The defense claimed that I was never refused service because I never placed an order for a beer with the bartender. The prosecutor again reiterated the case to the jury just as it happened in the bar. That Mr. Hudson told Mr. Green after ordering two beers that I can serve you, pointing to Mr. Green, but I can't serve him, pointing to myself. The jury, after deliberating for little over an hour, acquitted Mr. Hudson of the charge.

I am enclosing two confusing newspaper accounts of the case that appeared in the Marquette Mining Journal recently for your information.

I contend that the only reason I was refused service by Mr. Hudson in the Halfway Tavern on April 1 was because I am a Negro. Mr. Green, white, was not refused service in the tavern. Mr. Hudson twice stated to Mr. Green, "I can serve you, but I can't serve him, because he is already drunk." As I mentioned earlier and later verified by the Marquette State Police, I had not been drinking anything, including water, prior to entering the tavern.

This was not a test case for the City of Marquette. Two sincere people went to a public facility expecting to be accommodated by the proprietor, but I was refused service only because I am a Negro. I contend that if two whites had entered the bar they would have been served.

Any consideration given on the above case will be greatly appreciated.

Thank you.

Sincerely,

Clarence Underwood Jr.

As I was winding down my two-year stint at Northern Michigan in the spring of 1967, university vice president Tom Cook contacted me and said a friend of his who worked for the University of Wisconsin extension in Madison, Robert Dick, was interested in hiring someone with my qualifications. I asked for more details and Cook said he didn't know anymore then but if he should get more information he would let me know. He later told me the job still had not been defined.

I had committed myself to return to a teaching position in the East Lansing Public School system in August 1967. I had remained in contact with the new superintendent, Dr. Charles Young. He would call occasionally at my home to check on me. I appreciated our relationship.

I would stop off in Chicago that summer en route to East Lansing to work temporarily in a program administered by Dr. Robert L. Green. He, with the support of Dr. Martin Luther King, had been awarded a $100,000 grant to teach disadvantaged black adults how to read and write. The ultimate objective was to place those people in positions of employment. Dr. Green employed me as the job placement director. The program was well structured and the employees worked diligently to try and meet the program objectives. I worked in the program for eight weeks. We had modest success.

Detour to Milwaukee

We bought a three-bedroom house at 165 Gunson Street in East Lansing. Noreese and the children had moved there in June. We had some remodeling done, removing a wall to expand the living room. We had settled down by the time school opened in the fall. I resumed teaching elementary phys ed classes and was really enjoying the children. My family was getting re-acclimated to the community.

In October 1967, I received a telephone call from

Our house on Gunson Street in East Lansing

Robert Dick. He was the person Cook had mentioned to me at Northern Michigan who was trying to get a new job developed for the Milwaukee area. The university had a county extension office in Wawatoosa, a suburb of Milwaukee. Dick told me the job had, in fact, been established. It was for an assistant professor and agent who would work with urban youth.

I told Dick it wouldn't be fair to my family, the school district, and the East Lansing children if I were to pull up stakes again so soon and leave the community. He said he understood my predicament and explained that the youth situation in black Milwaukee was urgent and volatile. He said the university wanted to be pro-active now before things got worse. That was the time of the Civil Rights Movement and urban unrest was rampant. Milwaukee was having its problems with militant groups such as the Black Commandos, which was advised by a white Roman Catholic priest, the Rev. James Groppi.

Dick suggested that if I were interested he would write a letter to the East Lansing school superintendent, Charles Young, and explain the situation to him. I said he should try and find out whether Young would be interested in releasing me from my contract. I found myself in a most uncomfortable dilemma: On one hand I wanted to settle down in East Lansing and give my family some stability, and on the other hand the position in Milwaukee greatly appealed to me. Young presented Dick's letter to the board of education, which reluctantly released me from my contract on Jan. 26.

It wasn't an easy choice for me. I was hoping the school board would help make my decision easier by saying no to the release request. The children in East Lansing were truly beautiful and genuinely appreciated the challenging and fun physical education program I had developed. It was energizing for me to meet their eagerness each day.

During the 30 minutes I spent with each class twice a week I could easily detect which child needed a pat on the back, which ones needed some encouragement, who needed to have their ego adjusted, and who needed their ego stroked. I also could detect which child was being isolated by his or her classmates, or who was too intimidated to try some new game or activity because of fear of being ridiculed by the other students.

I used physical education classes as an active laboratory to address each of the issues with the children in every class and at every school. I would lie awake at night planning how I was going to help each student with their issues and made doubly sure I never embarrassed a child in front of his peers or privately. Often I would openly praise a child for trying something he or she was fearful of doing. I would challenge strong, egotistic children to get it right, to do their very best. I used all kinds of methods to teach the children, whom I loved.

Yet as much as I was reluctant to leave East Lansing again, I realized that I needed to take a more active role in the Civil Rights Movement to help minimize additional problems.

I kissed and hugged my family members and left by car for Milwaukee on Sunday morning, Jan. 28. It was a painful and tearful departure. They would join me in June when school ended for the year. I was to report to work Monday morning to Stanley Rynearson, chairman of community programs in Milwaukee County. His office and my new office would be at 9035-A Watertown Plank Road in Wawatoosa.

As I loaded my car to leave, I placed a wooden rod horizontally across the back windows, slightly rolled down, to hang my suits, sport coats and shirts. I must have had 30 pieces of clothing hanging on the rod, plus there were shoes and boxes on the floor and in the trunk.

Ripped off on first day

I didn't have a place to stay in Milwaukee. I planned to rent a hotel room for a day or two until I could find a room to rent. I drove to the downtown section of Wisconsin Avenue. I parked in front of what appeared to be a first-class hotel. It must have been around 3:30 p.m. I got out of the car, locked it and entered to register for a room. I must have been in the hotel 10 minutes, just long enough to register, then I got the surprise of my life when I returned to my car. The driver side back window was shattered and all of my clothes were taken. It was so devastating. For the first time in my life I knew the feeling of depression.

I returned to the hotel and reported the incident and called the police. Two officers arrived, examined the car and took a statement from me. I never did hear anything else from them and I guess I should not have expected more. It took several months of negotiating with All State Insurance Co. I had to get statements from J.W. Knapp's Department Store and other clothiers to verify my claims. Eventually they were settled. But when the only clothes you have left are what you are wearing, several months can be a long time.

I met Rynearson in his office at 8 a.m. Monday. He appeared to be a nice man. He was slightly taller than me and was a physical fitness enthusiast. He introduced me to the other employees, including a home economist, Karen Stamm; a financial planner; and a few other experts. Another employee, a black lawyer, had his office in the center of the black commercial district.

Stan put my office next to his. He told me the biggest problem was that there were very few programs in Milwaukee designed to service the needs of black youth. He mentioned there was heightened racial tension in the city and the university wanted to do something to defuse the situation, but didn't know what it should do. He indicated that I would work generally without a job description and be responsible for identifying what role the university should have in the black community with youth. Then my job description would be defined.

My initial reaction was, what have I gotten myself into? East Lansing looked more appealing, but I went to work, met with civic and church leaders, organizations, parents, and young school children. I wanted to get their take on what was going on in Milwaukee and determine the needs of the children and youth.

I discovered that the city was basically divided along racial lines. Wisconsin Avenue was the dividing line between the north side, where the majority of blacks lived, and the south side, where most white folks lived. It clearly had vestiges of Alabama, South Carolina, North Carolina, Illinois, and Michigan.

I was learning fast that racism exists everywhere and it is both insidious and overt. It is a very tough fight because sometimes you don't know with whom you are dealing. The Bible explains that God judges man by what's in his heart, while man judges on the basis of outward appearance. Man seldom knows with whom he is dealing because what he sees outwardly could be a mask, a cover-up. It takes more intimate relationship over time to get to know a person fairly well. Even then some people never learn about each other.

What was frightening about Milwaukee, which I hadn't observed in any other city, was the number of white policemen who drove through the black community with shotguns and rifles showing from the front windshields. During my time there I never saw a black policeman in the black community.

The public schools usually let out at 3 p.m. Unless students were involved in an extracurricular activity, there wasn't anything for them to do. I spent days observing many young children and youth in the age range of 10-18 hanging around the pool rooms, bars, and restaurants in the black community. There were prostitutes, pimps, and destitute people in the area. I was 35 years old then and it wasn't a section for me to be in because I never have enjoyed hanging around bars. I was there doing research for my job. But it was sad to see so many young kids hanging around with nothing to do.

One Saturday night the black lawyer who worked for the university extension office and whose office was in the black commercial section asked me to baby-sit for his children while he and his wife went to a social function. They got home close to midnight. On my way home I stopped at what I considered the best upscale black bar in the area. I hadn't been there before, but thought I'd go in, have a beer and leave.

I ordered a beer and the black bartender, who was the only person there, challenged me to a pinball contest. I said I wasn't interested, but he kept insisting that I participate. Finally, I got him to leave me alone by agreeing to play one game. He put a wager on it and if I won he would buy me a beer. If he won I would buy him a shot of liquor. Well, I knew I wouldn't be playing more than a game or two so I went for it.

I won the first game and the bartender paid for the beer I had already ordered. I won the second game and could see what was coming next. Sure enough, he won the third and fourth games and I paid him for two shots. He was collecting bets for the most expensive liquor in the bar, Chivas Regal. I didn't see him drink any of it. He was pocketing the money. I told him I was quitting and leaving and the bartender told me I couldn't leave. He became rather perturbed because I was leaving and he kept insisting I couldn't leave. At that moment a couple came into the bar and I left in a flash. I don't know what would have happened if the couple hadn't arrived. It was a situation that I never wanted to be in again.

Going into bars or bar hopping never has been something I enjoyed doing. The incident further reminded me to stay out of bars. I consulted with my lawyer friend about reporting the incident to the police, but he advised that without a witness it would come down to my word against the bartender's and that I should drop it.

Proposals go nowhere

By March I had formulated a proposal outlining my role and I presented it to Rynearson. I proposed that the extension services sponsor an urban 4-H program for black youth in Milwaukee, which would encompass youth from ages 10-19. It would operate under the leadership of paid coordinators and volunteer adults out of church sites or other community facilities.

The program would be designed for the needs of youth, providing sustained instruction in educational, cultural, recreational, and work-related projects. It would develop youth skills and leadership qualities and would operate after school and on weekends.

Rynearson tried to find funding for the proposal from the university and from the Milwaukee County executive director's office. He was unsuccessful, being told that all funds had been allocated for the year. That was disappointing because I was hired in January without a job description. I presented the proposal in March and surely they should have known that it would take money to address the gigantic and super complex problems with the urban youth.

I didn't create a clamor. Instead, I went back to work, continuing to meet and talk with parents and community leaders. I discussed with some youths the possibility of forming an organization to help other youths. There was an abandoned auto service garage near the inner city. It had nearly 20,000 feet of floor space. I contacted the owner and revealed my plans. I wanted the university to remodel the facility to the extent where it could be made into a teen-age center that we could use for roller-skating and dance parties. There would be a library and study rooms where students could get tutoring.

The youth group would operate the center. It would sell refreshments and charge admissions for dances and roller-skating parties. The owner agreed to rent the building for a nominal fee. The youth group and their parents were very excited over the proposal and I presented it to Rynearson.

However, once again the university and Milwaukee County executive office had no funds available. That was the straw that broke the camel's back as far as I was concerned. I felt as though I was being exploited. I couldn't understand why I was hired or what the university wanted me to do. Although I could understand that funds allocated the previous July may not have been available in the spring, I couldn't understand the absence of a verbal commitment for future funding.

I had devoted considerable time in the black community interacting with many different individuals and groups to sell the university's image in a positive manner, putting my credibility on the line for the university. In the end, I couldn't deliver on hopes that I had engendered amongst the people and I didn't want to continue in the role, so I resigned effective May 11, 1968. The university tried to retain me by offering various inducements, such as tenure, relocation of my family, and a salary boost. I was grateful for those efforts, but my mind was made up to leave Milwaukee.

Another challenge I encountered there was getting acquainted with some of the black militant groups. One of them was the Black Commandos, the group made famous by Father Groppi. He was their advisor for a while in the mid-'60s.

The Black Commandos had the reputation of speaking vociferously against racism and taking a stand for protecting the black community. Members were college aged and had a variety of backgrounds. I found them to be courageous and motivated to do what was right for the black community. I befriended some of them, trying to assist by either finding them meaningful employment or encouraging their enrollment in colleges. I was working directly with a few of them when I resigned from the university extension.

Doris Stacy, assistant dean for student services at Wisconsin-Milwaukee, was the administrator over a program named in her honor, Project STAY, which was designed to assist the welfare of minority students and to retain them at the university. I worked with her to recruit some of the Commandos and we were successful in getting a few to complete the admissions application. The process was pending as I left the area.

Dr. Martin Luther King assassinated

On April 4, 1968, I left work and drove to North First Street where I was renting a room in a house owned by Mrs. McIvory, who was in her late 60s. She was a good Christian lady and we often would engage in various discussions on current issues. I had just arrived and was preparing to call my wife when a special announcement came over the television. Dan Rather was reporting that

Dr. Martin Luther King Jr. had been shot on a balcony of the Lorraine Motel in Memphis, Tenn. A few moments later Rather said King was dead.

I finished the call to my wife and talked to our children. I wanted to be with them in the worst way. Besides being concerned about their personal safety, as a black man I felt insecure over the horrendous calamity of our black leader having been shot to death by a white man. There was no other reason for King's death other than hate and raw racism.

Richard Lutzke, my good friend at Northern Michigan, called to express his anger and regret over the senseless shooting. Ever since I first met he and his family in Spartan Village as a student at Michigan State he practiced fairness to all people. His call meant so much to me. His wife Betty, son Jim, and daughter Kathleen were good people.

The following evening there was a meeting called by some of the militant leaders in the black community to discuss what course of action blacks should take in Milwaukee to respond to the tragic event. Everybody was angry and grieving. The urge to do something out of frustration and the need to retaliate was extremely strong among the people assembled in the room that night. There were many heated suggestions and debates, with two of them being most prominent.

One suggestion was to recommend to the black community to protest the King killing by taking in unison one day off from work. The purpose was to temporarily impair the white businesses and employers. I was opposed to that idea because few black folks could afford to take a day off unless they used sick or vacation time. I couldn't understand how one day off from work would impair or disrupt the white community, with its vast resources.

The second suggestion was for blacks to form a human fence on each of the entranceways to the Milwaukee downtown section so whites could not get to work on a certain day. I know we all were frustrated and wanted desperately to send a public message. We wanted whites to know we were sick of racism and dehumanizing treatment from them, but the human chains on the ingresses were not the proper response. The thing that was most obvious to me then in Milwaukee and every other city I had lived in was that blacks generally were not empowered with authority. We were not in top leadership positions and we were mostly consumers. We didn't own any major financial institutions, department stores, utility companies, etc. So if the white merchants could not drive to their businesses to sell to blacks, who's hurting whom?

So what I proposed was that we should all go to work on that certain day and contribute a portion of that day's wages to a fund to start owning something constructive. I felt that suggestion, which wasn't accepted, would have done more than any of the others to get progress moving forward. To the best of my knowledge, none of the suggestions were implemented. If they were, it was done after I left the area. When I left the meeting and walked outside, I was struck by the number of police cars with shotguns very visible from the windshields, driving up and down the street. It was an intimidating sight.

I formally submitted my letter of resignation to Rynearson on April 14, to become effective May 11. It had been fixed in my mind to put it in writing ever since my last proposal was turned down in early April. I had mentioned my intentions to Stan, but was trying to wrap up a number of things and hadn't gotten around to writing the resignation letter.

Opportunity knocks at right time

A couple days after telling of my intention to resign, I got a phone call from Donald Lillrose, personnel director for the Michigan Department of Education in Lansing. I had visited him in his office on the fifth floor of the Michigan National Tower Building in 1964 during a day in which I visited two or three places in search of a job that paid more than that of my teaching position. We had a good visit, but he concluded that my educational experiences then weren't expansive enough to qualify me for one of their consultant positions. He asked me to complete an employment application and he would keep it on file. I figured I'd never hear from him again.

When he called in April he said he had been trying to track me down but every employer he called told him I had recently resigned. Lillrose said his department had an open position for an educational consultant, a job that would work in the compensatory education Title I program. I interviewed for the job with a core group of administrators and got a job offer April 17, with a starting date of May 13, at a salary of $12,820. I was earning $11,300 at the University of Wisconsin Extension Services. Soon I was back home with my family, which was waiting for the school year to end to join me in Milwaukee. I was grateful to Robert Dick and the University of Wisconsin Extension Services for having given me an opportunity to work in the Milwaukee area, but I was glad to return home with my family.

Bobby Husband and I soon regrouped on our music interests. He had written a new song and wanted me to hear it. We worked in his basement on the weekends, refining some of our previously written songs, as well as developing new ones. One of his songs had a good beat and we titled it, "Can't Help Myself." I identified a Lansing vocalist, Betty Johnson, to work with us.

After many rehearsals we decided to record the song. I wrote the flip side, "Opportunity Knocks Only Once." We engaged the services of a backup vocal group from Lansing and recorded the songs in October 1968 at the United Studios in Detroit. Miller Brisker, one of Aretha Franklin's road musicians, did the arrangements.

101

"Can't Help Myself" rose on the Lansing radio charts to No. 1, both at WILS and WJIM. It sold about 5,000 copies. Later on, Husband was the vocalist on another recording of songs we had written, "Man's Best Friend is a Woman," and the flip side, "Don't Lose Faith in Love." They were less successful. We continued to write additional songs but never wrote another one to our satisfaction that measured up to "Can't Help Myself." My love for music would continue throughout my lifetime.

CHAPTER 3:

MSU CAREER BEGINS

Opportunity knocks — after 'token' trial run

It is strange how a person's life can turn on a dime because of a chain reaction triggered by an unfortunate and unforeseen event. The regrettable stroke suffered by Michigan State Athletics Director Clarence "Biggie" Munn in 1971 provided the opportunity for me to return to my alma mater.

Today I can sit back and contemplate a rewarding three-decade career with the MSU athletic department and Big Ten Conference office, replete with the excitement, drama, and occasional controversy concomitant with big-time collegiate athletics. Yet for a time it seemed my career rewards, though satisfying, would be more mundane and confined to memories spent with the Michigan Department of Education and other great educational institutions.

But now I am able to chronicle 30 years of Spartans' athletics ups and downs from a seat at the head of the table, having entered in 1972 through the *front door* after Munn suffered a stroke and had to resign, prompting the promotion of assistant director Burt Smith to the athletics director's job — and providing an opportunity for me.

With few qualms, I had walked away from a career with the athletics department two years earlier and now I was getting a second chance at Michigan State, where I was an undergraduate and walk-on football player in the mid-'50s. In 1970 I abandoned an eight-month sojourn at MSU, which had whisked me through the athletic department as a result of demands from MSU black athletes in the wake of civil rights pressures that built up following the assassination of Dr. Martin Luther King in 1968.

My first "career" in the Michigan State Department of Athletics began in August 1969 when I left my educational consultant's job with the Michigan Department of Education to become an assistant ticket manager and also to help athletics academic counselor Smith, who was then the assistant athletics director and counsel to student-athletes. I was supposed to assist him with counseling black student-athletes, but I soon discovered that I was a "token" black who had few responsibilities and who was not particularly accepted by others in the department.

MSU ticket manager and a friend, Bill Beardsley, who interviewed me for the job, said the department was anticipating building an all-events center (what now is the Jack Breslin Student Events Center) — if a student referendum supported the proposal. I was to become manager of that facility.

Students defeated the referendum in the winter term of 1970 and with it my new managerial position vanished. However, it would not have been of much consequence to me if I had been given the opportunity to counsel black athletes. I cherished being in a position to have an important impact on their lives, a passion that stayed with me throughout my career.

Yet during those few months of that early MSU experience, Smith never shared his academic counseling

The Jack Breslin Center was officially dedicated Nov. 9, 1989, but was on the agenda in 1969 when I first joined the Spartans' staff with a promise that I would be the building's manager. But students defeated the initiative in a 1970 referendum.

work with me, even though I was able and had the time. I could sometimes finish my ticket office responsibilities in an hour. Munn even had me wandering through Jenison Field House and the men's intramural building once a month noting where the burned out light bulbs were located.

Isolation and few responsibilities

When students rejected the events center in 1970 it became clear to me that my already narrow role in the department was waning. I was becoming bored and frustrated both with the lack of responsibility and the isolation within the department.

An example of that isolation was evident during football season. All of the athletics administrators would travel with the team to the away games. *I never was invited.* In fact, I was the only person in athletics administration who never traveled on those trips.

Then, there were house parties given by athletics department staff members after home games. Again, all the administrators and their spouses were invited except for my wife and me. I *never was included* or extended an invitation. All was not negative, however. There were some head coaches who befriended me: baseball coach Danny Litwhiler, track coach Fran Dittrich and cross country coach James Gibbard, men's tennis coach Stan Droback, men's gymnastics coach George Szypula, men's golf coach Bruce Fossum, and basketball coach Gus Ganakas.

Perhaps the shunning had something to do with the climate of the times. After James Earl Ray assassinated Dr. King on April 4, 1968, in Memphis, Tenn., black student-athletes, sensitive to the civil rights movement in the South and most of the country, began to organize on their respective campuses and make demands for fair treatment from their administrations.

More than a hundred institutions with collegiate athletics programs were hit with demands — from the very student-athletes they had recruited, mostly for the sports of football, basketball, and track. At some universities there were more black athletes on campus than all other black students put together.

Generally, the athletes conducted protests because they believed they were isolated on the predominantly white campuses. Having personally experienced the isolation I could relate to their concerns. They were not encouraged to graduate and were given classes designed strictly for keeping them eligible for their sports, not with any goal towards helping them to receive their degrees. The lack of care and diligence was of grave concern to me as an educator. I had deep sentiments for the welfare of students.

Also during that time, black student-athletes in football and basketball, unlike their white teammates, didn't have the opportunity of playing every position on their teams. Most coaches in the '60s practiced a "stacking" system, which restricted black athletes to certain positions. For instance, even if a black recruit was an All-America quarterback in high school, if he was black, he was destined to be assigned to play defensive back, tailback, or wide receiver in college. If there were other black players starting already at those positions, the former high school quarterback would find himself "stacked up" behind them. He had to wait until it was his turn to play at one of those positions, which usually didn't happen until the starter either left school, became ineligible, or was injured.

Another concern that led to black student-athletes' protests in the mid-'60s was the dearth of black female students on the campuses. Unlike it is today, there weren't many black students enrolled at the university in the 1960s. Many of the black students were athletes who were popular on campus. Yet it wasn't generally acceptable in society for blacks and whites to date each other. If black athletes were seen dating white female students, those athletes were ostracized by the white coaches and were penalized in various ways.

Nationally, black student-athletes made the following general demands of universities:

- More black students must be enrolled.
- Blacks should be added to the cheerleader squads.
- Black counselors should be hired for the athletics departments.

Michigan State was hit by similar demands by the Black Student-Athlete Alliance, headed by Nigel Goodison, an All-America soccer player. It was that protest that resulted in my being offered the job in the athletics department in 1969.

Education job honed future MSU skills

Prior to that, I was with the Michigan Department of Education from 1968-69 working as an educational consultant in the state-administered Federal Elementary

107

Secondary Educational Act, commonly called Title I. I was assigned to work with eligible public schools in the southwest part of the state, covering districts from Battle Creek to Buffalo, Mich.

It was a great position that — like the one I was to accept soon afterwards with the same employer — unknowingly prepared me for duties that would come when I moved to MSU. To this day I am grateful to the administrators who gave me the opportunity to work there: Personnel Director Donald Lillrose; Lou Koscis, the chief administrator; Ferris Crawford, bureau chief; State Superintendent Ira Polley; deputy associate superintendent Leon Waskins; Bob Kerr, deputy superintendent for business; Norman Berkowitz, assistant superintendent; and Kenneth Swanson, my immediate supervisor. There were many other capable colleagues with whom I enjoyed working in that position and others working in different units within the department.

There were nine consultants in my unit, each of us assigned to a different part of the state. The job entailed reviewing program proposals from public schools that were applying for funds for a number of economically and educationally disadvantaged students. It was my responsibility to review the proposals in my district to insure they complied with state and federal guidelines (not unlike years later seeing to it that Michigan State complied with NCAA regulations).

Also, I recommended approval or denied the proposals and made site visits to the schools to validate their programs. Prior to that job I was with the University of Wisconsin, a job I will mention later.

In May 1969 I got a call from Beardsley, the Spartan ticket manager. I had been the physical education teacher for two of his sons in the East Lansing Public Schools system from 1961-65. I, with my family, also had served as a family camp counselor at Pilgrim Haven in South Haven, Mich., during a week for two summers each, with Bill and his lovely family: wife, Jean; daughter,

Paula; sons, Richard, Scott, and Doug. We had fun together.

We had lunch at a Lansing restaurant several times over a few months to talk about a job possibility in the athletics department at Michigan State. He told me about the planned all-events center, which would replace Jenison Field House as the home of Spartan basketball, as well as be a venue for concerts and other student activities pending the passage of the referendum. In the interim I would be an assistant ticket manager and supposedly work with Burt Smith in counseling black student-athletes.

I was earning $14,800 in my state job. MSU offered $14,000. It was not a tough decision to take the $800 pay cut because I was attracted to the promise of being able to help and counsel the black student-athletes.

As a former student-athlete in football for the Spartans during the 1955 season I recognized the need to have someone in the position who had the courage and sensitivity to help direct their lives. Many of my classmates and friends at MSU during my undergraduate days were black athletes, so I was well aware of the problems and needs of black athletes. I accepted the position and resigned from the Michigan Department of Education in August 1969.

Bill Beardsley

My office on campus was in the athletics ticket office. Beardsley was a good supervisor and we worked well together, but it didn't take long for me to realize how underutilized and underemployed I was. It certainly was a more relaxed job than any I had experienced. I had spent eight years teaching and working with children in crisis-oriented programs. My responsibilities in the athletics ticket office weren't challenging. I started to feel restless about going to work each day.

A waste of time — and university money

The ticket office had six to eight full and part-time employees. I counted and packaged tickets like everyone else. I accompanied Bill as he made his rounds on campus to make deposits with the office of the cashier and to deliver tickets to central administrators. He tried to do everything possible to keep me engaged in the ticket office, but there were many days when I would finish my work in one hour and spend the rest of the time reading newspapers and magazines. I felt I was wasting my time, not to mention the university's money.

There was one bright spot then in my association with the university: Vice President Jack Breslin. He was subsequently promoted to executive vice president when Dr. Clifton Wharton was named president in 1970. He was a friend of Beardsley and the three of us played racquetball each night in Jenison. Jack was highly competitive, tough to beat, and by far the best of the three of us in our cutthroat games.

Breslin was the vice president who had oversight responsibility for the athletics department. Theoretically, he was the boss. But the reporting lines between popular football coach Duffy Daugherty and athletics director Munn were split, Duffy reporting to the president of the university and Biggie reporting to vice president Breslin. Under that arrangement, most employees saw Daugherty as having the upper hand. The split had gone on for some time, I believe, when Munn resigned as head football coach in 1953 to become athletics director.

Munn was the American Football Coaches Association Coach of the Year in 1952 and his 1953

Spartans beat UCLA 28-20 in the Rose Bowl game. Munn, who was named to the College Football Hall of Fame in 1959, rode into the A.D.'s job with a seven-year football record of 54-9-2, including a 28-game winning streak from 1950-53. Daugherty succeeded him in the 1954 season and two-years later the Spartans again beat UCLA, 17-14, in the Rose Bowl game. Even with the notable achievement, it was Duffy's teams in the mid-'60s (19-1-1 record in 1965-66) that iced his reputation and propelled him to the College Football Hall of Fame in 1984.

Duffy Daugherty, left, and his MSU football coach predecessor, Biggie Munn, were responsible for bringing the Spartans to athletic prominence in the 1950s.

Athletics department employees were divided based on loyalties. It was a tight, closed department with no new openings and I saw no future there. I was the odd man out with nothing else to do but count tickets. So in March 1970 I contacted personnel director Lillrose at the Michigan Department of Education to see what the chances might be to get my old job back. He called me within a week or two to say my old position was filled, but he was working on a new position in his office for which I could apply.

Return to a more rewarding atmosphere

Sure enough, within two weeks Lillrose called to offer me the position of recruiter and training officer in the personnel office. I accepted and wrote a three-page resignation letter to Munn, sending copies to Breslin, Beardsley and later to President Clifton Wharton. I wanted them to understand what I had experienced in the department so hopefully they would show more sensitivity to the next black employee they hired.

Back once again with the Michigan Department of Education, I soon felt as if I were making a constructive contribution again. The job entailed developing a system to recruit professionals for every bureau and division opening in the department. There must have been about 250 positions that I had to keep filled with qualified professionals.

Additionally, I conducted training programs primarily for minority clerical applicants to pass the state civil service examinations. There was a big shortage of minority clerks in this area. I worked with the Lansing Public Schools and the Michigan Department of Civil Service in developing that program and we made great strides hiring minorities in all clerical categories within the department, although my recruitment included all sectors of the department of education.

My office was on the fifth floor of the Michigan

National Bank Building, the same floor where Dr. John W. Porter, the new superintendent, and his associates Philip Kearney, William Pierce, Ron Edmonds, Thomas Wilbur, Crawford, and Lillrose worked. Those were outstanding professionals who worked hard and demonstrated compassion to all. I felt I was contributing to the overall success of the department. Dr. Porter, just like Dr. Polley before him, had high expectations for each unit and we all did our part to meet the goals and expectations. But then Munn suffered a stroke and my rewarding job with the state would be cut short with the call from Breslin to come back to Michigan State.

MSU beckons again; I become an assistant A.D.

So in August 1972 I was back with the Spartans, not as a ticket assistant or underutilized counselor, but rather as assistant athletics director for student academic services. I didn't have to ask Burt Smith to siphon off some of his student-athlete counseling clients because now he was busy as the athletics director.

Clarence Underwood in the early '70s when he returned to work at Michigan State for a second time

I was now responsible for the academic eligibility of more than 700 student-athletes, administering athletics scholarships and other financial aid; serving with the human resources department; coordinating the book loan program; counseling athletes about their academic programs and personal issues; monitoring class attendance; reviewing certification for

113

competition; overseeing orientation of new student-athletes; and the interpretation of National Collegiate Athletic Association and Big Ten rules and regulations for the staff and the university community. Indeed, that was a huge job, but I always have been challenged by lots of work responsibilities.

There were two full-time clerks in my office. I trained one to handle procedures in financial aid, human resources and the book loan program. The second was trained to handle procedures in certification, preparing orientation materials and keeping track of eligibility.

Although I still was responsible for those assigned areas, delegating some of the responsibilities enabled me to focus on counseling services, orientation, the interpretation of NCAA rules for staffers, and whatever else came my way. Later on I was given another part-time clerical employee and the duties were then distributed among three people.

With so many student-athletes to monitor academically and counsel regarding their eligibility and personal problems, I had to establish a system to successfully meet their diverse needs. I collaborated with the office of the registrar and the assistant deans to establish a monitoring system to keep track of the student-athletes' class attendance. A card was sent to each instructor of the student-athletes several times during a semester requesting feedback on class attendance. I followed up on any athlete who had a problem. In addition:

- I met once a week to counsel each student-athlete with a 2.0 grade-point average or lower.
- I immediately met with any student-athlete who needed a tutor or who was experiencing difficulty with a course.
- I immediately met with any student-athletes experiencing a civil, criminal, or NCAA/Big Ten problem.

- I met with all other student-athletes at least once a term relative to their academic status.
- At the end of each academic term I sent congratulatory personal letters to each student-athlete who earned a 2.5 grade-point-average or better. The letter encouraged them to continue to make progress toward their degrees and to maintain their appointments with me for the next term.
- Letters were sent to all student-athletes who earned less than a 2.5 grade-point-average, encouraging them to improve their academic performances and adhere to the appointment schedule established for them. I tried to develop the foundation for a solid and effective student-athlete support services program.

There were many other personal reasons why the athletes would visit my office for assistance and I never got tired of seeing them. I spent many nights meeting with athletes about academic and personal issues that they were struggling with. I believed the only way I could be successful with them was to take an ownership attitude about their welfare. I felt they belonged to me on the academic side and I practiced tough love with them. I never interfered with a coach/student-athlete relationship or with a professor/student-athlete relationship unless there was evidence that the athlete was being mistreated. I would then get involved to get the facts and make a fair recommendation to the appropriate administrators.

There were times when I would ask the ombudsman for assistance with a professor who penalized an athlete for missing classes because of away competition. But generally I handled those problems alone. I felt honored to have the opportunity to try to counsel them in the right direction and I got more satisfaction out of seeing a student-athlete graduate than I did knowing he/she had earned All-America honors in their sport. Generally, most of the student-athletes were good people and were at the university for the right reasons, to earn their degrees, as well as excel in their sports. But sometimes a few got their priorities reversed.

Some resentment from coaches

Most coaches, I believe, accepted me and respected the work I was doing. However, there were a few who resisted and resented the interpretations I provided on Big Ten conference and NCAA rules and regulations. No one likes to be told that they cannot do something, but it was my job to give accurate information to the coaches, even if it sounded negative to them. To protect the athletics department, the university and myself, often I would put those interpretations in writing. That practice of documenting them didn't set well with some coaches.

In addition to my personal daily interactions with students, I spent an inordinate number of hours studying Big Ten and NCAA rules and regulations. I never wanted to give a coach or anyone else a misinterpretation. If I were uncertain about what a rule meant, I would call the conference office or the NCAA. Like everything else I did, I took pride in the work I performed for the institution. I struggled with trying to balance work and my personal life. My wife often would tease me, claiming I was married to my work. With me and 700 student athletes to monitor and counsel, the amount of time I could devote to anything else was minimal, so I could understand what she was suggesting.

Another practice I established was to inform coaches frequently, in writing, about academic performances of their players. I implemented the practice in September 1972 and my first letter was written to Daugherty. My secretary, Eddie Engle, whom I inherited from Burt Smith when he was promoted to athletics director, advised me not to send the letter. She thought that Duffy would have me fired for sending negative information to him about his student-athletes who were not consistently attending classes. I told Eddie to send the letter, which she did, and I never heard any feedback from Duffy. He was always congenial to me, but he seemed to intimidate some other coaches and department staff.

During the 1960s and 1970s there were few athletics administrators at Michigan State. When I returned there in 1972 to become assistant director for student-athlete academic services the department was led by Smith. Beardsley was assistant athletics director in charge of tickets. John Laetz was the business manager. Gene Kenney was the soccer coach and administrative assistant to Smith. And Carol Davis served as professor in physical education and was the assistant athletics director for the women's sports program. Later, in 1975, Dr. Nell Jackson, who was the first black female administrator, replaced the retired Davis.

Key issues ignored at staff meetings

In the fall and winter terms that year the six department administrators met every Monday morning at 8 a.m. in Smith's office. By the spring semester there were several important issues that needed resolution, but unfortunately many were not addressed appropriately at the meetings. Some very important issues, such as the development of the annual budget and fund-raising plans, were being delayed.

Breslin became highly frustrated with Smith's ineptness and lack of leadership and he began meeting with the director of athletics and his administrators on each Monday morning beginning in the spring term of 1973. He requested that I take minutes because he had grown distrustful of Smith. Jack, as well as other staff members and coaches, had come to regard Burt as having a penchant for stretching the truth. As one staff member said, "Burt could look you in the eye and not tell the truth."

Smith, although personable, had a quick mind that

could manufacture a plausible yet inaccurate story at a moment's notice. He was recognized as someone who could think quickly on his feet, but you may not be able to rely on what he said.

With all that said, I still have to say I liked Smith — who took credit for hiring me, even though it was Breslin and Beardsley who hired me in 1969 and Breslin who was instrumental in hiring me in 1972.

I used to see Smith in Jenison and at athletic events when I was a student. He was an assistant football coach under Daugherty and lectured in a football class I took as an undergraduate, but I really didn't know him well. We had never had a conversation prior to my employment in 1969. I talked with him formally the first time when I was hired in August 1969 and worked with him directly from 1972-75.

Smith's jackass references uncalled for

My office used to be Burt's and was next door to his when he became athletics director. Football players continued to visit him about their academic issues. Instead of referring them to me, since that now was under my purview, he would handle those visits himself.

I would hear him yelling at the players, calling them jackasses. I felt uncomfortable about that because Burt would phone my secretary and ask her to follow up on the problems of the athletes. I felt like my role was being minimized and unless I stopped Burt from doing the work that was assigned to me, my role would never get established with the student-athletes, coaches and the offices of financial aid, admissions, the office of the registrar, academic advisors and assistant deans, as well as other campus offices.

One day in September 1972, I decided to visit Smith's office and told him that as athletics director it wasn't professional for him to call student-athletes jackasses. He should, I told him, dignify his position by calling them by their proper names and that it would strengthen his leadership and organizational structure if he would refer to *my* office all athletes who came to see *him* on academic issues.

I told him if he continued he would be criticized for focusing too narrowly on a few students he previously counseled and for not being able to see the big picture. His first reaction, a familiar one to those of us who knew Burt, was to bury his face into his hands. Then he responded that student-athletes *were indeed* jackasses. He continued by saying he understood my position and he would change his procedures. To his credit, within a week he had arranged meetings between my office and representatives in other appropriate offices on campus. He did it to have me become familiar with the representatives and procedures in those offices so I could do my job.

Smith persuaded to make changes

Smith clearly had his shortcomings, but once I made him aware of issues that needed changing, in most cases he would attempt to change them or authorize me to make the needed changes. He did not have a written plan for the department and so he often had no idea what needed changing. But he was willing to listen and implement changes when presented with a plausible plan, if he agreed with the plan. I must repeat that Burt was good to me. He respected me and, in turn, I tried to help him in every way that I could.

Meanwhile, the weekly staff meetings continued with Smith's administrative staff and Breslin. I would put the agenda together and take the minutes, which I would then have typed and distributed prior to the next meeting. There were times when Breslin had issues that he felt were too sensitive to discuss at the meetings, so he would ask Burt and I to stay afterwards to talk privately about those matters. Most of those sessions focused on Smith's performance, such as his lack of support for a specific program, or erroneous information that Smith had allegedly shared with persons outside of the athletics department and which had made their way back to Breslin.

I found those special sessions stressful, but great learning experiences. I liked both Burt and Jack and found myself in the middle. Those discussions taught me how to be objective in a human conflict. I understood the issues that were discussed and tried to focus on the facts rather than get caught up with two personalities. Learning that technique later helped me as a compliance administrator. I had to sort through allegations and come up with the facts. I often would talk with Burt and Jack afterwards on an individual basis and tried to point out the issues from a factual viewpoint. They both seemed to appreciate the information I shared with them.

Breslin would start out those meetings by telling Burt about the information or situation that had come to his attention. Then Smith typically would either deny the assertion or give an explanation. Breslin would pin him down with specifics and the more Burt denied the assertion the more the vice president would put the full-court press on him. In most situations Breslin was clearly disappointed with Smith and, if the situation required action, he would give him a timetable to get something done.

One thing that still stands out in my mind about those meetings is that, although I never wanted Breslin upset with me about something I had or had not done, he was the most patient, understanding and compassionate person I had ever known. He was highly competent as an administrator and tried to help people in many ways. He tried to help Burt. He was wise and many folks both on and off campus sought his advice on various issues they were confronting. But once he got on your case for poor performance, you had a real problem on your hands. Jack and I became good friends. We later lived in the same neighborhood. Our families often socialized together. He was a great family man and his wife, Renee, and their three sons followed in their dad's footsteps by becoming varsity athletes at Michigan State. Jay and John played football and Brian was a starter on the basketball team under Coach Gus Ganakas.

Search begins for Daugherty's replacement

Duffy Daugherty retired from his head football coach job at the end of the 1972 season. One of Smith's first major assignments was to identify a pool of coach candidates from which would be selected the person to replace Duffy and put the program back on a winning track.

In December, Smith left campus to search for a slate of blue-chip coaches that he could eventually recommend to Wharton and his interviewing committee of Breslin, Smith, John Fuzak (who was the faculty athletics representative), and me. In order of priority, Smith recommended:

- Barry Switzer, an assistant coach at the University of Oklahoma.
- Johnny Majors, head coach at Iowa State.
- Lee Corso, head coach at the University of Louisville.
- Denny Stolz, defensive coordinator under Daugherty and former head coach at Alma College in Michigan.

To be truthful, Burt didn't recommend Stolz. Breslin and Wharton put him on the list. A few days prior to the beginning of interviews, Denny met with each committee member individually and explained why he should become a candidate. He promoted his candidacy with the committee. Other candidates applied but were not put on the priority list. The committee interviewed the top four on a Saturday and Sunday, but scheduled one non-priority candidate from the overall list — ex-MSU assistant Henry Bullough — for that Monday morning.

Switzer clearly was Smith's first choice and Burt promoted his candidacy with the committee. There was no question Barry was a viable candidate and had a very good chance of landing the job based on his qualifications, if only he could convince the committee. The program at Oklahoma was strong and successful, with the Sooners annually winning eight or more games and ranking high in the national polls. Switzer was the first person to be interviewed, getting the 8:30 a.m. Saturday time slot in Wharton's conference room.

Committee put off by long-winded Switzer

Wharton chaired the committee and, after members introduced themselves, he explained the job opening and asked Switzer to give a brief overview of his background. To this day it's a mystery as to what happened to Barry, but he spoke about one hour responding to Wharton's first question. On several occasions Wharton and Breslin attempted to interrupt him but each time Switzer would say, "I'm not finished. Let me continue."

When he finally finished and asked for the next question the committee members were reluctant to ask any more questions. Switzer asked the committee a few questions about the use of a university credit card for travel and private planes for recruitment, something the university didn't have in place at that time. There may have been one or two more from the committee to Barry, which were carefully worded so as to elicit a short response.

I saw Switzer in December 2001 at the College Football Hall of Fame banquet in New York and reminded him of his interview at Michigan State that December day in 1972. I told him that in my opinion the reason he didn't get the head coaching job with the Spartans was because he talked too long responding to the first question from Wharton. Barry said he remembered the interview but wasn't aware he had mishandled the first question. He said it was MSU's loss and his coaching record was the proof. He had an outstanding record at Oklahoma for many years. Iowa State had an 8-3 season in 1972 under Majors, but he was looking for a better opportunity. Despite a bad sore throat, he had a very good interview and was a desirable candidate. He was very hoarse, but performed well. His one big question was, how many non-qualifier student-athletes in football could he recruit each year. A non-qualifier is a prospective student-athlete who doesn't meet the NCAA minimum academic standards to qualify for eligibility and competition in his first year on campus (the minimum standard in 1972 was a 2.00 grade point average on all courses carried in high school. The standards have been significantly upgraded many times since then, including requiring a test score.)

Next up was Corso, who had developed football at Louisville into a competitive program. But Corso wanted to be recognized at a Division I-A program with more resources. He also did a very fine job during his interview. He was impressive and clearly articulated his support of student-athlete welfare issues. I think that was the first time I ever had seen a person wearing a suit that I imagined cost $200 or more. Keep in mind that was in 1972 and a good men's suit cost about $85. He had stylish shoes, as well, and was very articulate. The committee, though, still had one more priority candidate to interview.

Long-shot Stolz impresses committee

Stolz was considered a long-shot going into the interview. He had just come from small college power Alma to join Daugherty's staff in 1971. He was low key, not well known and had been defensive coordinator at a time when the Spartans program wasn't very good. It became obvious during the interview that he only needed an opportunity to present his case to make an impression, which he did.

123

Stolz had an advantage in that he was thoroughly familiar with MSU's program. He identified some lingering issues and offered solutions for improvement. He presented a logical plan to turn things around. When the interview concluded on Sunday, each of the committee members gave a preliminary assessment of the candidates and Stolz was at the top of everybody's list — except for Smith's. Burt still was pushing hard for Switzer.

There remained one more interview, the candidate who wasn't on the blue-chip list, Bullough, who couldn't be interviewed until Monday because of his duties as an assistant with the Baltimore Colts of the National Football League. The committee had received many calls in support of Bullough as a viable candidate because he was a former Spartan player, a graduate and assistant coach at MSU. He had been an outstanding player under Munn and an assistant coach under Daugherty (1959-69). Bullough left Michigan State for the Colts in 1970.

It was clear, based upon his recommendations, that Smith wanted a new coach who had no formal affiliations with the MSU football program. (Smith himself was an assistant coach under Daugherty from 1954-64.) At that time there were many former assistant coaches who had served under Munn and Daugherty who were working as head coaches at some prominent institutions, plus some assistants in the pro ranks. Burt didn't include any of them on the list.

After Bullough's two-hour interview, the committee met right away and again discussed each candidate. The consensus was to name Stolz to the position. He had made his case and Smith, the lone dissenter, still cast his vote for Switzer.

Smith snubs football program

Stolz would coach the Spartans from 1973-75 — all the while getting minimal attention and support from

Smith's office. Burt didn't promote the football program publicly and talked negatively about it in private. It was that lack of demonstrated support that caused him problems with Breslin, who called numerous meetings with him and to which I also was invited. Breslin lambasted Smith for his lack of leadership and support of the football program. Smith always would deny the assertions, but his behavior would not change for the better. Stolz was aware of Burt's attitude toward his program but he was committed not to allow Smith to interfere with what he was doing to move the program forward.

Stolz assembled a competent and hard-working staff. He retained Ed Youngs, Jimmy Raye and Sherman Lewis from Duffy's staff. He brought in newcomers Howard Weyers, Andy McDonald, Bill Davis, Dan Underwood, Ron Chismar, and Charlie Butler. Stolz was well organized, professional, and highly supportive of the student-athlete's academic program. He stressed class attendance and would discipline footballers who didn't abide by his team rules. He approached the management of the program as a business, attending to detail and making his coaches accountable for recruiting Big Ten caliber players. Plus, he was a nice guy.

Davis was the academic liaison with my office. We would meet each morning and discuss any academic problems that had occurred with any football player the previous day, including reported evening study hall problems. Davis would share the problems with Denny and the coaching staff. And there would be a follow-up. In 1972, athletics departments across the country didn't have compliance coordinators — that is, persons hired to interpret conference and NCAA rules and regulations, educate staff, monitor compliance, and conduct investigations of violations.

The Big Ten office trained academic coordinators of the institutions to interpret conference and NCAA academic and eligibility rules. The league office also sent all conference personnel written interpretations of its rules and those of the NCAA. Both the NCAA and Big Ten manuals of rules and regulations were distributed to all coaches and administrative personnel.

It was my responsibility at Michigan State to interpret those regulations for our staff. Along with my other myriad of duties, each week I would distribute interpretations from the NCAA weekly newspaper and reissue conference memos to the staff. In addition, staff members would visit my office or call me to seek interpretations. Smith, Fuzak, and I were the official representatives to the Big Ten and NCAA offices on those matters.

During Smith's tenure as director of athletics he never had departmental or coaches meetings. There never was an opportunity for our staff to come together to discuss NCAA rules.

Budget tightening; clerical confusion

I recall just two occasions when we brought together the head coaches and administrative staff. The first occurred on campus in a meeting room in Kellogg Center in 1973 when Smith, Breslin, and Fuzak discussed the financial status of the athletics department.

Since our football program had been struggling for six consecutive seasons beginning in 1967, attendance had steadily declined. Consequently we were experiencing a financial recession in the department. The meeting was called to announce a reduction in expenses, including, for example, making sure long-distance phone calls were limited to business. We were required to complete a form for auditing purposes for each call made.

We were similarly restricted from using athletics funds for entertainment purposes unless prior approval was given, and there was a restriction on travel that wasn't for recruiting purposes. Meanwhile, the annual pay increase for all staff members was nominal. Generally, though, the football program was given more latitude, but other programs, including men's basketball and ice hockey, were affected.

The second meeting took place in Smith's office during the fall of 1974 involving the many complaints from coaches about the work assignments of the clerical pool. Some coaches didn't know who was their assigned clerk. There were issues relative to the supervision of the clerical help when coaches were with their teams in practice, at competition and during travel away from campus. Some coaches made those complaints to Smith and several brought them to me.

I put together a simple plan that would put Smith's secretary, Sylvia Thompson, as the overall supervisor of the entire clerical staff. She would be responsible for keeping track of staff members and redistributing work from one to another when necessary. She would approve overtime, help evaluate the clerical staff, and report problems to me.

Smith accepted my plan and we called a meeting of all head coaches, supervisors, and administrators in Burt's office. It appeared that generally everyone except Beardsley, the assistant A.D. for business and tickets, accepted the plan. He thought his newly-hired secretary, Bert Boyko, would have been a better choice because he felt she was tougher than Sylvia. Nevertheless, we implemented the change and it seemed to work fine.

NCAA starts nosing around

While there were no formalized compliance programs among NCAA member institutions, Michigan State's efforts in that regard were as good or better than most universities around the country. I know that to be true from talking and sharing information with representatives from other Big Ten schools. I also received inquiries from some other institutions asking for certain information about our academics and rules interpretation procedures.

To be clear though, Michigan State University didn't have a comprehensive compliance education program to fully educate the coaches and staff of their responsibilities with regard to the rules. I don't believe I ever was asked to report any violation to the Big Ten conference or to the NCAA from 1972-75. We had submitted numerous eligibility petitions to the conference relative to a student-athlete's academic status, but no rules violation reports.

Smith told me in early February 1975 that a person from the NCAA was coming to campus to review some academic, financial aid, and eligibility information contained in files in my office. He asked me to accommodate him when he reported to campus. That person was David Berst, the chief enforcement investigator. He reported to Smith's office on Valentine's Day 1975. Burt called me to his office and introduced us. Berst was a young man, about 6-feet tall, 190 pounds. He talked softly and upon first impression seemed rather friendly and down to earth. He asked if he could review the financial aid, eligibility, and certification data in my office pertaining to all student-athletes.

At that time I had two very good clerks, Jamie Mick-Ruff and Patsy Kohagen. Jamie handled admissions and eligibility issues and Patsy handled financial aid and book loan procedures. Both were well organized and maintained accurate records.

Berst reviewed the records in my office for about two hours, never saying what he was looking for. But I believe he was checking to see if records were properly documented and to detect any irregularities that could have resulted in NCAA violations. Much of the record-keeping was required by the NCAA and, I believe, Berst was like an auditor verifying that it was intact.

When he finished his review he returned to Smith's office and told him he had to visit some stores in the area and would like one of Smith's staff members to accompany him. He said he wanted the visits to be done jointly by the NCAA and MSU personnel. Burt asked me to accompany Berst to the stores.

We started out around 1 p.m. and visited our first store, a record shop on Grand River Ave., directly across from campus. I was amazed when Berst told the store clerk that someone had purchased by credit card some record albums and other items there on a date and month he specified.

He asked the clerk if the store kept copies of credit card receipts and was told it did, whereupon he asked for and received two copies of the receipt for the purchase in question, one for the NCAA and the other for MSU. I was amazed when Berst requested receipts from memory and was shocked when the clerk found the exact receipt within minutes. As requested, the clerk gave each of us a copy.

Our second store was the MSU Bootery. Berst identified us and told the manager that someone had purchased some leather coats and boots there using a credit card on a specific date. Just like before, the manager retrieved the charge slips and gave them to us.

Our third stop, all within the same day, was at Sibley's Shoe Store in the Okemos Mall. Berst repeated the same procedure and the manager retrieved the charge slips requested and gave them to us.

Berst was professional and did not try to misrepresent who he was. He always identified himself and never tried to deceive anybody. It was surprising to see the cooperation the store representatives provided him without ever challenging his reason for needing the information.

During our travel between stores he and I discussed our families and our athletics backgrounds. I learned that he had played basketball and may have done some coaching at a small Division III institution. I asked him why was it that certain athletics programs like Michigan, Nebraska, Alabama, etc., appeared to be untouchable by the NCAA. Those institutions, with winning football programs in the mid '70s, seemed to be exempt from NCAA investigations and probation.

He said the problem they had as investigators was to get folks connected with those schools to talk about their dirt. Friends, boosters and staff of some universities do not put their business in the streets, he said, they keep it among themselves.

I remember Berst buying a box of candy from a store in the mall to take home to his wife for Valentine's Day. I made a mental note that a person who thinks of his wife during an investigation can't be all bad. When I reported back to the office later that afternoon, I immediately informed Smith what had transpired and asked him to inform Breslin and Wharton.

Tell the news media or not?

President Wharton later called a meeting with Breslin, Smith, Fuzak, general counsel Leland Carr, and myself. Wharton had received a preliminary inquiry from the NCAA notifying Michigan State that it would be conducting an investigation of allegations about our football program. The NCAA made certain specific allegations. Whereas Wharton felt the university had an obligation to release the preliminary inquiry to the media, Breslin believed MSU should conduct its internal investigation without notifying the media about the NCAA's investigation. That became a heated discussion.

Breslin wanted to keep the matter as quiet as possible and not say anything publicly until the investigation was complete. The president, however, believed the university could be accused of a cover-up if the matter was to be detected by the news media. Wharton felt it was necessary to make a public announcement, but not to share the result of the investigation until it was over. He called for a vote on the two options and the majority favored his recommendation, so the announcement of the investigation was made to the news media in the spring of 1975.

Things got boiling hot in East Lansing. Tempers were short and people began pointing fingers. The football program was impaired and a few coaches were under pressure because of the NCAA allegations. I had much compassion for the coaches because basically they were good people. This whole thing was very new to me and to them and I found myself feeling helpless. It was a difficult situation for everyone involved.

It was too late to correct what was being investigated and the institution was obligated to cooperate fully with the NCAA. Wharton formed a select committee to conduct the internal probe. It consisted of: Wharton; Carr; Dr. Fred Williams, professor of history; trustee John Bruff; Fuzak; and Dr. Jake Hofer, professor of agriculture. I served as liaison to the committee from the athletics department. Robert Wenner was the liaison from the internal auditing department. There may have been others assisting privately. The committee met over the course of many months gathering data, interviewing student-athletes, coaches, staff, and others.

That was indeed a difficult time at Michigan State. The media in Michigan were having a field day searching for leaks; writing headlines based on tidbits or fragmented information. The media were persistent in looking for information. Wharton, in order to protect the integrity of the investigation, mandated that staff could not make any comments to the media or others about the investigation.

My role was to respond to requests from the committee, such as to retrieve documents from files in the athletics department, bring student-athletes before the committee, assist in the on-campus interviewing process, and anything else the committee wanted me to do.

One day I drove to three cities in Ohio to interview four MSU student-athletes who had gone home for the summer and who had been implicated in a small way in one of the allegations. I continued to meet with NCAA investigators who came to campus to either interview MSU persons or to gather information. I was not involved in any off-campus interviews conducted by the NCAA representatives.

The general focus of the investigation was an assistant football coach, Howard Weyers, and his recruitment activities in the states of Ohio and Pennsylvania. There were numerous allegations asserting that he had provided extra benefits to several prospective athletes while recruiting them. Other allegations claimed that Weyers had access to money and a credit card belonging to Michael Doyle, a Lansing attorney, to help recruit the prospective athletes. Weyers and Doyle contested those allegations. Assistant coach James Raye was charged with arranging airline transportation for two athletes at a local travel agency on a credit basis. A few other coaches were involved in similar secondary violations, as was coach Raye.

The one thing that made it tough for the university in its defense with the NCAA was the total number of allegations, both secondary and major. There were approximately 160 allegations for which the university had to account.

NCAA penalties severe

The NCAA Infraction Committee dealt our football program one of the severest penalties in history to that point. The sanctions were:
- A four-year probation period.
- No television games over the four-year period.
- No post-season games over that period.
- The dismissal of Stoltz (an institutional decision).
- The dismissal of assistant coaches Raye, Weyers, and Charlie Butler.
- Ruling defensive back Joe Hunt ineligible for collegiate athletics.

- The suspension of tight end Mike Cobb for five games for the 1976 season.
- Reduction of annual scholarships over the four-year probationary period.
- Breslin removed himself from being overseer of athletics.

Those were some tough penalties for a program that had been struggling to be successful for more than eight years, suddenly having the legs cut out from under it. The team had won seven games both in 1974 and 1975 for the first time since 1966 when the Spartans won the national championship. The probation and resultant penalties were major setbacks for both the football program and the athletics department.

The football program had suffered brief probationary periods in previous years but nothing comparable to the 1976 probation. For example, the Big Ten and NCAA had penalized the program in 1953 for its affiliation with an illegal slush fund, The Spartan Foundation, operated by an MSU booster group. Then, in 1964, the program was hit with a three-year suspended probation for improperly using funds from a booster program allegedly abolished in the 1950s. The suspension was given when the university demonstrated that it had rectified the problem earlier.

Why was the stiff 1976 probation given? Many people speculated why the football program was hit so hard under the leadership of Stolz. Among the speculations were that:

- Stolz inherited a program that historically had taken liberty with NCAA and Big Ten rules and regulations.
- There was no comprehensive compliance education program.
- There was little or no institutional commitment to a strong compliance/enforcement program. Those concepts had just begun to emerge among NCAA member institutions.

- Coach Woody Hayes of Ohio State blew the whistle on MSU because our team defeated his in 1974.
- There were perceptions that the institution took an aggressive position during the investigation of defending itself instead of showing a spirit of cooperation with the NCAA.
- There was less than effective management/leadership in the office of athletics director.

Fallout and press leak doom Smith

After the investigation had concluded, the penalties were announced and the university had a postmortem about the future of the athletics department. All NCAA major violations have wide sweeping repercussions and usually staff members are at risk. Wharton and his executive cabinet were fully aware of the difficulties and the need to restore the department to a competitive position.

Burt Smith was leading the department. There were beliefs that his administrative ineptness had contributed to the violations and subsequent investigation and penalties.

One afternoon about 4:30 p.m., Wharton called a meeting in his office. Joining him there were Breslin, Smith, and I. Under the strictest confidence, Wharton asked Smith to step down from the athletics director position. He would be reassigned to assistant vice president in charge of the athletics department, along with some other duties. He would report to Breslin and his office would be in the Administration Building. Personally, I thought that was a very good offer to Smith. He could continue his involvement with the department without having the day-to-day disruptions. He would work closer with Breslin to help build trust between them and his salary would remain intact.

Wharton and Breslin explained there was an urgency to make that change, but wanted Burt to think about it overnight with his wife. The group would reconvene the following day to seek his decision. In the meantime, each of us agreed not to say anything to anybody about the proposal, with the exception of Burt discussing it with his wife.

I was shocked when Breslin came to Jenison around 8:45 a.m. the following morning wanting to have a meeting with Smith and me in Burt's office. It was easy to see that Jack was very upset. I was even more surprised to hear what Jack told Burt — that on his way home from work after the day of our meeting, he was listening to the *Bob Reynolds Sports Show* from Detroit on his car radio.

Around 6:15 p.m., after our previous day's meeting concluded, Reynolds announced the details of Smith's job proposal over the air. According to Breslin, Reynolds was opposed to the change and was trying to get public support for Burt. Naturally, Smith denied talking with his good friend Reynolds about the proposal. But who else would have a motive for doing it? Breslin called

Broadcaster Bob Reynolds

Reynolds to confirm the source of the information, but Reynolds only demonstrated his anger toward the university administration.

I mentioned early that I never wanted to be the victim of Jack Breslin's wrath. He basically was a peach of a man. But on that morning, his full wrath exploded out. He told Smith that he had to be out of Jenison Field House by 5 p.m. that day. He had to gather his belongings and move to a vacant room in Munn Ice Hockey Arena. Housed there, he would be isolated from everyone except for his friend, hockey coach Amo Bessone. Breslin told Smith to "collect your shit and get out." Burt had violated Wharton and Breslin's trust. The proposal was no longer on the table and Smith's job title, duties and salary were immediately downgraded.

It was a pitiful sight to see him in his office in the cold Munn Arena with scanty furnishings, no people in his vicinity and just sitting there in a chair. I visited him once or twice. It was painful to see him sitting in the office with minimal duties to perform. Most staff probably never knew why Smith was moved, and most associated it generally with the NCAA probation, which it was, but he was given a respectful opportunity to leave the department with favor. Essentially, Smith messed up a golden opportunity to retain his dignity at the university.

Smith was gritty. Despite his seemingly embarrassing demotion, he became the first commissioner of the newly formed Central Collegiate Hockey Association (CCHA). He conducted business from his office in the Munn Arena, but it never was the same for him at the university. He rapidly faded from the Spartan family scene of activities and events.

Wharton and Breslin assigned John Shingleton, the director of the MSU placement office, to serve as the acting athletics director on a part-time basis while he continued to administer the placement office. He was viewed as the person to create stability in an uncertain situation. Shingleton had a reputation as a no nonsense administrator. He was highly respected nationally among placement professionals. Prior to coming to the athletics department he had served in a number of other crisis-oriented roles on campus.

Shingleton brought his tough style of leadership to the athletics department for about five months and he did a good job of calming the waters. The NCAA/MSU football sanctions were in effect and the university began searching for a new permanent athletics director to move the department forward.

CHAPTER 4:

NCAA PROBE FALLOUT

Athletic department revolving door

WHILE JOHN SHINGLETON FILLED IN AS INTERIM director of athletics at Michigan State, university president Clifton Wharton wasn't sitting on his hands. Changes — from coaches to athletics directors — were imminent and, as history would show, they kept on coming for some two decades after the NCAA investigation and sanctions.

During the first seven or eight years after those tribulations I would find myself with new titles, new responsibilities, and several new jobs — including one that took me away from Michigan State and put me in the Big Ten office in Schaumburg, Ill., outside of Chicago.

First on Wharton's agenda was to find a permanent replacement for the deposed Burt Smith. Wharton headed the search committee and names were not to be revealed outside the committee. The president also would swiftly seek out a replacement for fired football coach Denny Stolz and basketball coach Gus Ganakas, who had been reassigned within the athletics department.

Wharton hired Joe Kearney from the University of Washington to fill the athletics director position. The president called me one day in early April 1976 to tell me the news and asked me to pick Kearney up at Lansing Capital City Airport. Although I did not know him, I instinctively recognized Kearney the moment he deplaned. He had a jovial smile and dressed in a relaxed west-coast manner, with an open-face shirt and a University of Washington varsity jacket. He was very friendly and we had a good conversation as I drove him to his university apartment, then to the grocery store and back to his apartment.

Kearney was a leader and a professional. He brought knowledge and experience into the department. Two of his most important challenges were to hire the replacements for Stolz and Ganakas. Just as with the A.D. search, Wharton chaired the committees to interview for the football and basketball jobs and, again, he wanted deliberations of the committees to remain private and confidential. To ensure privacy and confidentiality, interviews were held off campus.

Initially, the headquarters for interviewing the football coach candidates was the residence of Dr. Gwen Norrell, who was a faculty member in the Department of Counseling and Psychology. She had counseled many student-athletes and replaced Dr. John Fuzak

Gwen Norrell

as the faculty athletics representative to the Big Ten and NCAA. She was the first female faculty athletics representative to the Big Ten Conference. She was a very intelligent and politically astute person and we had an effective relationship. Eventually, she also became the first female vice president of the NCAA governance structure. On the committee,

138

besides Wharton and Norrell, were Kearney, Alumni Director Jack Kinney, Jake Hofer, and I. At Norrell's house, we interviewed Roy Kramer, the football coach at Central Michigan University; two NFL assistant coaches, Rollie Dotsch of the Green Bay Packers and George Perles of the Pittsburgh Steelers; and Ed Youngs, an assistant under Stolz.

The second round of interviews was conducted on a weekend in a hotel adjacent to O'Hare Airport in Chicago. Candidates there included Jim Mora, defensive coordinator at the University of Washington; Dick Crum, the coach at Miami of Ohio; and Darryl Rogers, the coach at San Jose State. (Crum eventually went on to a successful career at North Carolina and Mora had an NFL career that included a long stint as head coach of the New Orleans Saints.)

In my opinion, the best candidate we spoke with in the two interview sessions was Kramer and I said so during the assessment period. But I was the Lone Ranger in that regard. He was an outstanding high school coach at East Lansing. He went to Central Michigan and his 1974 team won the NCAA Division II championship. He was 10-1 in 1977 and then took over at Vanderbilt as director of athletics. He ended his career as an outstanding commissioner of the Southeastern Conference.

Kramer, more than anyone else, articulated the role of a student-athlete on a university campus. He believed the athlete needed to help himself academically by consistently going to classes, attending study sessions, and preparing himself to graduate. He spoke about how the coaching staff should monitor the conduct of their student-athletes, both on and off the field.

Another advantage Kramer had was that he was aware of the profile of about half the number of athletes on the MSU football team. He had tried to recruit them during his highly successful career at Central Michigan. He believed he could win consistently at MSU. Kearney was strong and showed much leadership during the assessment period. He made it known that he, too, thought Kramer was a good candidate — but his man was Rogers. He said he was already acquainted with Rogers from having observed him coach on the West Coast.

Kearney favors Rogers, Heathcote

There never was a confrontation by committee members over the qualities of the coaches and everybody was respectful and shared their opinions. Kearney recommended Rogers and supported him throughout the process. Most committee members supported Rogers, as well, saying they liked his articulated open offense, and he became the new coach for the 1976 football season.

But the committee's work wasn't done. It stayed in Chicago on Sunday to interview candidates for the basketball head coach position. Several candidates were interviewed. Among them were Lee Rose, the University of North Carolina-Charlotte coach; Virginia Tech coach Don DeVoe; Ohio University coach Bill Hess; and Jud Heathcote. There were no internal candidates. Just as in the case of Rogers, Kearney promoted the candidacy of Heathcote and that's who got the job.

Kearney was a highly competent and pleasant guy to work for. He related comfortably with people and was approachable. He had an open door policy and enjoyed a wide span of control. All men's head coaches reported to him, as well as the entire administrative staff. Dr. Nell Jackson was in charge of women's athletics and she reported to Kearney. All women head coaches reported to him through Jackson.

In addition to meeting with the administrative staff, Kearney met with the head coaches as a group once a month. He assigned Ganakas to coordinate the regional booster groups. The officers of those groups were invited to campus periodically to go through NCAA and Big Ten Conference rules education sessions.

Darryl Rogers, left, and Joe Kearney

Another major change occurred with the appointment of Kearney: He reported directly to Wharton and was a member of his council. Up until that point, the athletics director reported to a vice president.

Kearney and his wife, Doty, were involved extensively in the East Lansing/Lansing community. They frequently entertained staff and others at their home. He was effective as an A.D. and fit in very well at the university, as well as in the community. I thought he might retire from Michigan State.

Rogers, meanwhile, brought excitement to Spartan football with the passing game. Historically, we had been basically a running team. He was able to evaluate the players left behind by Stolz and turn them into winning teams two out of the four years he coached at State. His team was Big Ten co-champion in 1978.

In contrast to Stolz, Rogers was not a strong supporter or promoter of graduation for student-athletes. His attitude made my job as assistant athletics director for academics incredibly difficult. For example, we played Michigan at home on Oct. 8, 1977. Earlier that week on Monday, a football player came to my office and said, "Mr. Underwood, we don't have to go to classes this week." I asked him why. He responded, "Coach Rogers said this is Michigan Week and none of us have to go to classes." I confirmed that Rogers did make the statement, supposedly in jest. Whether it was jest or not, many athletes acted it out to the letter.

Short stay for Kearney, Rogers

At the 1979 NCAA convention, rumors were emerging that Rogers had accepted the head football coaching position at Arizona State University. It was further rumored that it would be a package deal with both Rogers and Kearney going together. I was surprised to hear that Kearney might be thinking of leaving MSU. Rogers was becoming a hot ticket and if he continued to build a strong program I understood that his coaching days were limited at Michigan State.

Kearney later told me he was struggling with the offer from Arizona State. He was becoming fond of MSU.

Now, though, he was reporting to a new president, Cecil Mackey, who recently had replaced Wharton, who had resigned to become chancellor for the SUNY (State University of New York) system. I appreciated the confidence Kearney had in me. We worked well together.

Joe and Darryl left for Arizona State in January 1980 and MSU had to search for its third A.D. and second football coach in four years. In the meantime, Heathcote, with the talent and leadership of Gregory Kelser, Earvin Johnson, and Jay Vincent, was having success on the basketball court. His overall record for the first three seasons, with a wealth of talent, was 63-26, which included two conference titles and a national championship. After Johnson left for the Los Angeles Lakers in 1979 following his sophomore year, and Kelser graduated, the overall record fell to 37-47 over the next three years.

Weaver takes the A.D. helm

President Mackey appointed Doug Weaver, a former MSU football player in the 1950s, as the A.D. He came to the university from the athletics director position at Georgia Tech. With the appointment of Weaver, the reporting lines shifted back to the A.D. reporting to a new vice president, Ken Thompson. Some faculty and staff called Thompson the most feared person at the university. They believed he would have no problem dismissing staff members. I got along well with him. We once went to Florida together and spoke at three alumni clubs. He appeared to be a decent guy.

Weaver, who had a law degree, was an astute man. He did not believe in regular staff meetings, preferring to meet with employees one on one and with his administrative staff whenever there was a crisis. He took copious notes during every meeting. At times he was very witty and at other times he was very reserved.

Similar to the chain of command under Kearney,

all the men's head coaches and the administrative staff reported to Weaver directly. But in contrast, Weaver preferred to work behind closed doors. He kept things close to the vest. Most staff, with the exception of the coaches of revenue-producing sports, had to make an appointment to see him. He administered the department at a time when the director of athletics had great control and authority. That was prior to the time when the university presidents took control of athletics in the early '90s.

Weaver was responsible for hiring a football coach to replace Rogers. There was no search committee; he had authority to make the decision. Perles, a Spartan and at that time an assistant with the National Football League champion Pittsburgh Steelers, was the sentimental public favorite. But Doug hired Muddy Waters, the head coach at Saginaw Valley State College, in February 1980. Some people had difficulty

Frank "Muddy" Waters, left, and Doug Weaver

understanding that appointment and couldn't understand why Perles wasn't hired. Waters, who had previously made Hillsdale College a strong program in small college football in Michigan, was a very friendly and down to earth person. His staff consisted of experienced collegiate and high school coaches. After three unsuccessful years with a record of 10-23, he was fired at the end of the 1982 season.

Perles era gets underway

Then, in early December 1982, Weaver hired Perles from the Philadelphia Stars of the new professional U.S. Football League, where he was the team's first head coach. I met George at a reception at Weaver's house. He told me there was nothing that he didn't know about football. He said he was going to put our football team back on the map. I believed him because he was a Spartan and wanted very much to be at the helm of the football program of his alma mater.

Perles had a pleasing personality and showed a determination that I had not seen since Rogers' departure. He mentioned that his athletes would go to class, have discipline, and graduate. I was excited with that philosophical bent. I told him that if I had known he would be the coach, I might not have accepted the associate director's position in the alumni office. Instead, I would have preferred to work with him as the assistant athletics director of the student-athletes academics support services.

One morning Weaver called me into his office after returning from a director's meeting with Thompson. I had recently earned my Ph.D. in higher education administration and felt the doctorate would enhance my opportunities to become an athletics director at the Division I level. Subsequently, I asked Doug for a raise in salary. I had taken two evening courses a semester year 'round. Weaver mentioned that Thompson inquired about my possible interest in a position in the alumni office. I told him that while my ultimate goal was to be an athletics director some day, I would be interested in discussing the position.

About a week later, I received a call from president Mackey asking that I come to his office. He told me that he wanted me to serve as the associate director for the alumni association. He said he had hired Dr. Chuck Webb as the executive director. He asked me to talk it over with my wife, Noreese, and we would talk again soon. I did discuss it with her and we agreed the position was an outstanding opportunity. It would further broaden my professional background, serve our alumni and friends directly, and thereby contribute to the overall mission of the university. I accepted the position and Mackey indicated he was pleased I had done so.

Resurrecting Alumni Association

The Michigan State Alumni Association had been abolished by the MSU Board of Trustees because of insurmountable differences between the trustees and the alumni board and wanted to become independent and autonomous, a move the trustees didn't endorse. To resolve the stalemate, the trustees abolished the association and started anew. It was the responsibility of Webb and I and staff to design a plan to resurrect it. We had an internal staff of approximately 14 people. Within a few months we had reorganized the association into 65 alumni clubs around the country (including a few in foreign countries).

Among the actions we took were to:
- Visit the clubs and help them in their organization.
- Invite speakers from the university to talk about their level of expertise.
- Sponsor alumni tours and re-establish the Alumni Homecoming Brunch.
- Form a board of directors.
- Re-engage with the degree granting colleges on

campus to get their alumni functions up and running.
- Hire Bob Bao to publish the alumni magazine.
- Host alumni functions at away football games, as well as post-season events in football, basketball and ice hockey.

The economy was sluggish in 1982 and unemployment was high. We undertook two new initiatives to assist our students and alumni. We brought back to campus some of our outstanding alumni in numerous professions to conduct seminars over a two-day period. The students learned from a practical sense the actual requirements of various jobs. The seminars complemented the theoretical education in the students' academic courses.

The second initiative was a job assistance workshop planned in several strategic locations in Michigan. The purpose was to assist our alumni in updating their résumés and sharpen their interviewing skills for employment purposes. We had other planned initiatives that were developed following my resignation in November 1983. The alumni association had been fully revitalized and our alumni and MSU staff were forming partnerships in a number of areas.

In September, Webb was hosting an alumni tour in Oxford, England, when I was approached by Big Ten Commissioner Wayne Duke to explore my interest in a position in that office. Noreese and I had just returned from hosting another alumni tour in Germany, where we had a great time. Wayne called Friday, Sept. 9, requesting that I meet him for breakfast Saturday morning at the Harley House located near campus. He and his wife, Martha, were in town for the Spartans' season-opening football game against the University of Colorado.

The assistant commissioner's position was open because Dr. Charles Henry recently had died. He was a giant of a man in character, personality, professionalism and intellect. He was appointed to the position from Grambling College by Duke in 1974 as an outgrowth of presentations made to the Big Ten by Dr. Robert L. Green, Dr. Thomas Gunnings, Dr. Joseph McMillian, and Dr. Gloria Smith, black professors at MSU who were concerned about racism in sports.

They met with Big Ten Commissioner Duke and conference representatives after a fight broke out at a televised men's basketball game between Ohio State and Minnesota. The black players were subjects of review by the media and the conference office. The MSU professors group subsequently requested that the conference create an assistant commissioner position to help address minority issues.

Henry was a dear friend and I had socialized and communicated with him many times, both from a professional and personal perspective. His death left a huge hole in the conference. Grambling later dedicated a gymnasium in his honor and I represented the Big Ten office at the ceremonies.

Big Ten asks Underwood to fill void

Duke was fully aware that I knew Henry, so we talked mostly about the job responsibilities, the conference governance structure, my salary, and a possible starting date if I were interested in taking the job. I found Wayne to be genuine, reasonable, and cautious. I had known him from my attendance at conference meetings. I liked and respected him. He had always been decent to me. We left breakfast that morning with the understanding that I would discuss the potential offer with my wife and he would call me in a few days to learn my decision.

It was one of the most difficult and emotional decisions I ever made. Noreese left the decision up to me. What made it so difficult was we were very much established in the community. All of our children lived in the Lansing area. Noreese was satisfied and

148

entrenched in her position with the state of Michigan (Michigan Employment Security Commission) and I had been working with the MSU Alumni Association less than one year and was involved in some exciting programs.

What I found appealing about the Big Ten position was the opportunity to work with Duke; return to

I enjoyed my brief time in the Big Ten office

athletics to continue my goal of pursuing an athletics director's position; to be given the chance to learn the structure and operations of Big Ten athletics departments; and, hopefully, use my knowledge, creativity and hard work to make a contribution to the conference and all collegiate athletics.

Although I was familiar with Duke and his top assistant, John Dewey, I didn't know the inner workings of the conference office. I wanted to know Wayne and John better and understand the office. I resigned from the alumni association and drove to the Big Ten office in Schaumburg on Nov. 1, 1983. I was excited about the opportunity but had sadness in my heart. It was tough to leave my family, friends and my position in the alumni association. President Cecil Mackey and former president John A. Hannah both called to wish me well in my new assignment. I also received a congratulatory letter from former president Clifton Wharton.

I found the conference office to be a great place to work. Duke had assembled a highly competent staff and everybody showed commitment to doing an excellent job. Dewey was the associate commissioner in charge of the budget, compliance, personnel matters, support to the faculty athletics representatives, and other duties. Phyllis Howlett was an assistant commissioner with the women's sports, championships, meeting logistics, and had additional duties as well.

As assistant commissioner I was assigned as liaison with the directors of athletics, all men's sports, all officiating matters, advisory commission, team physicians and trainers, band directors, and had other responsibilities. Jeff Elliott and Mark Rudner handled sports information services. Mary Masters was the assistant to Howlett and Eleanor Jessup was the assistant to Dewey. In all, there were 22 staff members, plus four supervisors of officials who worked outside the office.

Some of the major services performed by the office were the promotion of fairness and uniformity in the interpretations of rules and regulations; the sponsorship of championships; the negotiation of broadcast contracts; establishment of eligibility and certification standards; and enforcement of the policies, rules and regulations.

We were always busy attending meetings for sports groups, administrators, and faculty representatives, plus writing minutes and meeting results. We met with external sports groups, responded to telephone calls, and attended regional and national meetings. Each of the central administrators would attend a different campus football game each week and our office would plan the annual Rose Bowl trip for the joint group, consisting of the faculty athletics representatives, interested directors of athletics, women's athletics administrators, and central administrators from the office, as well as an advisory member representative.

There always was more work than any of us had time to do. We normally would report to work at 8:30 a.m. and work until 6 p.m. or later. We had internal staff meetings and a "to do" list that was turned in weekly to the commissioner. The associate and assistant commissioners' tasks typically consisted of working with groups. For example, I would solicit agenda items from the athletics

Noreese and I with Gov. James Blanchard at the Big Ten meeting on Mackinac Island in 1985

directors and the Big Ten office staff would add items to the agenda. I would prepare the meeting workbook and mail it to each A.D. and give our staff a copy.

I met with the athletics directors and commissioners and the football and basketball coaches and other groups assigned to me. I took notes at meetings; wrote minutes and gave them to Duke for approval; mailed minutes to the A.D.s and other groups following approval; did follow-up work, including writing letters, making phone calls, notifying persons and groups who had recommendations needing action; and start preparing for the next group. In comparison to my first role in the MSU athletics department in 1969, my conference office position was challenging and I felt like I was making a contribution. When you have 10 groups to service in this manner, you stay busy. Each group had its own chairperson who rotated annually. Some groups required more leadership from the conference office than others. Again, as an example, the football coaches had their own chairman but they relied on me to guide them through the agenda. In contrast, the chairs of the women's and men's track and field coaches were much more independent. They would conduct their own meetings and use the conference office staff basically as consultants.

I found the corporate style conference office had a much different atmosphere and culture than a university campus. There was more opportunity to develop friendships on campus, obtain assistance with issues, and more public scrutiny. The Big Ten office relationships were relatively confined to our colleagues. There was more formality, administrative accountability, and less communication among the internal staff in the conference office. Contrary to the perception of some critics, the Big Ten office was not a passive place to work. There was much work involved trying to meet the needs of conference representatives and institutions.

In addition to my challenging responsibilities, I found the time to serve at community functions. Noreese and I were faithful members of Gammon AME Methodist Church in Chicago, where I participated in the choir and Bible study. I transferred my membership from the East Lansing Rotary Club to the Schaumburg Rotary Club. I served on the board of Habilitative Systems Inc., a social services agency for the underprivileged in Chicago. I volunteered at a senior citizen's home, Sisters of the Poor, where I coordinated shuffleboard tournaments.

I remained a member of the national Sigma Pi Phi fraternity. I was initially inducted into the Alpha Chi chapter of the fraternity in Lansing in 1978, then transferred my membership to the Beta chapter of Chicago, and then back to Alpha Chi when I returned to Lansing. Furthermore, I was a charter member of the Chicago chapter of the National Association of Guardsmen Inc., and transferred my membership to the Detroit chapter when I returned to Michigan State. I served on the MSU Alumni Board. In addition, I was in demand as a public speaker for many high school and civic functions. Noreese and I met some outstanding people in the Chicago area and continue to maintain friendship with many of them today.

Duke an ethical, honest commissioner

Wayne Duke was a great person to work with who delegated and let the employees do the work. He was honest and ethical. He would do his homework and offer broad views on issues. Critics accused him of being a procrastinator at making tough decisions. I can understand that perception and believe Duke would agree with it to some degree. It originated from his style of management, where he was thorough and yet at times felt the need to touch base with many people before rendering a decision.

Whenever you rise to a high level position such as commissioner you had better be certain that the information you give is accurate, complete as possible and of substance. People always are looking for ways to challenge your position. They expect your very best at all times and Duke usually would provide an informed opinion on complex issues. He did his homework well.

One of his greatest strengths was his ability to work with people. He was highly communicative and a pleasure to deal with. He demonstrated much compassion for people. I have seen Wayne be nice to folks who treated him disrespectfully. He had a beautiful blend of ego and empathy and could adapt to all situations. He trusted athletics directors and would share anything with them and had a professional and psychological need to bond with them.

As open and resourceful as he was with people, however, I couldn't understand why he couldn't resolve the barrier between himself and Indiana basketball coach Bobby Knight, who is one of the most intelligent, but most misunderstood men, in America. I never asked Duke the source of the problem, but I do know he could easily become irritated and agitated with the mentioning of Knight's name in the conference office. I know Wayne has a big heart and will, if he has not already done so, resolve that issue — although neither he, nor Knight, are in the Big Ten any longer. Duke retired and Knight was fired by Indiana and became the basketball coach at Texas Tech.

Early in January 1989, Duke told me, after 18 years as commissioner, he was going to retire. I was not totally surprised by his decision but I had expected him to work for another two to five more years. He didn't give a reason and I didn't intrude by asking him why. I had come to understand that being commissioner is a tough job in a conference like the Big Ten. There are many factions that need servicing and it's difficult to please everyone. As compassionate as he was, I could understand how addressing complaints and personal criticisms over many years could wear down a person like Duke. Most folks are affected by such general fault- finding.

He left quietly: no ceremonies, no cake and ice cream, and no pat on the back. One day in the spring we came to work and the next day he was not there. It had become quite clear that the presidents wanted a change in leadership. Some of the faculty representatives were complaining about the slow pace in which the meeting minutes were approved and distributed to them. In addition, there was concern about the delay in updating compliance procedures. The procrastination claims came on the basis of those issues.

New commissioner is presidents' man

Conference presidents announced in March 1989 that James Delany, who had been commissioner of the Ohio Valley Conference, was the newly appointed commissioner of the Big Ten. I didn't know him but I was aware he had worked for the NCAA on its enforcement staff. Later on that March I spoke with him for the first time at an NCAA men's basketball tournament site in New Jersey where one of the Big Ten teams was appearing and he was representing the NCAA.

He reported to the office in Schaumburg in May. Unlike Duke, who aligned himself closely with the athletics directors, Delany was the presidents' man. He was not modest in saying upfront that he was hired by the Big Ten Council of Presidents and not by any other conference group. Initially, that dramatic shift in protocol created some tension. Delany was new and unmistakably delivering a message from the presidents that it was a brand new day, with a revamped governance structure. The power base had shifted to the presidents' council and away from the A.D.s, faculty reps, and women's administrators (a joint group).

That new shift came in a surprising discovery that Penn State had been voted membership into the conference. Delany had been involved with the presidents in the deliberation that led to that decision and had been sworn to secrecy, yet he was their front man with the governance groups. Delany was operating in a delicate and difficult role, walking a very thin line. He had to work very closely with the joint group members and yet not break his trust with the presidents.

I thought he handled the situation with class. The joint group soon felt its authority slipping away. Delany was the only leader between the presidents and the joint group. The athletics directors were used to being the decision makers, as was the joint group, and were not accustomed to having secret decisions thrust upon them. Duke had made sure the A.D.s were informed on almost every issue. They had developed an effective working relationship, although it was a little rocky at times.

Delany's initial meetings with conference groups, including the football and men's basketball coaches, were quite contentious. Those groups were accustomed to working with a commissioner who would share most information openly. Access to that information was now controlled totally by the presidents' council and Delany.

I give Jim credit for intelligently handling a confounding situation with all its potential for discord. He refused to take the bait when confronted or challenged about the transformation going on in the conference and there were several occasions that had the potential of going bad. He was smart and attempted to explain over and over that he had been sworn to secrecy by the presidents concerning Penn State's membership in the Big Ten. He challenged the groups to consult with their individual presidents, who voted in favor of admitting Penn State. He would have violated their confidence if he had talked out of turn.

Over the years, I have learned that, like everything else in life, no matter how difficult things may be at the time life moves on and when you have good leaders at the top people will adjust to critical issues and move on in time, as well. All problems are made for human growth and improvement, if we work to resolve them. An adversarial situation, irrespective of its intimidating or horrifying fear, can be a good thing if we learn to grow from it.

So sure enough, through the commissioner's calmness, leadership, and communication, the Penn State membership matter was fully accepted in the Big Ten with some phasing in components regarding eligibility and financial issues. Although the joint group was upset over the presidents' confidential process and erosion of their authority, I don't believe anybody in the entire conference was opposed to the Nittany Lions' membership. They had great people and successful programs that clearly enhanced the conference image. Folks were annoyed with the process in which the membership was granted, but not with Penn State.

Dewey bows out; reorganization retreat

Delany began his tenure in the conference office by sponsoring an office staff retreat in his cottage in Buffalo, N.Y. The senior staff was there for about five days with a challenging agenda. Each staff member had to conduct research on a predetermined topic or two and present our findings to the total staff. We had to come up with a strategic plan that would reorganize staff functions and help set a new direction for the office. We worked well together, had fun, and it was a great way to get oriented with the new commissioner.

Prior to the retreat, long-time staff member John Dewey retired. He had been a conference employee for 45 years. Similar to Duke, he, too, left the conference office unobtrusively. He was an intelligent, hardworking, and organized person who was known as "Mr. Big Ten." He had performed almost every professional job in the Big Ten office and was a great resource to the staff and to representatives of the universities.

For years Dewey was the auditor and chief investigator for Big Ten and NCAA rules violations. He worked with the faculty reps, A.D.s, and the women's administrators. He was promoted to associate commissioner in 1984. I will always be thankful for the generous assistance he provided to me in the office. Noreese and I appreciate the friendship of both John and his wife, Ann, and wish them the best life has to offer.

Kevin Weiberg was hired from Maryland to take Dewey's position. At the retreat, Delany made some additional organizational changes. I was previously the liaison with all men's sports. Weiberg would now have the athletics directors and another new hire, Richard Falk, would handle men's basketball coaches, as well as another one of my duties, administrator over men's basketball officiating. In addition to my remaining assignments, I was given two of Dewey's responsibilities: the compliance program and liaison with the faculty representatives.

Sports Information Director Mark Rudner, meanwhile, was promoted to a new position, assistant commissioner for media communications. There were a few other changes, but Howlett continued to serve in her role.

The staff worked well together and the office was busy and productive as ever. The conference (still called the Big Ten, even though the admittance of Penn State gave it 11 universities) purchased a building in Park Ridge and it would be renovated. The conference office would be relocated there. (A new Big Ten logo was designed so that the number 11 could be seen within the lettering of the words, "Big Ten").

Big Ten Commissioner Jim Delany and I

Dave Parry was hired to serve as supervisor of football officiating. He had worked as an official in the NFL for many years and the conference was fortunate to hire a person of his caliber. Parry significantly improved the technical and professional aspects of the officials and instilled public trust in the officiating program. He is a top-notch professional.

The conference also hired Carol Iwaoka to manage a number of areas of responsibility, including eligibility, rules interpretations, as liaison with the faculty representatives (when I resigned in August), student-athlete welfare issues, etc. She was hired from California-Berkeley and was a good addition to the staff, bringing experience to those areas.

SCORE scores with Chicago pupils

Delany was highly motivated to achieve all of his initiatives for outreach activities in a Chicago elementary school in a low socio-economic neighborhood. He wanted to sponsor a reading program and delegated that project to me. Mary Masters, a most capable young woman who was managing editor and special projects director, collaborated with me on the project. (Mary now is an ordained priestess.) We developed a plan that involved our entire conference office staff with the adopted school.

We conducted a contest among staff to come up with an appropriate name for the project. Administrative assistant Janice Lowing came up with the name SCORE — Success Comes Out of Reading Everyday. It was a hit and she won the prize and the SCORE program was implemented at Melody Elementary School on Chicago's west side. We purchased books for grades five and six. All of us, including the commissioner, would go there to read to the children and let them read to us. It was an effective partnership between the conference office and the elementary school.

We sponsored contests and gave awards to the

students who read the most books in a period of time. We took the students on a field trip to Northwestern University. They had an outstanding time running around on the athletic fields and then we provided them with lunch. The SCORE program was successful and was expanded to a second elementary school after I left the office.

Michigan State beckons again

In March 1990, I started receiving telephone calls from Perles, Michigan State's head football coach and recently appointed director of athletics, who wanted to know of my interest in returning to the university. He had an opening for assistant athletics director for compliance and student services. I told him on two occasions that I was not interested in returning to my alma mater, where I had departed and returned twice before.

I had no ill will against my alma mater but my focus was on obtaining an athletics directors' position. My work was going very well in the conference office and my market value was increasing, as evidenced by the series of inquiries about my interest in different positions. I wanted to wait to see if I could find such a position that was the right fit for me and the institution.

At the May conference meetings, Perles asked me once more to consider visiting the campus for an interview. I agreed that I would at least interview for the position, but had little or no interest in taking it if it was offered. On the other hand, Noreese wanted me to take the position, if offered, because our children still were in the area. I said to her that I would interview for the job.

In the meantime, I had already been contacted directly by the president of Morris Brown College in Atlanta. He wanted me to interview for the position of commissioner of the Southern Intercollegiate Athletic Conference (SIAC). It was comprised of 14 historically

160

black colleges in the South. I did interview and was offered the job, but I had not committed myself. Moreover, I was contacted by a headhunter to inquire about my interest in another athletics director position in Georgia. I never did receive full details of the opening because I expressed no interest in it.

I visited Michigan State in June and met with the committee chaired by Dr. Larry Sierra, a former classmate in physical education classes, who was then the director of intramural services. Others on the committee were Dr. Michael Kasavana, faculty athletics representative; Sam Chatterjie, director of the Instructional Media Center; Dr. Lonnie Eiland, a professor in natural science; and Terry Fossom, assistant director of the Ralph Young Fund.

Following that formal interview, I spent some time with Perles. Up to then I had never engaged in much conversation with George. We attended physical education classes together as undergraduates and were colleagues during my brief stint as assistant ticket manager in 1969. He was an assistant football coach on Duffy's staff. Even back then in the 1950s and '60s at MSU, it wasn't customary for blacks and whites to socialize off of the playing surfaces. We were in the same classes together, played sports together, but informal time was devoted to folks who resembled you. That was just the way it was back then in these United States of America. Blacks went one way and whites went another.

I was among the persons who wanted Perles to become the MSU football coach when Waters was hired in 1980. Even then I didn't know Perles personally. I was aware of his outstanding work with the Pittsburgh Steelers and he was a Spartan. I thought he was exactly what the university needed to get our football program back on track.

When Weaver hired him for the position in 1983 I was ecstatic. I was working at the MSU Alumni Association then. I met Perles at a reception at Doug's house and I remember telling him that if I had known he was returning to Michigan State as head football coach I never would have left the athletics department. I had the feeling he would be a great coach at the university. He wanted very much to work for his alma mater and he wanted his teams to be successful like in the days of Biggie Munn and Duffy. He saw himself as the most likely bridge to make it happen.

Not only was he a strong coach, I was delighted that he was coming back for another reason dear to my heart. I believed he would be committed to requiring student-athletes to attend classes and study sessions regularly and thought he and I would have made a great pair, he as the coach and I as the team's academic counselor. I imagined the football team's graduation rate would be the best in the history of the university, perhaps setting an example for other institutions.

Later, I worked with Perles when he attended the head football coaches meetings in the conference office.

George Perles

I prepared the agenda, guided them through it and kept track of their meeting minutes. George was strong in these meetings, an excellent representative for Michigan State. Annually in May, at the end of the coaches' regular agenda, he asked only the head coaches to stay in the room to discuss their football staff's salaries. He would ask conference office staffers to leave the meetings. Perles conducted those sessions just with the coaches so they could be open about the compensations they and their staffs were paid.

During all those meetings, I never heard Perles speak

with conviction on subjects like compliance, raising revenue, student-athlete welfare issues, gender equity, etc. The drifts of their agenda never went in those directions. In our June interview he floored me with his philosophical views on those subjects. He wanted a strong compliance program; articulated a plan to raise revenue to improve our sports and construct new facilities; and was passionate about student-athletes graduating. He also wanted to bring the department in compliance with gender equity requirements.

I sat there awestruck because he was saying exactly the model plan I had put together over time in the conference office in case I interviewed for an athletics directorship. I left Perles' office with my head spinning and went directly to a pay phone and called Noreese in Schaumburg, Ill., telling her George had done an excellent job on me and it appeared we might be returning to East Lansing. Naturally, she was happy about that.

Perles did call and offered me the position at $70,000. It was the same salary I was earning in the conference office. I accepted then met with the president of Morris Brown College, not for the purpose of negotiating a higher salary, but to tell him directly that I was going to accept the position at Michigan State. I believed I owed it to him to give him my decision face-to-face. He did not like it, but I wanted to be fair and honest with him.

All the while I kept Delany informed of my activities. He initially asked me to remain in the conference office. Later, he indicated he would not stand in my way if I wanted to leave, so I decided to resign. Delany sponsored an administrative staff going away dinner at a restaurant in my honor, giving me a $1,000 bonus for meritorious services and leaving me a very nice note the evening prior to my departure from the office. I received other mementos from the staff, which I really appreciated. The conference office was a great experience for me. It certainly expanded my knowledge of college athletics vastly in many different areas.

I met some outstanding people in my role as assistant commissioner in the Big Ten and learned a lot from them. I shall never forget how gracious athletics directors Don Canham of Michigan; George King, Purdue; Ralph Floyd, Indiana; Bruce Corrie, Northwestern; and Neil Stoner, Illinois, were to me whenever I visited their campuses. Others who befriended me were faculty athletics representatives Kasavana and Norrell of Michigan State; Hayden Murray, Indiana; Yvonne Slatton and Sam Becker, Iowa; Carol Kennedy, Ohio State; Mildred Griggs, Illinois; Philip Nelson, Purdue; and Paul Gikas, Gwen Cruzat and Percy Bates, Michigan.

Add to the list other athletics directors like Christian Grant, Robert Bowlsby, and Bump Elliott, Iowa; Jack Weidenbach, Michigan; Weaver, Michigan State; Rick Bay and Chris Voelz, Minnesota; Hugh Hindman and James Jones, Ohio State; Elroy Hirsch and Pat Richter, Wisconsin.

There were a number of women's athletics administrators who supported my efforts in the conference office: Isabella Hutchinson, Indiana; Sandy Barbour, Northwestern; Carol Mertler, Purdue; Phyllis Ocker, Michigan; Phyllis Bailey, Ohio State; Joni Comstock, Purdue; Kit Saunders Nordeen, Wisconsin; and Kathy Lindahl, Michigan State. There were many other conference representatives who came into the governance structure after I left the conference office.

To all of them and to all the athletics directors, women's administrators and faculty athletics representatives with whom I served and worked with, and members of the conference office staff, I wish to express my thanks. I also am grateful for the association I enjoyed with the football coaches, men's basketball coaches, team physicians and trainers, band directors, baseball coaches, the other coaches groups, the advisory commission, and the men's and women's officials and supervisors. I continue to appreciate their acceptance of me

Perles, a stickler for punctuality

I returned to MSU in August 1990 as the assistant athletics director for compliance and student services. My office was in Jenison Field House with the other administrators. Perles, now the football coach *and* athletics director, had his office in the Duffy Daugherty Football Building. Perles became A.D. on July 1, 1990, replacing Weaver.

Administrative staff meetings were conducted weekly in Jenison at 8 a.m. I recall my first staff meeting. It gave me a little insight into the man to whom I would report. I had jogged in Jenison from 6:30-7:30 a.m. and then showered. While dressing, I realized I had forgotten to bring a dress shirt. As I was leaving the parking lot en route to my home to get a shirt, George was entering the lot. It must have been nearly 7:45 a.m. I mentioned to him what had happened and indicated I might be a little late for the meeting. He responded, "You will be on time." I returned 10 minutes late. I could tell by the tone of his voice that reporting late for meetings and appointments did not set well with him.

Perles drilled the value of punctuality into both his players and staff. And he was an excellent personal role model in that regard. There were numerous examples when he demonstrated that quality, but two stand out. The Big Ten and NCAA both require each student-athlete to complete multiple financial and eligibility forms before a team's first organized practice of the season. Typically, the director of compliance services is the one who administers the meeting. Some coaches at MSU also used the meeting to review team conduct rules. That was the case in August of 1990 with Perles.

There must have been 110 players and a combination of 35 coaches, graduate assistants, student managers, trainers, equipment staff and administrators crammed into the auditorium of Wilson Hall for the two-hour meeting. It was a warm night and Perles spoke first to the team. He was halfway through reviewing team rules when the door opened. It became extremely quiet and all heads turned to the young player who entered the room and walked down the aisle toward the back of the room with his head down.

It surely seemed that everybody but me knew what was coming next. I am sure most of them had seen it before or maybe had been a victim one time or another. Perles asked the young man why he was late. He responded that he had overslept. He was then asked whether he had an alarm clock. The player said no. George asked whether he had a roommate. The young man said yes. Perles bellowed out some very strong language at the player for what appeared to be 10 minutes.

I am sure it was much less time, but it was so intense. He was, I was certain, using this occasion as an example to the team. I thought he unquestionably got his point across to the young man and to the team. He then continued to review the team rules. Discipline is a major component in the lives of athletes. Without it, a person has little chance of accomplishing individual and team goals.

The second example of Perles' commitment to punctuality related to persons traveling on the team charter for away football games. It was understood that no passenger could arrive late and board the aircraft. That was his mandate. He would stand outside greeting each passenger as they climbed the steps to board the charter. But whenever he boarded the plane, the doors would be closed. I never observed them reopened for any latecomers.

Joe Farrell, who is probably Perles' best friend and who was his undergraduate roommate, fell victim to the mandate. Farrell was riding to the airport with a friend, Gene Scott, a big booster of Spartan athletics. They arrived a few minutes after the aircraft door had closed, but prior to takeoff. Perles would not permit the door to open. Joe and Gene served as examples to those of us who already boarded the plane.

Perles had some very definite life skill values that he tried to instill in his players. One of them was never to be late for an appointment. Being late showed signs of irresponsibility. During the five years I worked directly with him, I never witnessed him arriving late for an appointment, unless he was detained by central administration prior to his next meeting. Even now, when we meet for lunch or for some other reasons, he always is an early arrival.

I shock folks when responding to the question about who was the best A.D. I ever worked for at Michigan State — and there were some good ones. I tell them George Perles and they look surprised. Then I tell them why I feel that way. You will find few people with Perles' people skills. He is adept at cultivating loyalty, showing compassion, empowering staff with responsibilities, and holding them accountable. He was highly organized and a strategic planner who believed in the chain of command and was a master of those areas.

Another quality he exhibited, to my liking, was his direct approach to tackling problems. He hit them head-on. There was no beating around the bush. Staff members knew where they stood with him. I have always respected folks who were direct and upfront with me. I can take the worst of criticism and remain humble if it's given to me with honesty and without any political agenda. I never have liked backbiting and deceptions. Noreese will tell you that I don't like to hear much unconfirmed gossip about other people, so we seldom have such discussions in our house. I have seen Perles' genuine compassion on display. He would rip an athlete unmercifully one day for a misdeed and the next day he would be hugging him showing how much he cared. He was a leader who knew how to get the very best out of people.

Perles understood finances and budgets. His personal style of management was not conducive for everyone.

He had his share of opponents. I know that when the president at that time, John DiBiaggio, gave him the mandate in 1991 to either surrender the head football coaching job or the A.D. position, a majority of coaches and administrators hoped he would remain the A.D. I know he wanted to end his career at the university in that role, but it was the worst of the two options. Perles had six years left on his 10-year coaching contract. His total compensation was approximately $500,000 annually. The athletics directorship was for three and a half years, with significantly less money, and required a presidential evaluation after the first year of any new contract. He had to choose the option after the evaluation of his already-served one-year athletics directorship in the position for the 1990-91 year.

In anticipation of that review, one of the first initiatives I implemented when I was hired in 1990 was a monthly review of the activities in the department. I contacted each administrator every month to obtain a listing of the accomplishments for the individual units. I would chronicle them by dates in a report under the signature of Perles and send them to Provost David Scott, who was responsible for heading up the one-year evaluation. When the time came for Perles to prepare a narrative summarizing his accomplishments for the evaluation, we already had an up-to-date history. The coaches and administrators were requested to provide their evaluation of Perles' performance and results of the reports showed most wanted him to continue as the athletics director, but he remained as head football coach.

'Associate director' promotion first for MSU

He promoted me to the rank of associate director in June 1991. It was the first time such a designation had been established in the department. The position elevated me to second in command. I would be in charge whenever Perles was out of town or unavailable. We worked very well together and respected each other. We would meet frequently to review agendas, discuss concepts, resolve issues, and plan strategies. There were other staffers upon whom Perles depended for appropriate services, such as promotions director Ganakas; Sports Information Director Ken Hoffman; Don Loding, ticket manager; marketing director Breslin; Terry Braverman, director of the Ralph Young Fund; and Peggy Brown, business manager.

Perles had many ideas about fund raising and other concepts that he was unable to develop in his one year as A.D. One of the concepts he asked me to develop was a Code of Conduct for Student Athletes. Some coaches in the 25 sports were having difficulty applying consistent disciplinary measures to athletes who committed offenses. The proposal identified 34 possible violations, divided into three categories: minor, serious, and gross misconduct. It met Perles' approval but was not adopted by the university. There were issues regarding double jeopardy and penalties for off-campus offenses in which the university generally had no such policy. The board of trustees subsequently developed a policy that covers off-campus offenses. The trustees also developed a policy that prohibits a student-athlete with a felony record from participating in the intercollegiate athletics program.

Another concept we were successful in implementing was a hall of fame. I did the research and developed the concept into a proposal that Perles approved. We appointed an internal committee to get it established. George no longer was the A.D. when the first induction ceremony occurred in 1992. Merrily Dean Baker was appointed A.D. in May of that year by DiBiaggio. The inductees consisted of 30 athletes, coaches, administrators, and players, including Breslin, Daugherty, Munn, Earvin Johnson, Bob Carey, Don Coleman, Lyman Frimodig, Earl Morrall, Bubba Smith,

Gene Washington, Ralph Young, Gloria Becksford, and George Webster.

The 1993 football team took a 6-4 record into the last regular season game of the schedule — in Japan against Wisconsin in what was called the Coca-Cola Bowl. Going into the game, the Badgers needed a victory to qualify for the Rose Bowl. We were bowl-eligible because we had won six games, but we could not be selected for a bowl until the season was over.

Wisconsin was riding a crest of popularity. It had a good team and was ranked high in the polls. At the sold-out banquet on the eve of the game, every Japanese speaker was overwhelmingly in favor of Wisconsin. Little mention was made of Michigan State. Coach Barry Alvarez spoke for Wisconsin and Perles spoke for MSU.

Feeling slighted, as most Spartans in attendance were, Perles told the crowd, in part, "This game don't mean shit to Michigan State." I understood why he said it, but it was wrong for him to say it. There were trustees, administrators and a few alumni there. As political as the university is, I knew the statement would come back to haunt him.

McPherson targets Perles for dismissal

The Spartans got a bid to play in the Liberty Bowl, Dec. 28 in Memphis, Tenn., against the University of Louisville. About a week before our team and the official party departed for Memphis, M. Peter McPherson, the new MSU president who took office Oct. 1, 1993, from Gordon Guyer, called my home on a Saturday night and said he was thinking about firing Perles immediately after the bowl game. He said he believed George had lost the inspiration to win and had become too content and satisfied with mediocrity.

McPherson stressed he wanted a winning team and asked for my reaction. I told him I was surprised by his stance. I believed Perles still had the fire to win and should

170

have a much better team in the 1994 season because seniors would dominate the lineups. I explained that after a successful 1990 season, the 1991 squad was loaded with freshmen and sophomores. I think the team should have won more games in 1993 and next year's team should win more than six games.

He asked, "What if we lost the Liberty Bowl?" I responded, "We should not lose to Louisville, which is known as a basketball school. But if we did lose, it would send a bad signal for next season." The president thanked me for my comments and said that unless he made changes soon he would be viewed as part of the problem.

In Memphis at the Liberty Bowl pre-game brunch, McPherson approached me and asked if I had given more thought to his position on Perles. But before I could respond we were interrupted. Later, in the press box with a minute or two left in the game (which we lost 18-7), McPherson and trustee Joel Ferguson, who was chairman of the board of trustees, invited me to join them on the staff bus. As we sat in the middle section, athletics ticket manager Loding boarded the bus and subsequently the conversation about Perles never took place.

McPherson called my home in early January asking whether he should hire a consultant to search for a new football coach. I suggested Canham. There were several reasons for my suggestion. Canham was a friend and man I deeply respected. Although he had a University of Michigan background, he was no longer formerly affiliated with U-M and was a professional businessman who was available to conduct the search. He had recommended Alvarez to President Donna Shalala at Wisconsin. Canham, nationally known for his accomplishments while director of athletics at Michigan, was a friend to MSU.

(Crisler Arena in Ann Arbor was packed with his admirers in May 2005 for a memorial service after his untimely death from a ruptured abdominal aortic aneurysm that caused him to crash into a tree while driving near his home in Saline. He was 87.)

I advised McPherson that it was important to hire a proven successful coach. The university and its alumni deserved the very best. We did not need anyone with fewer credentials than Perles because that would further alienate Michigan State's friends and supporters. McPherson thanked me for the advice. A few days later the president called at my home and said he didn't feel comfortable using Canham as the consultant because some MSU people might view Canham as a negative because of his association with Michigan. I understood his point but didn't agree with it because a consultant works quietly behind the scenes and the university has veto power over all suggestions put forth.

Nevertheless, I told him there were other competent professionals who could perform very adequately in the role. I told McPherson I would be attending the NCAA convention in San Antonio. He asked for me to quietly feel out some potential consultants and try to get the names of some coaching candidates. Among those I spoke with at the convention was Joe Kearney, the former MSU athletics director, who was the commissioner of the Western Athletic Conference. He suggested two possible football coach candidates.

I also approached Roy Kramer, commissioner of the Southeastern Conference, about whether he would be interested in serving as the consultant. He was interested, so when McPherson called me and asked if I had spoken with anyone about the job or gotten the names of any coach prospects I told him what I had done and assured him Kearney and Kramer would keep the information confidential as I had been instructed.

McPherson later called at my home requesting the telephone number of Kramer and wanted more background on him. Also, he wanted to know if Big Ten commissioner Delany should be involved in the search. I advised against his involvement because he was too close to the scene.

McPherson agreed and said Kramer would be better because he could make contacts with candidates without them knowing for whom he was working.

McPherson then acknowledged he had already spoken with Delany relative to the search, mentioning that Delany had sought the opinion of consultant Rick Bay. Indications were the head coaches at Miami University in Florida and Boston College might be available and both institutions, I indicated, had successful teams.

Trustee Joel Ferguson; Robert Green, former Dean of Urban Affairs; and I at my fraternity retirement party

The president then asked whether a professional coach could be successful at Michigan State and he mentioned the possible availability of Joe Gibbs of the Washington Redskins. Gibbs would be suitable, I said, but might be very expensive. McPherson was prepared to pay the cost if we could land him and he asked how much compensation Perles was getting. I didn't know specifically, but told him I would research it.

McPherson said he would review Perles' contract

173

and that Ferguson was aware of all that was going on. He asked me to continue to maintain confidentiality. I was working on that mission without the knowledge of my supervisors, Athletics Director Merrily Baker, and Roger Wilkinson, who was vice president for treasury, operations and finances and who also had oversight responsibilities for the athletics department. They, along with Perles, had no role in the process.

Later in January, I received two phone calls from McPherson on consecutive Friday nights. He said Kramer would telephone him each of the next two Saturdays at Cowles House, the residence of the president, to bring us up to date on the search. He invited me to join him. At the meeting were McPherson; his wife, Joanne; the president's administrative assistant, Jay Morris; and myself.

The first Saturday, Kramer reviewed the list of possible candidates and McPherson told him to follow up with each one of them and determine their interest. He also requested that Kramer continue to search for other prospects. Kramer failed to call the second Saturday, calling me instead at my office Monday morning to explain he had a conflict and wasn't able to follow up with the president.

Later that evening, McPherson called at my home and sounded annoyed, saying Kramer had called suggesting it would be best to wait until fall 1994 to search for a quality coach to replace Perles. Kramer thought a change in February would create too much disruption at the university and at the institutions where the candidates were located.

He said he understood Kramer had called me and I acknowledged that and offered to share our conversation, but Kramer had requested the opportunity to tell McPherson first hand about his recommendation. I got the feeling McPherson didn't like it because I had not told him sooner about Kramer's call to me. He wanted to know whether there were any remaining coach alternatives and I said I totally agreed with Kramer's recommendation and we should wait as the SEC commissioner had suggested.

I didn't participate in the development of the "expectations" McPherson decreed to Perles for the 1994 season. I found out in a press release March 3 that Perles was supposed to have an unspecified "outstanding" season or suffer the consequences. I knew such a mandate was a no-win situation for George, his coaches and players. The runaway train was moving down the track fast and no one could stop it. Perles was rapidly losing support from central administration, the board of trustees, and some alumni. The athletics director and a few others in the department wanted his head. It was a highly antagonistic environment for anyone in Perles' situation to simply survive, let alone have the mandated outstanding season.

The "expectations" legitimized the pent-up negative feelings some people had against him. I heard ugly comments about the program and I'm certain the coaches and players heard similar ones. No coach can have an outstanding season when he is looking over his shoulder trying to see what may be coming at him. Perles is a strong man, but even the strongest would buckle in such a situation.

Despite the unsettling climate, Perles and his coaches worked very hard to overcome the adversity. They prepared the team well for each game. The Spartans had lost their best running back, Steve "Batman" Holman, in the summer. We lost to Notre Dame in South Bend, 21-20, with one of our receivers dropping a touchdown pass in the end zone. We also lost a very tough game at Iowa, 19-14.

I didn't attend the news conference March 3 when the "expectations" were announced, nor did I go to Perles' last news conference when he was fired. I was aware that it would be painful for everyone connected with the program. When it was all over, a good and decent man, a

175

one-of-a-kind guy who gave it all he had and did so with integrity, had fallen from the throne. He is a man of rare dignity who works hard and I'm glad to call him my friend.

More new duties — and long, long title

In September 1992, our department was having a meeting with the coaches and administrators in Kellogg Center in anticipation of the upcoming academic year. During the meeting, Baker was called to President Gordon Guyer's office. Returning about 45 minutes later, she pulled me aside and said she was going to expand my job description. (DiBiaggio left on Aug. 31 and Guyer was appointed as president, serving a little over a year, until September 30, 1992.)

Baker wanted me to continue as associate director of athletics for compliance services and as administrator for student-athlete support services, but out of the meeting, added to the mix, was a role with the office of the provost. The title would be, *Assistant to the Provost for Athletics Compliance, Standards, and Academic Services.* I would attend the provost's staff meetings on Thursday mornings and meet with the Council of Deans on Tuesday mornings.

Baker is a highly intelligent person who I had known and worked with when I was in the Big Ten office. She was the women's A.D. at Minnesota. She and Christine Grant, the women's A.D. from the University of Iowa, met with the men conference athletics directors and so Baker was no stranger to me when she was hired in 1992. I respected Baker and harbored no ill will toward her.

Initially our working relationship was good. Then it declined steadily. One issue was she wanted me to heal the problems existing between she and Perles. I did try to help but was unsuccessful. Both persons were too stubborn and egotistical. Another barrier was how she wanted me to communicate with her and still another was related to a memo I wrote about Jud Heathcote.

She wanted me to come to her office often and chat informally about matters, frequently reminding me that the other two associates, Greg Ianni and Kathy Lindahl, communicated with her in that fashion. I respect Greg and Kathy. I don't know how they communicated with Baker outside of our structured staff meetings. It was not my style to interact with Baker in the manner that she suggested.

Any supervisor with whom I ever have worked for or with will confirm that is not my style of relating on the job. First, my job kept me extremely busy. I like it that way otherwise I get bored and lose focus. Second, I seldom use work time to visit socially about personal matters or to gossip. I always felt, rightly or wrongly, that I was being paid a handsome salary to deliver effective services and it did not include personal issues. I tried to keep her informed as best I could about my job duties. There were some things I couldn't share with her because the president asked me to keep them private. I know there are folks who will strongly disagree with my style in a working environment, but I always have tried to separate work time from personal time. That doesn't mean I was a recluse on the job. I was civil, cooperative, and did a few brief periods of office visitations. But I kept focused on my responsibilities.

That wasn't the first time I encountered Baker's management style. I once worked with a consultant at the Michigan Department of Education who advocated that colleagues should customarily interact with each other informally in the office to get better acquainted and to reduce cultural strain. I always have believed that there are other ways to accomplish those objectives than by doing so during regular working hours.

Baker never did invite me to lunch. Nor did she ever entertain her three associates together in a relaxed atmosphere after working hours. The four of us took a half-day off from work once to play a round of golf. Using working hours to communicate socially or to chitchat never was my style.

Baker, Norvell don't last long as A.D.s

Using working hours to communicate socially wasn't my style, but there was a time when four of us from the office took some time out for a round of golf to get better acquainted in a relaxed atmosphere.

Overall, Baker was a good person in the wrong place at the wrong time. The A.D. position at Michigan State just wasn't meant for her. Just like Perles trying to work under "an outstanding season" mandate in 1994, her destiny was fixed the day DiBiaggio resigned from the university Aug. 31, 1992. Baker worked in an adversarial environment in which everything she did was under scrutiny. She made some mistakes along the way. But even if she had been perfect, she would have caught hell.

A week before she arrived on campus in May I received a call from DiBiaggio, who wanted to know whether I had any problems with Baker. He wanted a supportive cast around her. I responded that I had no problems with her and had known her for several years, mentioning that I believed I could help her get acclimatized to the university. He said he believed I was an honorable man and hoped things would work out between the two of us.

It's impossible to speculate whether our relationship would have grown from good to best under DiBiaggio but, as it turned out, I was told by Wilkinson during a fiasco involving a memo I wrote about Heathcote, that

I was one of the persons Baker wanted transferred out of the department. When she left it was without any fanfare. I read about her resignation in the newspaper. She was paid for the remainder of her five-year contract and relocated to Florida. I do see her occasionally at some post-season athletics events and we treat each other cordially. I don't have any issues with her. I wish she and her daughter the very best in everything they do.

Baker was an experienced athletics administrator who was aware of sports culture and nomenclature. She was acquainted with many athletics folks and had her supporters nationally. Her successor, Merritt Norvell, who was hired by McPherson in December 1994, was lacking in that understanding. He was a former football player at Wisconsin and had served

Merrily Dean Baker

on its athletics board. He was a former IBM employee. I knew it would be a real struggle for him when he first addressed the department at Kellogg Center upon his permanent arrival at campus in July 1995.

He repeatedly claimed ownership of the coaching staff by using the phrase, "my coaches." Every time he would use the term I would see new football coach Nick Saban and other head coaches sitting in front of me cringing. The coaches looked at each other shrewdly. Those independent, powerful coaches belonged to no one at the university, especially an unknown newcomer.

Norvell had polished public speaking skills and was a man of integrity, with some marketing skills, as well. Normally such qualities are sufficient to carry a leader through most jobs, if he leaned on his staff for expert help. Norvell, however, was too egotistical himself to rely upon staff for advice. He gave instructions rather than receiving advice from his experienced staff members.

Eventually it was obvious that he had lost the respect of his staff and could not provide adequate information to solve problems. As a consequence, staff members worked around Norvell in order to make progress in their jobs. Many more were turned off by his haughty manner. One illustration occurred during the first away football game in 1995, against Louisville, when he violated a traditional MSU travel rule: never be late for the team plane.

At the stated departure time, everyone boarded the team aircraft except Norvell and his wife. They arrived five to 10 minutes late. The flight attendant asked Norvell in a rather loud manner who he was to delay the departure time. He said, "I'm the boss." Norvell's response and tardiness did not set well with Saban and the trustees on the plane. The tradition at MSU allowed coaches to be responsible for team travel and departure time, so the "boss'" statement was in conflict with the belief of a coach who felt he was in charge of the plane.

At Cardinal Stadium against Louisville, a torrential rainstorm started just before kickoff. It is protocol for the visiting A.D. to be given a private box in the press box, usually accommodating six to 12 persons. MSU historically uses the box for its officials traveling to the game. Norvell, failing to act with any political astuteness, used the box to accommodate some of his relatives. Mrs. Saban and some trustees were left out in the rain. A political disaster was looming.

The working conditions steadily declined under Norvell's leadership and he was forced out of the job. Upon his resignation, he was quoted by the *Lansing State Journal* as saying the A.D.'s position was too complex. He was paid the remainder of his five-year contract, plus a $100,000 consultant fee. McPherson was the person who made the decision to hire Norvell. It was DiBiaggio who hired Baker, but McPherson who paid both Norvell and Baker the buyout money. I wish Merritt and his wife, Cynthia, the very best in life.

Merritt Norvell

CHAPTER 5:

THE HEATHCOTE MEMO

Leaked private advisory
creates year of turmoil

LATE IN THE 1994 SEASON, A SERIES OF EVENTS
began that snowballed into an avalanche of negative
publicity for me, loss of a few acquaintances, and even
death threats. They came after I suggested in a memo
to President M. Peter McPherson, somehow leaked to
the news media, that basketball coach Jud Heathcote
should resign.

Along the way I learned some painful lessons about
balancing honesty and discretion, and the importance of
reinforcing the chain of command, even when it seems
difficult to do so and others do not. I also found out how
persistent the media can be.

First, let's go back 19 years earlier to 1976 when I
served on the interviewing committee that recommended
Heathcote as the coach. President Clifton Wharton
headed the committee. Others on it were faculty athletics
representative Gwen Norrell, Alumni Director Jack
Kinney, professor Jake Hofer, and Athletics Director Joe
Kearney. The interview took place in Chicago at one of
the hotels adjacent to the airport.

Heathcote was hired, but our relationship seemed to sour early and we didn't see eye to eye on some NCAA compliance issues in the department. There were a number of relatively insignificant incidents in which we had unfortunate discussions. Once he came to my office and yelled at my secretary, Jamie Mick, because she had returned a recruitment reimbursement voucher to him for additional information. I took exception to his behavior because Jamie was only doing her job by following procedures. It was her job to reconcile recruitment expenditures with the requirements of NCAA rules and university policies so the basketball program would be in compliance. I told him he should have come to me with his complaint but he didn't respond. There were many similar incidents.

He once called me on the telephone for an NCAA rules interpretation. Because he didn't like the one I was giving to him, he slammed the phone down while I was talking to him. At the time, my office was on the third floor and his was on the main floor of Jenison Fieldhouse. I immediately headed to his office to tell him I didn't appreciate his behavior. I was a colleague, not his enemy, and we were supposed to work together in the athletics department and respect each other.

We met in the lobby. He was on his way to see Athletics Director Doug Weaver. I told him I didn't appreciate him slamming the phone down in my ear when I was responding to his question. He didn't say anything and continued walking toward Weaver's office. About an hour later, Weaver phoned and asked me to come to his office. Jud had gone. Weaver said he didn't know what he was going to do with me and Jud and that we couldn't seem to get along with each other.

When I entered Weaver's office, I observed from his window that there was a work crew across the street in winter weather digging a ditch near Demonstration Hall. I told Doug I'd rather be one of the ditch diggers than to infringe upon my integrity by deliberately giving an erroneous NCAA interpretation for the convenience of coach Heathcote. Weaver never again brought any issue between Jud and I to my attention.

In 1977, Heathcote sponsored a party at his home on a Friday night and my wife and I were in attendance. At the time, he was trying to have an academically at-risk junior college student admitted to MSU for the winter semester. There was a problem with the student's transcript, which made him temporarily inadmissible to the university (I believe some of his credits hadn't been recorded, so Jud sent assistant coach Bill Berry to the junior college to have the transcript updated). Hours later, Berry arrived at the party with the revised transcript and gave it to Heathcote. When Berry arrived, I was outside on the deck conversing with some of the guests.

Jud Heathcote

Jud, who was in the living room that was full of people, sent for me and when I arrived he overtly handed me the transcript, saying in a dictatorial manner in front of his guests that, "You had better not f_ _ _ it up." I suppose he meant that since I was the assistant athletics director responsible for the academic counseling of student athletes and liaison with the office of admissions he didn't want any more delays with the athlete's admission for the next semester.

I was angry by his disrespectful and rude behavior

185

toward me and left the party abruptly with my wife. I called Jud early Saturday morning at his home before he took his team to the Lansing airport for an away game. I told him I didn't appreciate the way he treated me at the party. I felt he should have been more civil because I wasn't responsible for the admission of the transfer athlete. That was a responsibility that belonged to the office of admissions. Neither was I responsible for the deficient transcript. I felt like he was blaming me for the initial incomplete transcript, which had been sent to the office of admissions and denied. He never apologized during our phone conversation. He just held the phone until I finished talking. I presented the revised transcript to the office of admissions Monday morning and the athlete was subsequently admitted for the winter semester.

Then there was the issue at the 1991 post-season men's basketball banquet when I was the compliance officer. Heathcote had ordered awards for some of his athletes and planned to give them out that night. The NCAA places a monetary value limit on the awards a university can give to an athlete. Anything in excess of the monetary limit is considered an NCAA violation. Jud never consulted with me about the value prior to ordering the awards, figures that were listed in the NCAA manual in his office. He acted on his own.

Around 5 p.m., about an hour and a half before the social hour, I received a telephone call from the athletics business manager, Peggy Brown, who informed me that Jud intended to give some student-athletes awards that would exceed the NCAA limits. That would mean a violation that had to be reported to the conference office and the NCAA. I immediately called Heathcote and told him not to exceed NCAA limits otherwise I would have no choice but to report the violation to the NCAA.

When Heathcote started giving out the awards at the banquet, he asked me to stand up in the audience. When I did, he made comments to the effect that I was the reason all of the awards couldn't be given out that evening to the student-athletes. I got angry and felt his behavior was totally inappropriate and unprofessional. I visited his office the next day to better understand what he was trying to say about me. That time he did apologize to me, plus he got some other letters and calls requesting that he make a public apology to me. He sent me a letter reiterating his apology.

Two years later, in 1993, he resented the way I conducted thorough investigations regarding allegations of Big Ten and NCAA rules violations associated with the men's basketball program. He preferred that I work to deny the allegations instead of searching for the truth. I only knew one way to seek the truth and that was to look aggressively for the facts in all investigations that I conducted. I didn't allow those and all of his other slights to interfere with my working relationship with him.

I always have taken the position that, although I may have a contentious relationship with a fellow employee, I was being paid to cooperate with that employee on the job. However, because we weren't close personal friends, I didn't feel I could talk to him about sensitive issues, which might be misconstrued. And I felt no obligation to socialize with him personally after working hours.

Complaints mount against Heathcote

In early 1994, I had been given the title of Senior Associate Athletics Director, with responsibility for compliance, athletics academic counseling, and the three revenue-producing sports: men's basketball, football, and ice hockey. After the men's basketball team started slowly in the 1993-94 season, I started getting phone calls and visits from people complaining. Such complaints from fans, parents, and alumni are a normal part of athletics culture. The complaints said they were tired of an average men's basketball program and advocated that

Heathcote retire. His conference record at the time was a mediocre 172-164 and, at that point of the season, the Spartans had a 5-7 Big Ten record. They would end up with a 10-8 mark, good for fourth in the conference, and a 20-12 overall record.

While our men's basketball team was struggling early in the Big Ten portion of the schedule that winter, Heathcote said publicly he *might* retire at the end of the season — or remain for another year. For a head coach of a revenue-producing sport to raise the question of retirement and be indecisive about the date is a kiss of death for the recruiting season because the coach is the most important factor in attracting prospects. Few will commit to a program if they don't know whether or not the coach will still be there.

I never understood why it was necessary for Heathcote to make such a wishy-washy statement so early in the season, fully aware that it would affect future recruitment. Most coaches don't announce their retirement until they have agreed on a definite date and the announcement usually comes at the end of the season.

It already had been difficult for MSU to recruit blue chip urban prospects with Heathcote as coach, although that wasn't well publicized. (That statement may seem puzzling to the reader who remembers Heathcote taking the Spartans on to win the NCAA championship in 1979 with Earvin "Magic" Johnson, Greg Kelser, and Jay Vincent leading the way. But Gus Ganakas and his staff heavily recruited Johnson and Vincent before Heathcote's arrival and Kelser already was a sophomore in the program.)

Heathcote is bright, entertaining, and articulate, but his program had been able to attract only a few blue chip urban prospects from the urban areas in Michigan. Yet he did have success recruiting such prospects as Steve Smith, Shawn Respert, Mark Montgomery, and Kevin Willis from Detroit; and Matt Steigenga from Grand Rapids. However, during his tenure many other blue chip urban prospects in the state either went to the University of Michigan or to institutions outside the state. The failure to consistently attract blue chip student-athletes from urban areas in your own state can cause long-term damage to a basketball program that is difficult to repair.

Generally, moderately successful athletics programs can't consistently attract blue chippers from other states. At best, they may occasionally land one blue chip urban student-athlete and some secondary players. Most blue chip urban prospects attend institutions in their own states so their parents, relatives, and friends can see them compete. That is, unless a university has a nationally renowned program. Then it can recruit the urban blue chippers from anywhere because they and their parents want to be associated with championship programs.

Even when Heathcote's team won the NCAA title in 1979 he couldn't capitalize on the success when it came time to recruit. In the 1979-80 season, the team won just six Big Ten games, lost 12, and finished ninth in the conference. MSU was just 7-11 in the league the following season and finished eighth. Then, in 1981-82, the Spartans again were 7-11 in the Big Ten, finishing seventh. It is better for coaches to focus their recruiting on top players in their own state and use the other states to recruit whatever good prospects they might be able to get.

In-state recruitment hadn't always been a problem at MSU. Ganakas, who was the head coach from the 1969-70 season through 1975-76, was successful recruiting blue chip players from Michigan's urban areas. About 80 percent of his prospects were recruited from the state of Michigan, compared with about 58 percent that Jud recruited from the state. Gus snared such blue chippers as Kelser, Ralph Simpson, Mike Robinson, Lovell Rivers, and Lindsey Hairston from the Detroit area; Terry Furlow and Bill Glover from Flint; Bill Kilgore from River Rouge; Bobby Chapman from Saginaw; and Edgar Wilson from Dowagiac. He also was instrumental in the recruitment of Johnson and Vincent

Player walkout blemishes MSU program

Ganakas was establishing a solid recruitment base in Michigan before he was unexpectedly reassigned to another position in the athletics department after the 1975-76 season. That was about a year after one unfortunate incident during his coaching tenure, one that some fans wouldn't put behind them: the walkout by MSU men's black basketball players in January 1975 in protest over Ganakas' decision to start forward Jeff Tropf, a white freshman, in place of one of the more experienced black

The 1974-75 basketball squad of Gus Ganakas had a 17-9 record, but 10 black players, including, from left, Lindsay Hairston, Terry Furlow, and Bill Glover, walked out in protest over a decision to start a white freshman against Indiana. After suspending them, Ganakas reinstated the players after they apologized.

players, for the upcoming home game against Indiana. The black players believed Tropf couldn't help the team win against the Hoosiers, who were ranked No. 1 in the country.

MSU President Clifton Wharton appointed me to serve as the liaison between the student-athletes and coaching staff during the protest. Athletics Director Burt Smith was out of town attending an ice hockey meeting in Colorado during the walkout. Ganakas suspended the 10 black varsity players for the game and played junior varsity players, including Tropf, instead. Indiana won 107-55.

I met with the players Sunday in a classroom in Jenison Fieldhouse and reported the questions, concerns, issues, and decisions of the athletes to Ganakas and his staff. After several hours of discussion, the players decided they had made an error in judgment and requested to be reinstated for Monday night's Ohio State game. When I relayed their decision to Ganakas he said no and that the players would continue on indefinite suspension. I told them of Ganakas' decision.

By that time the players were in agony over their walkout and didn't want to miss any more games. They decided to go down the hall to Ganakas' office and meet as a group with him. Hairston spoke for the team, telling Ganakas they all wanted to play Monday against the Buckeyes and would do anything to get reinstated. Hairston apologized for their behavior and for causing embarrassment to the program and the university.

Hairston's apologetic words were music to the ears of Ganakas, who immediately lifted the suspension and accepted the players back. Some folks resented the protest and Ganakas' subsequent decision to allow them to return to the team without disciplinary consequences. In my opinion, he did the right thing in both instances and I publicly supported him.

The protest, which made national news, harmed the basketball program. To continue the suspension would have, in all probability, made a bad situation worse each passing day. I learned from the athletes that the reason for the walkout wasn't confined to the decision of Ganakas to play Tropf. There were other issues, such as how the players perceived their treatment by the athletics department as compared with that given to football players. They felt their program was financially short-changed relative to the quality of training table meals and for away games meal money compared to the football program. They also felt there were communication misunderstandings, but that was corrected by the coach.

The players already had suffered a lot by missing the Indiana game and stewing over their decision to walk out. But they were men enough to admit their mistake, apologize to the coaching staff, which included Ganakas, assistants Vern Payne, Dick Versace, and Pat Miller. The coaches, in turn, were men enough to accept the apology and give the players a second chance

The Heathcote era was next and later, when he resigned, assistant Tom Izzo succeeded him and resumed placing special emphasis on recruiting in-state blue chip student-athletes. About 70 percent of Izzo's squad members graduated from Michigan high schools, including such successes as Mateen Cleaves, Morris Peterson, Kelvin Torbert, Antonio Smith, and Charlie Bell from Flint; Jason Richardson from Saginaw; Jason Klein from Grosse Ile; and Marcus Taylor from Lansing, to name a few.

Coach's indecision tough on recruiting

Izzo was virtually unknown to the public when Jud anointed him in 1994 as his successor, before Heathcote knew when he was actually stepping down. As one of our top recruiters, Izzo was in a tough spot because Jud was wavering about his retirement date. It would seem disloyal and confusing to prospects and parents for Izzo to recruit them to play for Heathcote but the young athletes might wind up playing for Izzo instead, or some other coach, particularly when there already was much confusion about Jud's retirement date.

It was almost impossible for Izzo to recruit blue chip urban athletes while standing in the shadow of Jud. Why should they commit to a program that was struggling against Big Ten competition when they didn't know precisely who the head coach was going to be? Jud created this uncertain climate by not being decisive about his retirement date. Blue chippers go to championship programs and those in which they believe in the coach. You can't put much confidence in a coach who is publicly wavering about his tenure in the program.

None of the negative comments really mattered to me because fans complain all the time about a coach. Either he isn't winning enough games, can't recruit well, or just didn't make the right call on a certain play. It goes on and on. I always have tried to defend coaches against such public criticism. I made it my duty to respond to all complaints I received about coaches, without the coach having knowledge about them.

However, considering the whole situation and the future of the men's program, it seemed best for Michigan State if Heathcote retired and let the ambitious Izzo take over. Since Jud was eligible for retirement, leaving the university a year earlier wouldn't harm him financially, and he was considering retirement anyway.

I wrote a confidential memorandum to the president on the matter, asking to speak privately with him about it and also seeking permission to speak with Heathcote about his status. I indicated, among other things, that the coach should be fully compensated for the one year remaining on his contract. I wouldn't have recommended the retirement if there were any resistance from McPherson about paying Heathcote for the year that was left. I thought the issue could be handled in a professional and dignified way, without fanfare and without anyone getting hurt.

I told the president — who regularly sought my

advice and consul — that I wanted to ask Jud to retire at the end of the season, or be terminated. I had previously played the role of confidential advisor to presidents and chief executive officers without incident. I never imagined a problem would occur with the memo. It was written at a time when the atmosphere in the department, and between it and central administration, was cloudy.

Authority riff encumbers role

My duties seemingly were being expanded in a re-organization. Yet in actuality they were encumbered by a conflict in authority that was developing between Athletics Director Merrily Baker and myself.

President John DiBiaggio hired Baker in May 1992 but announced his resignation a month later to become president of Tufts University in Medford, Mass. The board of trustees in September then appointed Dr. Gordon Guyer until they hired a president to serve on a long-term basis. Baker was left to fend for herself in a den of wolves. Many people initially were opposed to her being named athletics director. She wasn't known inside the Spartan family and had little support. Some trustees, coaches, staff, and alumni felt that as a woman she couldn't succeed in a traditional man's world.

MSU President
John DiBiaggio

Our relationship didn't get much better as time

194

passed and when it was most important for me to confide in her as athletics director I didn't feel I could rely on her judgment or support. Yet I continued to communicate with her generally about departmental business.

Usually when a new department head arrives, people in the department look to him or her for reassurance that things will be OK. But early on, Baker made some faux pas. For example, she placed the same significance on each sport, judging them to be of equal worth. She considered golf or women's swimming to be just as important to the department as football. Although she may have been motivated by the noble sentiment that all sports are equally important at MSU, the fact of the matter is that without earnings from football and men's basketball many of the 26 varsity sports wouldn't exist at the level they do today.

When football coach George Perles requested that we hire a graduate assistant to perform non-coaching duties for his program, Baker checked with me to determine if the position was permissible under NCAA rules and regulations. The position George wanted wasn't a coaching job so it could be funded at the annual cost of a scholarship, $12,000-$15,000. I told Baker the job could be established and funded. However, she told Perles I said it *could not* be funded. When George told me what she said, I wrote a memo to both he and Baker confirming what I had initially told Baker, but the upshot was that Baker had mis-communicated my message.

She also spent a good part of her first year on the job speaking all over the country. When she was gone, it wasn't clear who from her staff was in charge, leaving the department vulnerable to a leadership gap.

McPherson succeeded Guyer in October 1993 and it wasn't long before he was getting complaints and pressure to fire Baker. McPherson came to MSU from the Bank of America in San Francisco. He was deputy secretary of the U.S. Treasury Department from 1987-89, the second-highest Treasury Department official in

President Ronald Reagan's administration. From 1981-87 he was the administrator for the Agency of International Development where, among other things, he oversaw U.S. aid to Africa when some areas of the continent were having a food crisis.

Although he was a Michigan State graduate, McPherson wasn't too well versed in either academics or big-time collegiate sports. When he first arrived on campus he lived in the Kellogg Center and devoted the weekend interviewing academic deans and central administrators.

Confidant to new president

Joel Ferguson, who was chairman of the board of trustees, had promoted my candidacy for athletics director when Baker was appointed. He arranged for me to meet with the new president. Ferguson was trying to get McPherson to consider me as secretary to the board and administrative assistant to the president. That, combined with Baker's bad start, put me in a position of closeness to McPherson, which was the start of my informal administrative role with him. I am pleased to note that he sought my advice also on matters outside of athletics. I was emboldened in my perceived role as his advisor.

On the Sunday afternoon of McPherson's first weekend on campus, he and I met in the Kellogg Center lobby and took a walk around Jenison Fieldhouse. He asked me many questions about athletics, including how to improve our football and men's basketball programs, the price of tickets for those sports, how many sports there were, and the size of the budget. Then he asked what I thought his initial actions at the university should be. I was grateful he was seeking my suggestions.

He ought to speak to the faculty and staff and offer them some financial hope, I mentioned, since budgets were tight and annual salary increases were at the 3 percent level, or less. Also, I said he should motivate them into believing they were important and that they were contributing significantly to the university's mission, the state of Michigan, and indeed the world. With his broad array of experiences, he surely knew what to say to motivate the staff, I said. We arrived back at Kellogg Center and went our separate ways. It was a pleasant visit.

McPherson said he wanted to get to know me and, after moving to campus in October, he began to call me three to four times a day, both at the office and my home, seeking advice and enlightenment on many issues. Meanwhile, Baker continued to have problems. In 1993, our football team played against Wisconsin in the Coca-Cola Bowl in Japan and we all attended. Baker apparently neglected to thoroughly read the bowl contract, which required a number of blonde cheerleaders. We didn't meet the quota and while we were there McPherson had to

A stipulation in our contract to play in the Coca Cola Bowl in Japan in 1993 required a certain number of blonde cheerleaders.

meet with bowl representatives to straighten out the oversight. He tried to find Baker but to no avail.

The next morning, the day before the game, he asked me to have breakfast in the hotel restaurant with him and his wife to discuss the bowl contract. I said I hadn't had a chance to see it. Baker had not shared it with me. McPherson said Baker left the area with her daughter and he needed to see the contract.

We followed that game by playing Louisville in the Liberty Bowl in Memphis in December 1993. There was a joint reception honoring official parties of the two institutions prior to the game. Whether by accident or design, Baker wore Louisville Cardinals colors (red and white) to the reception, as did Louisville representatives. All other Michigan State official party members wore Spartan colors (green and white). Baker sure didn't enhance her credibility with her faux pas.

When I was at the NCAA convention in January 1994 in San Antonio, I got a call from McPherson. He told me he was going to restructure the athletics department and have all staff members, except for Baker, report directly to me. That would include all administrators and coaches. Baker would be in charge of fund raising for the department, he said, adding that if the restructuring didn't work, Merrily and I would be in trouble. I was highly pleased the president had sufficient confidence in my abilities and credibility to promote me to such an elevated and expanded role in the department. It was totally unexpected and I looked forward to returning home to get the process moving forward.

Conflict over new job responsibilities

About a week after the convention, Baker met with me in her office and said she decided to reorganize the department. She said my title would be changed from an associate to senior associate athletics director. I'd have responsibility for the three revenue sports (football, men's basketball, and ice hockey), controlling their day-to-day operations. I also would handle compliance and student-athlete services. There would be no increase in salary, Baker said, because I already was getting paid more than any of her other administrators in the department. Soon, though, there would be problems with the implementation.

A few days later, Baker scolded me for visiting with the three revenue coaches about the changes before she had the opportunity to do so, but I explained that the coaches already were aware of the changes and she never asked me not to tell them. Perles had asked me about them and I didn't feel the need to lie to him. He said he felt good about my new duties. Heathcote and hockey coach Ron Mason also had been alerted about the changes from someone else, prior to my conversation with them. They both congratulated me. An issue soon emerged about what, precisely, my new responsibilities entailed. The university released a press statement on Jan. 24, 1994, from the public relations office of vice president Terry Denbow, which read:

Clarence Underwood will become senior associate athletics director with operational responsibilities for revenue sports.

Six weeks later, however, after much discussion, the university issued another press release. It read:

Merrily Baker, as director of athletics, has full responsibility for administration of the department. She reports to vice president Wilkinson.

Clarence Underwood has operational responsibilities for revenue sports (football, men's basketball, and hockey), compliance, and student services. Within these duties and fully accountable to director Baker, Underwood has day-to-day financial and personnel responsibilities within established policies and budgets.

When Baker provided me with a written job description on Feb. 2 she described my duties with the revenue sports as that of coordinator. She would retain authority for their budgets, approving expense reimbursement, travel vouchers and expenditure requests. Her interpretation of my duties was confusing and appeared awkward to administer. I couldn't understand what I was supposed to do with those sports.

The original press release said I had day-to-day operational responsibilities for the three revenue sports, yet, according to her, I could not approve reimbursement/expenditure requests, nor could I approve travel vouchers. Those requests from the coaches had to be processed through me to Baker and back to me and then to the coaches. I found that unacceptable.

According to her, I had no more authority over those sports than a clerk and it was insulting and confusing to me. I was experienced and the number two administrator in the department. I couldn't understand why she wanted me to function as a messenger between the three sports and her office. It took many meetings with McPherson, vice president Roger Wilkinson, Baker, and I to work at it. I never compromised or yielded to Baker's point of view. It would have been a step backwards for me in the overall progression of my duties and professional career.

During most of those meetings the discussions were between Baker and me while the president and Wilkinson listened and observed with occasional comments. It was a difficult situation. Baker was fighting to retain control of the revenue sports and I was trying to figure out my new relationship with them, other than the message boy role she had prescribed. I don't believe we ever came to a clear working understanding over this issue and the president didn't reconcile it. The situation was left hanging for Baker and I to work out the best we could. We managed to work it out under awkward circumstances.

Since I was now, by title, the second person in command of the athletics department, on Feb. 16 I was included in one of the meetings with Wilkinson and Baker. Among the items we discussed then was the status of

Heathcote. Wilkinson said Jud's retirement uncertainty was an issue and McPherson wasn't sure what to do about it.

I already had written a draft memo on the subject. But I hadn't delivered it. I believed I had a solid relationship with the president and felt very comfortable in writing him that confidential communication. I believed I had a better relationship with McPherson on athletics matters than either Wilkinson or Baker since he called me frequently to seek my advice on athletics issues.

A friend advises against memo

I mentioned my intentions to Ferguson, who called me on a Saturday night to discuss an unrelated matter. Ferguson considers himself to be an expert on athletics matters and he never was modest about expressing his views regarding issues important to him in the department. He is very astute and usually did his homework on the issue he would call about.

During our brief conversation, I told him I intended to write a letter to McPherson recommending that Heathcote be asked to resign or be fired. I mentioned that Jud's indecision about retirement was hurting our basketball recruiting and asked him whether he was bothered by my intentions. He said he wasn't because there was much public sentiment against Jud's program and his indecision about his retirement date.

I refined my hand-written draft that Saturday night and on Tuesday of the following week read it to a close friend who was an administrator at the university. My friend advised me not to send the memo because he believed the university was too political and I would get little or no support from central administration. Regretfully, I later found out that he was correct.

I have been privileged to work with chief executive officers at some of America's finest institutions and be supervised by some outstanding leaders who were very supportive of me and my work. In turn, I was loyal to them. I always have tried to do the very best work in all of my jobs, with integrity, giving more effort than what was required for the salary I received. Because of my past communications in that manner and the fact I felt comfortable in my relationship with McPherson, I considered my action to be acceptable. I felt more justified writing the memo after hearing Wilkinson say that Jud's indecision was also a problem for McPherson. I was confident my memo would help the president address the issue.

I know now that it would have been wiser to just speak to McPherson about the Heathcote issue rather than documenting it in a memo. But writing memos about important issues was normal procedure for me. In the past, executives over me were part of busy, productive organizations and at times were too involved in business or travel and weren't readily accessible. That's why I sometimes would write confidential letters or memorandums to make them aware of something or to offer suggestions. I have followed that practice every place I've worked and it always has been met with an expression of appreciation for my alertness, advice, and suggestions.

Initially, I addressed the memo to Baker and copied one for the president, but I changed it to McPherson. Merrily, being on shaky ground in the department with some coaches and staff members, was trying to get personal support from Jud. Baker and I already were at odds over my duties and I didn't have the confidence that she would not leak the memo to Heathcote just to be vindictive and get his endorsement on what she felt my new job duties should be. I had my secretary type the memo. Both the envelope and stationery were labeled confidential and I hand-carried the correspondence to the president's office in a sealed envelope and gave it to one of his regular secretaries on the morning of Feb. 17.

McPherson called me later that afternoon and

sounded upset by the contents of my memo. His voice was raised and sounded strained. He asked me to process the memo through Baker because he wanted to get Wilkinson involved. The four of us could then sit around a table and discuss it, he said. However, I didn't process the memo through Baker because I didn't think that was a good idea. I wasn't defying McPherson's request, I simply had no faith in the relationship Baker and I had established. After speaking with the president, I asked my secretary to change the name on the letter in the computer from McPherson back to Baker, but I then changed it back to McPherson and finally had her delete the memo altogether. I didn't retain a copy for myself. I was getting a sixth sense to drop the whole matter.

Reporter sniffs around, breaks news

Well, sure enough, the memo was leaked.

While there may have been many leak sources, my suspicions always have returned to a meeting I had with Kyle Melinn, a sports writer for *The State News*, the university's student newspaper. On Feb. 23, I received a phone call from Melinn. I had never heard of him. He said he wanted to do a biography on me for a Black History Month article. I tried to schedule the meeting for the afternoon of the 25th, a Friday. He claimed he was leaving town at noon that day en route to his hometown and needed to see me that morning, so I agreed.

Melinn visited my office about 11 a.m. The interview that followed was strange. He focused mostly on my background, but asked what I considered superficial questions for about 30 minutes. At one point I left briefly to go to the restroom. My secretary's office was across the hall. She was there and could see the reporter from her window. I mention that now because it had been rumored that the reporter took papers from my desk or wastepaper basket when I stepped out of the room. I didn't keep a memo for my files.

Melinn would have been a bold person and skilled thief to search my office while I was away for about three minutes or less. In my opinion, he already had a copy of my memo to McPherson regarding Heathcote when he visited me and was just trying to check me out by asking some pretense questions. The interview concluded about five minutes after I returned to the office. Since the reporter said he was leaving East Lansing at noon on Friday to go home, you can imagine how surprised I was to see him the next day (Saturday) working at a fast food restaurant in town. He spotted me and tried to hide, behaving as though he was frightened to see me. He immediately went to the back room so I couldn't observe him. The behavior was bewildering to me and I wondered why he had lied about leaving town Friday afternoon to go to his hometown.

One day later, Sunday at about 5 p.m., I got a call from Melinn asking me to make a comment regarding my memo. Naturally I was upset and wanted to know how he got a copy of it. He wouldn't tell me and I eventually hung up on him. So began an evening that turned my work life upside down.

Immediately I called McPherson at home and his wife told me to try his office. He answered the phone. I told him of the call from *The State News* reporter and that we had a serious leak. He said he also had gotten calls from *The State News* but did not talk to anyone and he wanted to know what I told the reporter. I said that I told Melinn I had written the memo and asked how he got a copy of it, but he wouldn't tell me. The president said he didn't know either, but it created problems because it looked like there was something going on between us regarding Heathcote's status. In the meantime, the basketball team had just beaten Ohio State to win its fourth game in a row and that, McPherson said, made the timing seem inappropriate.

Our conversation was short because there wasn't much else to say. McPherson said he would call vice president Terry Denbow, the public relations expert for the university, and get back to me shortly. About an hour later, Denbow called and seemed surprised by the revelation of the memo. He asked about its origin and to whom I had given copies. I told him I had given the original to McPherson and there were no copies. Denbow said he spoke with McPherson and he would prepare a statement for him indicating he received the memo but didn't act on it. He said McPherson told him he tore up the original and put it in the trashcan. Terry said that whole incident was unfortunate and he would try to search for more information.

I soon got another call from McPherson, telling me he would call *The State News* to say he got the memo from me and that he told me to go through channels, which I had refused to do. He asked me to tell *The State News* the same thing, but I said I wasn't sure I would say that I refused to follow channels. My next call was to Heathcote. I wanted to explain why I wrote the memo. His wife said he wasn't home but was out playing racquetball. I left word for him to return the call but he never did.

Anti-Underwood bandwagon begins

Board of Trustees member Bob Weiss from Flint called me at home around 6:15 p.m. sounding very upset. He said I had overstepped my authority; that the board of trustees had dealt with the issue last year; and Heathcote had one more year left on his contract. He wanted to know what was going on and why I had written the memo. I explained my

Trustee Robert Weiss

205

reasons, but Weiss said angrily that he was mad and somebody better say something publicly to support Heathcote. Weiss said he was going to call McPherson.

Baker was in Arizona when all that was going on. I called to tell her what had happened and she told me Wilkinson already had called. She asked who leaked the memo and said we would discuss it when she returned.

After talking things over with my wife, we decided it was best to share the story with sports reporter Jack Ebling of the *Lansing State Journal*. Ebling had written many articles in the past in which he sought my comments and advice and we felt he had been fair. We didn't want *The State News* to have an exclusive. I wasn't pleased with Melinn for lying about leaving town Friday afternoon and trying to hide in the restaurant when I saw him the next day at noon. I also believed he already had a copy of the memo when he visited with me that morning. I didn't trust him and felt it was better to share the story with *The State Journal* in order for the readers to get a balanced perspective.

I called Jack at his home and relayed the story to him. He appeared bewildered and shocked as I told him about the memo but he seemed highly pleased that I was sharing the story with him.

McPherson called me again at 11 p.m. and said he had been visiting with members of his family and that some of them were very fond of me, but a few were suggesting that I be fired, along with Perles, Heathcote, and Baker. He assured me that while he did not appreciate receiving the memo he could understand why I addressed it to him. To his credit, McPherson acknowledged that he had used me as an advisor. I had given him some solid advice on many issues, he said. He asked me to keep pushing for budgetary and personnel matters with Baker and that I was a good man and the memo wouldn't hurt our relationship. I thought it was generous of him to make the call. It was timely, comforting, and highly appreciated.

On Monday morning my name was in headlines in both *The State News* and the *Lansing State Journal* and over the radio and TV. Baker still was out of town. She was contacted by the media and made some premature disparaging comments about the memo and that she would deal with me when she got back. McPherson and I had to attend a meeting with the athletic council at 7:30 a.m. Monday. It was quite uncomfortable for me because I needed some quiet time to think carefully about what was happening and try to figure out how the memo was leaked. McPherson addressed a few agenda items and made some brief comments about the memo story, which now was spreading rapidly across the country. I made a few remarks, though nothing of consequence because I was in no mood to talk about it.

Media circus includes concealed cameras

The media had a field day with the story over the next two weeks. They called my office and home day and night trying to get me to comment. They sent reporters to my home and office with concealed cameras and tape recorders trying to get an angle for a story. I wouldn't talk to them. A few of them followed my car after work hoping I would stop and give them an interview. I never did.

The first couple days after the story broke I did provide follow-up comments to Ebling and also appeared in a live interview from my home with local TV sports anchor Tim Staudt for the 11 p.m. news. We had agreed in advance not to discuss the memo. Then I got a visit in my office from Wilkinson, who said he wanted to see how I was holding up. He said he had reviewed videotapes from television reports, particularly reporters' comments from Baker, and felt the media had damaged me. Wilkinson mentioned he had talked with Baker and she was angry and wanted me transferred out of athletics, but he was trying to calm her down. Also, Wilkinson said, McPherson was concerned that my comments to the media would prolong the story, suggesting on behalf of the president that I refrain from talking further with them. That was good advice that I heeded.

Wilkinson expressed compassion for my welfare. I explained to him the frequent communications I had with McPherson, of which Wilkinson was not aware, that led me to believe I could comfortably write to McPherson. I told Wilkinson I would file a complaint with Dr. Bruce Benson, chief of the MSU Public Safety Department, and have his office conduct an investigation to find out how the memo got leaked to *The State News*. Wilkinson had no problem with that but said he would run it by the president first and if there were a problem he would contact me.

I did what I could to find the source of the leak. With an investigator's background, I questioned some staff and replayed different scenarios. I thought I should at least engage professional help from the MSU Police Department. I made an appointment with Benson on March 1 and met with him in his office where I provided background information about the memo. He said he needed to talk with the prosecutor's office and get back to me. He called back two days later to say the prosecutor's office reported there was no apparent evidence that someone broke into my office.

Without such evidence, Benson said, his office would have no authority for an investigation. Even if there were evidence, he said, his office would have to get permission from Wilkinson to conduct an investigation because the vice president was his superior. There were two other hand-written memos from me to Wilkinson. One had been sent via campus mail seeking his assistance in resolving the stalemate between Baker and me relative to my new job description. I don't believe the second one, on the same subject, was sent — but both mysteriously appeared in *The State News* in articles written by Melinn.

I don't know how the paper got the memos. My

first inclination was they had been taken from my office and I reported that to Benson, who called back within a few days and told me he would conduct the investigation. He said the prosecutor confirmed there was a basis for it and the complaint will be "Entry Without Permission." He asked me to check with Wilkinson to get university authorization.

The vice president then called to say McPherson was advising against a police investigation because it would prolong the story and create additional negative publicity, so it was called off. Wilkinson said McPherson wanted him to talk with me in person over the weekend and try to figure out how the memo was leaked. He asked if changing the locks to my office would solve the problem but I said no because those who had keys would also have the new keys.

Today, I don't know how the memos were leaked and by whom. Some people have suggested Melinn. Others have suggested staff in the athletics department and perhaps the president's office. I'm not sure and probably never will know how the unfortunate leak occurred, although in 2003 a sports writer told me a former *Lansing State Journal* sports reporter told him Melinn had gotten the information by rummaging through the trash bin outside of Jenison Fieldhouse. If that is true, I wonder what would have inspired him to search through the trash in the first place. How did the memo get in the trash bin when I never retained a hard copy. We did not have shredders then in the athletics department but I had a habit of tearing my papers into small pieces before discarding them in the trashcan. I seriously doubt that Melinn had the intuition and skills to search the trash bin, find my torn up waste papers and piece them back together for his story. Up to that point I had never been the victim of media scrutiny.

A few weeks after Baker returned from her trip she called a meeting with me to address the situation. She was basically hung up over my breach of protocol and what the appropriate discipline should be. She wanted to know why I had gone over her head with the memo. I told her I felt that sending it was consistent with the role McPherson wanted me to play. She seemed determined to give me a written reprimand, which she did.

I must admit it was an awkward situation for both of us. She was trying to get me fired or transferred, while the president was calling me numerous times a week asking about her performance and discussing other pertinent issues in the department. She had no clue relative to what was transpiring during those discussions with McPherson.

When I had first written the memo it was addressed to her, I explained, but I later changed it to the attention of the president because she was struggling badly in the department and had little or no support. She was trying hard to establish a rapport with Heathcote, Mason, and a few other high profile people on campus. I believe she felt her edge was slipping away. Based on the internal politics surrounding our working relationship, I believe it would have been just as chaotic for me if I had given her the original memo.

Group of black faculty tries to help

While the buzz over my Heathcote memo lingered, I got a call for another meeting with McPherson in early March. Also attending were Denbow, Perles, Baker, and Wilkinson. The president wanted to discuss the announcement of a new defensive football assistant for the Spartans, Henry Bullough. Right after that meeting, McPherson asked to see me in his office. He said he had gotten a call from MSU professor Thomas Gunnings, who had told him the Black Faculty and Administrators Association had met and decided to conduct a press conference to help counter the negative publicity I was getting — unless the president made a public statement of support for me.

McPherson explained that he liked me and he had said some nice things about me at an alumni gathering recently in Flint and that he also planned to make similar comments at the City Club that very day. Additionally, he planned to talk positively about me over an MSU radio program the following week.

He asked that I tell Dr. George Rowan, the president of the black faculty and administrators group, what he had done and planned to do, and I said I would do that. I did, and Rowan said he would report that to the association. I never heard anything more about that matter and the press conference never was held. After the basketball season ended I got a request for an interview on the MSU Student Radio Network. I agreed, as long as we didn't discuss the memo. After that broadcast I received calls from former university president Guyer and others commending the way I handled the interview.

On March 12, McPherson called to let me know that the *Lansing State Journal* had printed a nasty article painting me as the bad guy and that McPherson had to publicly support Baker in the media but wanted me to know that he would support me when he had the opportunity. The president wanted me to understand that Baker still was in control of the department as far as the public was concerned and as such he had to support her. He was suggesting that he appreciated the advice I was giving to him and if some auspicious opportunity arose for him to praise me without deflating Baker's ego he would do so. I don't know if the compliments ever were bestowed upon me. I never was in a position to hear them but I appreciated the gesture.

My colleagues in the athletics department demonstrated their loyalty through their behavior. I didn't expect or want them to show compassion for me and they didn't. They would meet me in the hallways and drop their heads. I figured their loyalties were split between Heathcote and me and they didn't know how to handle the situation. I understood their positions and fully realized it was a matter I had to bear alone. I never tried to put any of them in a compromising position. Unless they mentioned some aspects of the situation to me I never brought the subject up to them. I wanted each of them to have the liberty to form their own conclusions, whatever they might have been thinking, without interference from me.

Religious convictions bolster spirit

I tried to focus on my religious beliefs and understand in a very small way how Jesus must have felt going through the crucifixion. I internalized lyrics from the hymn, *Amazing Grace*, which says, "There is a cross for everyone and there's a cross for me." I kept wondering if the memo was my cross to bear. That situation caused me much anxiety and turmoil. I had difficulty coping with the fact that my initial intentions were to help alleviate a problem and it later hurt me trying to figure out how it had turned out so negative. Then, too, I was frustrated by not knowing how the memo was leaked to the *State News* and why there wasn't a formal investigation.

It never was my plan to hurt Heathcote and his family. He already had announced his desire to retire. For the good of the university, I felt he should have retired at the end of the 1994 season, with full compensation paid to him for the one year remaining on his contract. That was a common occurrence at the university. However, I wasn't alone with my burden. There were many supporters, some I didn't even know, who wrote letters offering to assist me in some manner. Many letters of support in my behalf were written to McPherson, who passed some of them to me.

On March 30, I returned a call from Wilkinson's office. Baker was with him in his office and said Heathcote told her that he had decided to coach one more year, the 1994-95 season. They wanted my reaction. I said I had none, except to be pleased to know that Jud had established a definite retirement date. I wouldn't have any more to say on the subject, I told them. I was asked to prepare a statement I could use as a quote in case the media contacted me. Two days later, Denbow came to my office at McPherson's request and said the president didn't want me to make a public comment about an article in the *Detroit Free Press* regarding Heathcote's decision to coach another year. The president, through Denbow, further requested that I not comment on the possibility that basketball player Shawn Respert might withdraw from MSU and enter the NBA draft. I assured him I would honor both requests.

Then Denbow, to his credit, apologized for the manner in which he slanted MSU media releases about the memos and the reorganization, affecting me. He said he had recently become aware of my on-going relationship with McPherson and said if he had known about it earlier he would have given a different angle to the stories. I thanked him for telling me that.

Trustee Ferguson called me once during the media frenzy and asked me to visit him at his television station. The media had made me look like a bad guy, he said, and I asked him to tell me what I had done wrong or unethical. He said I had done nothing wrong. This, too, shall pass, I told him, and I was not too worried about it. He said Wilkinson should be doing more to help my situation because he was the central administrator over athletics.

More trustees bail out

On March 24, trustee Dee Cook called me. She said my career was winding down in athletics and I would soon retire. She wanted to know who had authorized me to write the Heathcote memo. I said, no one, it was done of my own volition. She said I had done a good job over

213

the years but she was concerned about Ferguson's influence in athletics and she encouraged me to disclose soon the genesis of the memo to get the mess off my back.

Trustee Dee Cook and I

There was other fallout, as well. My relationship with McPherson changed. Instead of getting up to four calls a day from him, I got perhaps two a month. And trustee Weiss turned negative toward me and stopped speaking to me altogether. Four years earlier, when I returned to Michigan State in 1990 from the Big Ten office, he appeared to be one of my strongest supporters. He and Ferguson advocated my candidacy for the athletics director's position when it was open in 1991. When he lost his job as prosecutor for Genesee County, Weiss asked for my assistance in finding him another position, which I did try to do, though unsuccessfully. To the best of my knowledge, I never have done anything to harm him.

In 1995, I called Weiss to ask him if I could visit with him to try and iron out whatever differences existed between us. We met for lunch at Grand Blanc Country Club near Flint, where I told him I always had supported him, contributing to his financial campaign when he ran for re-election for the prosecutor's office and also, at his requests, in trying to find a job for him, as well as his daughter when she graduated from MSU. I had also tried to get NCAA Final Four men's basketball tickets for him, again at his request. I wanted to mend the fence between us.

Weiss said he didn't like the way the memo was handled and I countered that I didn't like the way it was leaked to the media. I wrote what I considered a confidential memo to McPherson, I said, and had no idea how inappropriately it would be handled.

He said he was told I had made some disparaging remarks about him when I went on the MSU Student Radio Network shortly after the memo was released to the media. I told him I never made a negative comment to anyone about him and had no motive for doing so, particularly on a public radio show. Whoever made such a statement about me was telling a bold-faced lie, I said, and there were audio tapes at the station which easily could be retrieved and checked.

Weiss said he didn't like it when I asked his wife, Vickie, who was a photographer at the MSU-Minnesota football game in Minneapolis in the fall of 1990, to take photos of the host school's athletics director's box when basketball recruiting prospect Chris Webber and some others were visiting there. I told Weiss that happened four years ago and there was nothing that could be done about it now. I did it out of convenience. As Michigan State's compliance officer I was more interested in having the pictures taken and not so much as to who took them.

NCAA recruiting rules prohibit a prospect from sitting in the press box on a visit to a university. The prospect may walk through, but he isn't allowed to eat or sit in the box. Since Webber and company were sitting in the press box for nearly half of the game, I requested Weiss' wife, who was a field photographer, to take some pictures as evidence that an NCAA rule was being violated.

Heathcote had told me earlier that he did not like my involvement with the photos because it caused MSU to lose Webber to Michigan. I don't think that was true because Webber never really committed to MSU. Clem Haskins surely thought he had Webber committed to the University of Minnesota and he told me so during the MSU-Minnesota football game. The University of Michigan always was prominent in Webber's mind and there is where he ended up as a collegiate student-athlete. During our lunch, Weiss said that was one of the issues that made him turn against me. We shook hands and left, but the relationship hasn't improved.

As I reflect back on my controversial memo, I would have to say the media tried to crucify me and all the while the university didn't offer any support, just the way my administrative friend at MSU had said it would happen. I relied on a few close friends, the Lord, and my family to get through the ordeal.

Baker gave me a letter of reprimand. But the way I feel about it now is basically the same way I felt then, that it was an awful lot of political noise about nothing. You can bet your bottom dollar that if I had done something illegal, unethical, or immoral I would have been fired, and rightfully so. I was put under great media scrutiny after doing nothing except to write a private memo to the university president suggesting ways for him to deal with an average Big Ten coach who was hurting our men's basketball recruiting program. Michigan State was too good to continue to sponsor an average program.

Anger, threats resurface a year later

I received many mean-spirited letters — some from members of the faculty at the university — from folks I

216

never heard of during that stretch. Heathcote continues to maintain a negative attitude toward me. My name was the focus of sports talk shows. I received nasty phone calls — and a few that threatened my well-being. That animosity from the nameless still was prevalent a year later, March 11, 1995, when Heathcote coached his final scheduled basketball game at MSU and the university threw a farewell retirement celebration for him in the Breslin Arena.

Just past midnight prior to the game I got a call from a man who told me not to show up because if I did I would not live to remember it. When I asked who he was he hung up the telephone. I reported the incident to the East Lansing and MSU police departments. It could have been a prank call, but I was not taking any chances. At the game I noticed a uniformed MSU policeman at the entrance of my seating area. He was there the entire game.

Some lessons learned

Some valuable lessons were reinforced in me with the memo fiasco:

- Sensitive information should be verbally communicated one person to another on a need-to-know basis.
- Be careful about trying to help someone with a problem unless he first seeks your assistance. Good deeds don't go unpunished.
- Always do your job to the very best of your ability. That is why you are paid. Be loyal to your superiors, but don't put much trust in having that loyalty reciprocated. It seldom is.
- Don't get too caught up over what the news media and others think of you as a person, as a professional, or as an employee. The media and other folks, through gossip and innuendo, try to influence public perceptions against certain

217

people. They rarely know all the facts and they surely don't know you. Hold your head up and keep marching forward.

- Always live with integrity and take the high road on issues of difficulty because not many people can climb the hill without being exposed.
- Finally, the phrase "political correctness" is in vogue today. It means, in simple language, behaving in a manner that is acceptable to most people. Instead, listen to the advice of trusted friends and relatives before making decisions that have the potential of affecting others.

Chapter 6:

ETHICS AND ACCOUNTABILITY

Erosion of compliance issues can be devastating

How ATHLETICS DEPARTMENTS ARE RUN AND how colleges and universities play the game depends directly on the governing boards and their appointed presidents.

The NCAA makes it clear under Article 2 of its constitution, which concerns principles for conduct of intercollegiate athletics, that, "It is the responsibility of each member institution to control its intercollegiate athletics program in compliance with the rules and regulations of the association. The institution's chief executive officer is responsible for the administration of all aspects of the athletics program, including approval of the budget and audit of all expenditures."

The governing board has the most important first step in the development and implementation of an effective compliance program at the institution. It should establish standards of moral and ethical leadership, as well as policies of institutional control, for all personnel affiliated with the institution. The board should hire a president who shares those moral values and who has a working philosophy and proven administrative background that is ethically compatible with the board's policies.

The board should understand that normally when a major NCAA violation occurs there has been a breakdown in the policies adopted by the board. There has been a failure in the vertical monitoring of the program involved and a lack of proactive correction and discipline. Such failure may suggest that required communication and supervision for compliance has not been properly performed. Fixing the system must start at the top with the governing board and delegated to the president.

Every person in the organization's vertical structure must be held accountable initially when a major violation occurs. Too often in the scenario presidents take control, exonerate themselves and other administrators in between, and places blame on the coach, compliance director, or some other lower level employee within the chain. Those employees become the scapegoats while the president and others go wholly unscathed. There have been numerous cases nationally where an ethical coach or compliance director was blamed and fired for a faulty compliance system that was long overdue for correction by those in charge of the institution.

The responsibility of the governing board, especially in public institutions where members are directly elected and held accountable by the citizens, cannot be summarily ignored or dismissed when a major NCAA compliance problem occurs. The most prudent action the governing board can take during a crisis is to review the conduct of the chief executive officer in providing leadership and the necessary monitoring of the program involved. If the board is satisfied with its review then the president should review the behavior of those persons connected with the crisis to pinpoint the problem.

Presidents' neglect engulfs programs

Presidents play a fundamental and critical role in the design, development, and oversight of NCAA compliance programs. In carrying out the governing boards' policies they set the tone and athletics departments follow. Athletics directors carry out the wishes of their respective presidents. Intercollegiate athletics directly reflect the values of the governing boards and university presidents. Few presidents, if any, want to personally get involved in the operations, especially if they are enjoying winning programs. They react only when a major crisis erupts and they are forced to do something.

Instead of being proactive, even when they suspect that things are going on that shouldn't occur, they remain quiet. They play a wait and see game, hoping that unsavory athletic situations will not be exposed and that they will not have to handle a scandal. And if they do, the athletics director, coaches, and compliance director can take the heat. The presidents need a scapegoat. Hear no evil; see no evil; speak no evil is the presidents code in the compliance area. And that makes for a dicey athletics situation.

Six MSU presidents were gathered here during the tenure of President John DiBiaggio. From left, Edgar Harden, DiBiaggio, John Hannah, Clifton Wharton, Cecil Mackey, and Walter Adams.

The benign neglect of university presidents; their willingness to compromise educational values; their readiness to live with rules that they know are bent, broken, and ignored, are signal reasons for current problems plaguing intercollegiate athletics. Presidential neglect has resulted in the myriad of unacceptable ethical and institutional control issues now engulfing university athletics programs. And because of the unrelenting pressures to win — and to win now for financial reasons — the situation will likely get worse before it gets better. That, regrettably, is the current situation of intercollegiate athletics affairs.

The number of NCAA probations involving ethical conduct and institutional control issues that have emerged over many years are a disgraceful and shameful blot on higher education. The country reacted with alarm and disgust over the recent dishonorable management practices at major corporate giants, such as Global Crossing, Enron, Kmart, WorldCom, Arthur Anderson, and others. Their conduct was puzzling, eroded public trust, and shook financial markets. Yet, in 2003-04 there were 41 institutions of higher education on NCAA probation and no similar outcry occurred on the part of the universities themselves, or the public. Instead, those unethical activities were merely accepted as a matter of course.

Historically, according to 2004 data from the NCAA, 554 probationary penalties have been meted out to 259 collegiate institutions and 164 of those colleges and universities have been hit with multiple NCAA probations. I wonder what would be the public reaction if, for example, one of our local banks or investment companies were found guilty – twice – of fraud? Would we continue to do business with that company? My guess is we would not. Then I wonder what would be the public's reaction if one of the publicly funded universities lost its accreditation because of mismanagement? Undoubtedly, such public embarrassment and damage to the academic reputation would cause the institution, and the state, to demand an investigation and long-term administrative oversight to correct the problem. There would be on-going internal reviews, possibly with outside consultants, to help insure the problem never reoccurred. Yet the same scrutiny often isn't given to an athletics program on NCAA probation.

Most of the sanctions at NCAA institutions originated from unethical conduct and institutional control issues. In nearly every case an athletics representative was involved. That means the institution didn't have the proper organizational structure or administrative oversight in place for its compliance program to function effectively. There is some fear among institutions that an enforced, comprehensive compliance program will damage the winning revenue programs.

Most compliance programs are shams

The compliance programs at most institutions always were and remain shams. They used to consist of one full or part-time professional and a secretary. A few programs today have upwards of five staffers. The compliance staff then, as today, has a heavy responsibility to the institution. It must:

- Uphold the integrity of the institution with the NCAA and the conference office. That is supposed to be done by educating the athletics department coaches and staff on NCAA and conference rules and regulations. The education regarding regulations further includes student-athletes, faculty and staff, boosters worldwide, alumni, and friends.
- Monitor the compliance activities of all those groups.
- Interpret all rules and regulations to individuals in those groups.
- Conduct preliminary investigations of all

223

allegations of NCAA and conference violations and write up each case for processing.

- Prepare and submit student-athlete waivers and eligibility petitions to the NCAA and conference office.
- Review the financial aid, annual certification, awards, transfer procedures, as well as anything else that falls within the 460-plus pages of the NCAA rules book, the institution's rules, and the conference's manual.

Those are demanding responsibilities for an office with few staff members. Many believe that those small staffs were created to give the semblance of compliance and to meet minimum paper expectations. It is a method of shifting blame and isolating the focus on the athletics director, coaches, and compliance director when something goes awry.

Since the late 1980s, the institutions and their presidents have been formally entrusted, through enacted legislation, with the responsibility of insuring that their institutions comply with the rules and regulations of the NCAA. The presidents always have had that authority delegated to them by their governing boards, but mostly ignored it.

For too long, many presidents abdicated their responsibilities and weren't held accountable. They shied away from problems in athletics and pretended to be shocked whenever allegations of major NCAA rules violations surfaced on their campuses. For too long the presidents put their heads in the sand and tolerated the antics of powerful revenue coaches out of fear of alienating coaches, alumni, and wealthy supporters.

Why? The presidents fear, even worse, the wrath of an angry employee and the governing boards, which hold the employment contracts. So what did the presidents do? They sat in their ivory tower offices and put the onus for compliance on the backs of their athletics directors. And many of the athletics directors, afraid of their jobs, chose not to report major infractions on their campuses. They waited until the infractions were made public and were investigated by the NCAA. They, like the presidents, acted innocent and professed no awareness of the charges. The result of such hierarchy of cascading fear is to isolate athletics from the mainstream of the institution thereby avoiding accountability from the A.D. on up the chain of command.

Cavalier treatment of compliance problems

I once worked as a compliance coordinator for an athletics director who told me not to bring him any compliance problems and not to report any to the NCAA. I didn't abide by the intimidation and continued to report in writing known violations to him. Without a written record, no violation would ever have been reported, which is what that athletics director wanted. And the first time there would have been a major violation, I couldn't have defended my behavior without the written record. All negative fingers would have been pointing directly at me.

I learned a valuable lesson from the A.D. — never get so intimidated by a person's power, position, prestige, or money so as to cause me to lose my integrity. So I have taken the position throughout my professional life to do what is right and ethical on the job. And if doing the right thing causes me to get fired, I can walk away with my head up and seek another position. But if I act foolishly and lose my job and reputation for being unethical, I have no one to blame but myself and must suffer the consequences.

Strangely, the A.D. never made additional comments to me about the written records of the violations and I don't know if he ever submitted them to the NCAA. I never received any feedback from him or the faculty athletics representative, both of whom would have received a written response from the NCAA enforcement staff relative to each reported violation from the institution. Knowing the A.D.'s attitude toward compliance, I was constantly aware of the need to be vigilant and report all known violations to him. I never wanted to fall into the trap of ignoring a violation and then being fired for not reporting it.

There were some powerful athletics directors up until the late 1980s who believed they were above the rules. I became acutely aware of the immense power of the athletics directors one day in a Big Ten Conference meeting where I served as the conference's staff liaison with the athletics directors. They were discussing a subject and at one point I said, "You guys can't do that". One of the A.D.s looked at me and said, " We can do anything we want to do."

I had never before heard anybody make that kind of bold assertion at the institutional level. But that's the way it was back then when the athletics directors were in charge of the athletics departments, until the presidents were mandated to take control in the late 1980s.

Concerned with the number of NCAA unethical conduct allegations occurring in the decade of the 1980s, low graduation rates among athletes, the stir over inequitable resources for the women's athletics programs, and how those issues, among others, were publicly casting negative integrity perceptions at the institutions, the presidents took over the athletics departments. They did so by attending NCAA conventions or by mandating that their institutional representatives, usually the faculty athletics representatives, vote on legislation as instructed by the presidents.

By taking over, the presidents reduced the power of the athletics directors and that of the faculty athletics representatives. Such restructuring in the governance structure caused some restlessness among those previously in power in the athletics departments.

Although that shifting of power and authority moved more to the presidents, the accountability did not — it stayed at the lower level of the hierarchy.

Generally, the athletics directors often found themselves between a rock and a hard place in compliance. They needed to fully support the revenue coaches and maintain alliances with them and turn their heads away from wrongdoings while assuring the presidents that their coaches weren't doing anything worse than other coaches nationally. The athletics directors contended that there were too many silly rules and nobody could follow all of them and remain competitive.

Many of the athletics directors had coaching backgrounds and didn't want their coaches to be disadvantaged in the recruitment wars. Usually, the A.D. was talking out of both sides of his mouth. It was a simple ploy to justify whatever cheating was going on at the institution, while telling the president everything was fine.

The one thing I could never understand about most coaches though was that they claimed to know which coaches at other institutions were cheating in recruitment, yet they never wanted to turn those coaches in to the NCAA. When I asked for the evidence, they refused to disclose the information. Instead, they continued to complain and request similar unfair advantages for their programs. A lack of cooperation made me wonder whether the coaches were simply blowing smoke or if they were afraid of reciprocal behavior by their opponents? The athletics directors usually sided with their coaches.

I have never known compliance to be a high priority at many institutions. I discussed the subject with numerous compliance directors nationally and they all had similar views. If compliance over the years had been high on the agendas at the institutions, there is no way that we would be seeing so many prestigious academic institutions annually going on NCAA probation. Some of the most intelligent and creative professionals work at institutions of higher learning. Surely if they have the expertise to advise world leaders and executives of major corporations about how to resolve complex problems, unquestionably they could figure out how to fix their institutions' compliance issues.

I've learned that compliance is something merely to be tolerated at NCAA institutions. It isn't a popular subject among athletics people. Yet, being inattentive to its enforcement has caused serious embarrassment to many educational institutions. It has tarnished institutional images; ruined reputations; embarrassed universities and their leaders, state legislators, alumni, and taxpayers; and caused crippling damage to the financial stability of the athletics departments.

Stigma of NCAA probation

There are few things more harmful to a university and its athletics department than several consecutive years of NCAA probation. An institution hit with NCAA probation due to irregularities in its football or men's basketball program will suffer academically from the reduction of admission applications. To be excluded from post-season events and the opportunity to showcase your team on television is devastating to recruitment generally and demoralizing to the athletes on the team. Probation can cause fan interest to wane. The stigma can linger for years, especially if the scholarships and recruiting visits were reduced. It may take years for a team to recover from the devastation and regain its image to attract quality athletes. Two years of NCAA probation in football, for example, including sanctions of no post-season events and no television can cost an institution an estimated minimum $8 million. That is calculated as follows:

- $1 million for the investigation.
- $4 million in lost bowl revenue ($2 million for each year).

- $2 million in lost television revenue (to the conference or institution over the two years)
- $1 million in lost gate receipts, marketing, and donor giving ($500,000 each of the two years).
- Plus the loss of tuition, fees, room and board from prospective students who chose other institutions.

There is just too much at stake for an institution not to take control of the compliance program and bring some stability and predictability to it. Despite what we hear and read in the news about ethical conduct problems and lack of institutional control at other institutions, most of us think it never will happen to our colleges or universities. When such incidents happen elsewhere we may give our programs a cursory review. Finding nothing of any consequence we feel insulated and reassured, then continue to do business as usual. Apparently, the situation is such that some universities feel that the rewards of non-compliance outweigh the costs of complying with the rules. Apparently, the saying that "cheaters never prosper" doesn't always hold true for intercollegiate athletics.

Well, I have some startling news for anyone who still is living in make-believe land. The reality is that most athletics departments are a nightmare waiting to happen. Most of them engage in improper activities and they know it. It is just a matter of time until something improper going on now will get out of hand. What happened at the University of Michigan with basketball booster Ed Martin and the players is not an isolated incident, nor is it uncommon, to degrees, at other institutions. U-M rightly ended up providing its own sanctions, pending the NCAA's investigation of allegations involving improper financial support between Martin and some players. The NCAA later provided some of its own additional penalties. Furthermore, the firing of Jim O'Brien, the Ohio State University men's basketball coach, was a shock to many people. He was fired by his A.D. for allegedly keeping secret a $6,000 transaction between him and a prospective student-athlete that happened five years previous. The A.D. found out about the deal when the prospect's name surfaced in a deposition taken in a civil lawsuit filed by a woman seeking $510,000 in expenses and damages from two Ohio State boosters.

The pressures to recruit the best athletes, keep them contented on campus, and to win big now have put coaches in a difficult situation. They are paid big money to keep the victory banner waving on the institution's front lawn for everyone to see. Most of them get uptight over an average season and start thinking short term instead of thinking long term about their programs. They know the consequences of allowing the banner to drop for a period of time, irrespective of the reasons, can be devastating, so some coaches feel the need to take short cuts in their programs. They know the administrators will not stand up to the pressures applied by unforgiving alumni, particularly the big donors.

Coaches keep things under their hats

Coaches know things are going on but they don't want to bring harm to their programs, offend the star athletes, or insult the big boosters. So they turn their heads and pretend it's not happening and hope everybody remains quiet. Coaches know the backgrounds of their athletes better than anybody else on campus. They recruit them, visit with their families, coach them 20 hours a week during the season, meet with them throughout the year. They know the athletes' personal problems, academic problems, and even their social problems, so they know when athletes' lifestyles change, when they get new wardrobes, where the automobiles come from, and where their new-found dollars come from.

If a big time respected booster in the community is involved, the coach will close his eyes. But surely he knows what is happening in his/her program. If not, he/she should. But like the case of former student-athlete

230

Roosevelt Wagner (who made NCAA allegations to the media and to the NCAA enforcement staff against the football program at Michigan State, as well as other similar cases nationally), one day something will happen to expose the situation. Either an athlete will become disgruntled about something in the sports program and tell the wrong person about his/her situation, or an athlete will see another athlete being treated better than him and expose the wrongdoings, or a booster will get careless.

Or it could be a jealous girlfriend speaking out of school. Or perhaps it's a gambling issue. One never can be entirely sure how it's going to happen until it is revealed. The point is that it will come out. I learned after 15 years of NCAA compliance work that folks who are cheating are smart enough to test you first with little things to get your reaction. They will tell you bits and pieces of something small that you have to piece together or they will tell you about another institution's problem to elicit a response. Whenever it happened to me I believed they were hoping I would not react negatively or be surprised by the information they shared with me. Unfortunately, I wasn't the one to be tested because when I figured out the puzzle and could prove the allegation, I always reported the little violations to the NCAA. It was my way of trying to control the big things.

I don't believe there is a clean athletics program in America, although some programs operate better than others. There are too many rules, coaches, boosters, student-athletes, alumni, faculty, staff, agents, and sports fans for everyone to be in complete compliance with NCAA rules and regulations at every institution. It's impossible.

Perhaps more importantly is how fast, efficiently, and honestly the improprieties are handled on campus whenever they are detected. There needs to be a swift system of due process and proper resolution in place to handle every allegation. No secondary violation should ever be swept under the rug. As a compliance director I never was smart enough to discern which violations should be reported to the NCAA and which ones should be ignored, which, at times in the latter case, I was asked to do. I surmised that the first time I took matters in my own hands and failed to report a violation I would be in trouble. What do I tell the same staff member, booster, or student-athlete the next time he/she committed a violation? What if they told me to get lost?

Every institution has a group of high profile athletes who everybody wants to be around to feel good about and for bragging rights, as well as to enhance their own personal images. The boosters want their children and grandchildren to personally know those athletes and the boosters interact with them in various ways, clamoring for their attention and inviting them to their homes.

Some of the boosters have athletes as their guests for meals at restaurants, which is an NCAA violation. I was surprised one Sunday afternoon when, as A.D., I was eating brunch with my family at a private club and one of our star athletes at Michigan State and his girlfriend entered the club to have brunch with a member booster. Naturally, I reported the incident to our compliance office, which took appropriate action.

On another occasion, I had to intervene quickly and aggressively one day when a male athlete came to my office all excited with an offer from a female professor who wanted to buy him an automobile. I learned they were not romantically involved. The athlete, who lived off campus, went to the class late one day and explained to the professor that he was having car problems. After the next class session she visited with him and offered to purchase him a car. I had difficulty convincing the athlete that he could not receive the car and maintain his eligibility.

Such benefits always have been available to athletes everywhere. Sports are big worldwide and the practice of giving athletes benefits is pervasive. Folks are fascinated with sports and star athletes. Athletes are heroes in our country. All types of folks gravitate to them. Why do you think professional athletes are paid millions of dollars by the merchandisers to wear their items? The answer is: so others will be sold on the advertisements and buy them. And it works. And why is it that most local newspapers have more news on sports than any other single subject? The answer is: sports are the second most talked about subject in America next to sex.

Boosters and unethical benefits go hand-in-hand

If people connected with an institution think their boosters are not giving extra benefits to athletes they need to wake up from the dream. Years ago, when I was the compliance officer for the Big Ten Conference office, Commissioner Jim Delany asked me to spend two hours with a group of star athletes who had come to Chicago for the annual football kickoff luncheon. He wanted me to talk to the athletes about the general problems in sports associated with agents, gambling, substance abuse, and improper sports conduct.

I consider myself a forceful speaker before a group of people. Shortly into my presentation, a few athletes raised their hands. I acknowledged them. They told me rather rudely that they didn't want to hear about ethical behavior issues. What they wanted to know was how could they get a share of the funds their institutions grossed from the athletes' sports participation. I have always been opposed to paying college athletes for their sports participation. I told them in clear terms that I felt the full scholarship, Pell Grant for those who qualified, summer employment, and now the NCAA special assistance fund, provided them adequate funds as students. I also suggested they have to learn to budget the money they receive and further suggested they needed to focus on earning a college degree so they could get a job when they finished their eligibility.

Those few athletes, who were from various institutions, countered by stating they needed money now and would have no difficulty risking their eligibility to accept it from an agent, booster, or anyone else. Some of the other athletes who had not spoken agreed with them, maybe out of peer pressure. Anyhow, we kept discussing the agenda items, as well as their issues, and when we finished the meeting I felt like I had been through a washing machine. I was disappointed to know some of the athletes were more concerned about getting quick money and thereby jeopardizing their eligibility than they were about earning their college degrees and learning about ethical conduct issues. I was surprised they would be so open about it to a conference office representative. But at least I believed they were honest.

We never will be able to stop improper behavior in intercollegiate athletics. Given current social mores, the urgency to win and financial pressures, it will always be with us. After many centuries we have not learned to prevent fraud in our sophisticated society. But we need to learn to put controls in place and minimize such behavior in college athletics before the ship sinks.

I applaud the National Association of Basketball Coaches for requiring NCAA Division 1 men's head basketball coaches to attend a summit in October 2003 to discuss ethical conduct and accountability issues moving rapidly in the sport. Over the previous year there were a number of Division 1A men's basketball programs socked with NCAA ethical conduct problems.

It's admirable that the basketball coaches addressed those issues, but such a meeting would have been much more effective and certainly more meaningful if the institution presidents had the courage and foresight to call the meeting. At least, it would have been wise for the presidents to participant in the coaches meeting and require the athletics directors to attend as well. Such joint participation would have permitted those with decision-making authority to help frame the ultimate

234

recommendations to NCAA member institutions. Basketball coaches, like other sport groups, are limited in their authority to effect change in isolation. At best, they can make some recommendations that may or may not be heeded by the power brokers (the presidents).

Presidents start to accept responsibility

Since the early 1990s, I believe the presidents have shown some evidence of gradually coming front-and-center in the compliance area, particularly at institutions hit with NCAA probation. They are beginning to accept the responsibility to set the compliance tone on their campuses. There is recent positive evidence at numerous institutions. To set an effective tone of compliance, the presidents need to exercise leadership and explain the need for everyone associated with their institutions to do the right thing. They need to educate boards of trustees, university officers, faculty and staff, students, boosters, and friends about their presidential responsibility to have the institution comply with NCAA rules and regulations.

Presidents need to be involved in establishing broad operational policies, procedures, and plans for the athletics department to establish the standards of conduct for staff. The athletics directors should be fully accountable to manage the day-to-day responsibilities. Presidents must display the courage, conviction, and commitment to route out wrongdoings and support the recommendations of the athletics department director whenever wrongdoings are uncovered. To do less is to return to the old ways and shirk responsibility. The difference between today and yesteryear is that everybody now knows about the broad power presidents hold over the athletics department. The media and public will hold them accountable for major athletics problems.

Presidents need to be strong and true in the compliance area and not just pay lip service to it. One of

235

the serious problems in the compliance program is a lack of consistency in the enforcement of NCAA rules and regulations. Presidents need to demonstrate intestinal fortitude by standing up firmly to a coach, booster, or trustee member and by setting the proper compliance culture to help staff and boosters understand that noncompliance is not an option. They need to make sure not to leave it to chance that athletics directors and coaches are on the same page with the compliance director.

Presidents need to stop coaches and athletics directors who don't get convenient rules interpretations from their compliance directors from going around them in search of flexibility from the president and board of trustee members. That means inappropriate pressure is applied to the compliance director to be more flexible in rules interpretations.

What chance does a low-level position compliance director have in enforcing the rules when powerhouse coaches, the president, and trustee members are overruling him/her in matters of NCAA rules interpretations? Absolutely none. The compliance director's only means of redress in such a situation is to put the interpretation in writing and hold tightly to a copy of it because someday he'll need it.

Presidents have to put a stop to such antics and they need to know that wavering in enforcement of conference and NCAA rules will only exacerbate the problem. Looseness will weaken the trust and confidence that coaches and staff must have in the compliance program.

Mackey expected rules to be followed

I shall never forget when Cecil Mackey was hired as the president at Michigan State University and I was the compliance director. He asked to meet with the entire athletics department. His message left an indelible impression upon me and I believe every other staff member. A few staff members who were in attendance still mention it today. Mackey said he expected all staff to fully comply with all rules and regulations of the Big Ten and NCAA, and policies of the institution. In instances where inadvertent violations were made, he expected staff members to step up and report them promptly to the compliance director. He continued by saying he expected staff to work with integrity in all phases of their responsibilities.

He could understand a staff member having one or two inadvertent secondary violations, but three would be a problem, he said, and surely one major infraction would be a reason for dismissal. He challenged the staff to test him if we did not believe him. It was a simple and dynamic message and staff listened to every word. It was so quite in the room we could have heard a feather drop on the hardwood floor. We knew

Cecil Mackey

that he meant business. We had not heard anyone say that to staff before with such conviction. I don't ever recall having any major compliance problems at the institution under Mackey. Staff frequently requested interpretations of rules before implementing an action, often asking that they be put in writing.

Another example was Chancellor Charles Reed in the Florida higher education system. Long before the NCAA mandated the self-study and peer review process for its member institutions, the innovative educator conducted his own process for at least three years, starting in 1988. Reed hired external athletics consultants to review the athletics programs at each of the Florida state institutions. He devised criteria and allowed the consultants the latitude, over a three-day period, to thoroughly review every aspect of the athletics department.

I was involved on two occasions with a team that included Cedric Dempsey, the A.D. at Arizona who later became NCAA executive director; and Barbara Hedges, associate athletics director at Southern California, who was the A.D. at the University of Washington. Our team was assigned to the University of Florida, Florida State, and Florida A&M universities. Other athletics consultants had assignments at different Florida institutions. We reported our findings to Reed, who in turn briefed the governing board of our findings and further reported the results to those executives reporting to him. It was a model that the NCAA later refined and mandated in the peer review program for its member institutions. In this program, the NCAA assigns a team of representatives from member institutions to evaluate another institution's athletics program.

Two contrasting compliance examples

The two exemplary compliance examples by Mackey and Reed contrast sharply with some other practices existing in higher education. I have known presidents to demonstrate a lack of understanding about their roles that contributed to the misconceptions of coaches and staff in the compliance program. I will present two case studies, both of which happened at Michigan State University during the tenure of President M. Peter McPherson.

• The case of the concealed weapon:
A student-athlete was charged with carrying a loaded pistol in the glove compartment of his automobile. He was arrested and claimed he had been hunting some

wildlife and neglected to remove the gun from his automobile. Since carrying a concealed weapon is a felony, the case was under the jurisdiction of the prosecutor's office and was processed through the courts.

The university also took action based on precedent involving similar cases with students at the institution. McPherson convened a meeting with the vice president of student affairs, the athletics director, the vice president of finance, the campus police chief, the athlete's coach, and the compliance director to discuss the case. The vice president of student affairs reviewed the files of similar student cases and provided information to help the president determine the university's penalty for the student-athlete. The president suspended the athlete from practice and competition in his sport for several weeks.

Since the incident occurred in the early part of the season, the student-athlete missed two-thirds of the season. But he was able to continue to work out in the weight room and attend supervised study sessions for student-athletes. He was not permitted to eat at the training table with the team during his suspension. The student-athlete rejoined the team after serving the suspension. The court sentenced him to a year of probation, plus community service. He was not kicked out of school.

• The case of the substitute exam taker:

In that incident, a professor alleged to the faculty athletics representative that a student-athlete, not enrolled in the class, had taken an exam for another athlete enrolled in the course. The professor had waited until the non-enrolled student-athlete was exiting the room before challenging him. The professor asked the student-athlete his name and he gave the name of the athlete registered for the course. The professor asked for identification and the student-athlete said he had none on him. The faculty athletics representative notified the athletics director, who had a strong background in NCAA investigations.

The professor had noticed the size of the student and surmised he was an athlete. She reviewed the athletics department website and identified the student-athlete from the pictures of the athletes. The athlete duly registered for the course was a teammate of the student-athlete alleged to have taken the test. He lived out of state and had missed the last day of classes to visit his family for Thanksgiving and had not personally taken the scheduled exam that day.

After receiving the information from the faculty athletics representative, the athletics director notified the coach and his boss, a vice president, about the incident. The athletics director then met with the faculty athletics representative and the compliance director to plan a strategy to interview the student-athlete who allegedly took someone else's exam. He lived in the area.

The athletics director also planned a strategy to interview the athlete who went home for the Thanksgiving break. The A.D. and his team waited for the out-of-state athlete to return to campus to start the interviewing process. The second athlete claimed in his interview that he was having lunch on campus in a central location and talked to an unknown man and mentioned to him that he wanted to leave campus a day earlier than the start of the Thanksgiving break to visit his family, but had an exam on that day. Allegedly, the man offered to take the exam for the student and information was exchanged.

The athlete said further in the interview that he was fully aware his actions were wrong but he needed to get home to visit his family. He had requested permission from the professor to either take the exam earlier or after he returned to campus, but was denied. He claimed that he didn't know the name of the man who had taken the exam for him. It was later determined after the interview that the athlete and the other man both were roommates who were on the same team. The person who was registered for the course had lied to the interviewing team when he claimed he didn't know the man who took the exam for him.

The student-athlete identified by the professor as the person who took the exam was interviewed next. He said the night before the exam was given he drove to his family's house several miles from campus and didn't leave the premises until late in the afternoon of the next day (the exam was given at 10 a.m.). He said his father, who was home most of the day, could corroborate his story. The father was called and verified his son's story.

The son agreed to visit the office of the professor, with the interviewing team on hand, to clear his identity. The professor got cold feet when she saw the student-athlete and she acted neutral. She wouldn't give a positive identification. Yet the professor later told colleagues in the college that the student-athlete she observed with the interviewing team was the actual person who took the exam. It later was indicated that the professor believed the athletics department would not penalize the student-athlete for his part in the wrongful act, even if the professor had given a positive identification.

Meanwhile, the college got involved, reviewing the incident separately from the athletics side. At that point the interviewing team was mostly concerned about both athletes giving false information during formal interviews, which is considered unethical conduct under NCAA rules and regulations. The interviewing team requested permission from the athlete who allegedly took the exam to have a sample of his handwriting analyzed and compared with the written name on the test. He agreed. The samples were sent to a nationally renowned graphologist who said the same person wrote both samples.

The student-athlete who took the exam, and his father, were called to visit the interviewing team. Earlier they had denied involvement, and during their visit together with the interviewing team they vehemently continued to deny it, even though they were told the results of the test from the graphologist. They were made aware that knowingly furnishing the institution's representatives with false or misleading information concerning the individual's involvement in or knowledge of matters relevant to a possible violation of an NCAA regulation constituted unethical conduct, an egregious violation of NCAA Rule 10.1.

The father and son were given every opportunity to tell the truth but failed to do so. They threatened to obtain legal counsel, as well as to seek assistance from the president of the institution. And they were encouraged by the interviewing team to do so.

The athletics director, after consulting with the interviewing team and the university vice president who was his boss, decided to immediately and permanently dismiss both student-athletes from the athletics department: the one who took the test for his roommate and the one who initiated the infraction by having someone else take the test for him. The A.D. made the decisions mainly because the two deliberately and consistently lied during an investigation. The father of the athlete also lied.

In a few days the father and son started calling the athletics director asking for a second chance, while still holding on to their story of innocence. They said they weren't aware that the decision would be so swift, definite, and harsh. They claimed they weren't aware of the magnitude of the allegation and requested an appeal. The athletics director referred them to his boss, the vice president, but the A.D., in turn, never was notified of the status of the appeal request.

The student-athlete who took the exam had played well in his sport and was projected to play extensively the next season. McPherson became involved and told the athletics director he felt the dismissals were too severe and compared the athletics director's decisions to the decision the president had made in the gun case. According to the president, he believed that carrying a concealed weapon in a glove compartment was a worse case than lying and academic fraud. The president said academic fraud was a term created by the faculty and did not have much meaning outside of the institution. McPherson reminded the athletics director that he only suspended the student-athlete with the gun for several weeks.

The president felt lying during an investigation deserved a much lesser penalty and he hounded the athletics director on numerous occasions about his decision, citing it as being too harsh. The A.D. told McPherson that lying during an investigation is among the most serious ethical violations in such a situation. He reminded the president that the father and his son had been given many opportunities to be honest and they continued to lie, even when confronted with hard evidence. Although the president disagreed with the athletics director, to his credit he didn't countermand the decisions and both student-athletes were dismissed by their colleges.

McPherson later asked the athletics director whether he would object if the student-athletes appealed both their academics and athletics dismissals and were readmitted to the institution by their colleges. The A.D. said he believed he had taken the appropriate action based on the violation, but he wouldn't object if the student-athletes were successful in their appeal and could get reinstated at the institution and resume their participation in the athletics program.

Both student-athletes transferred to other institutions. After a few months, the student-athlete who took the exam, and his father, once again called the athletics director requesting to return to the institution's athletics program, if successful in their re-admittance request. Both confessed they had lied during the interviews and said they did it to try to protect the son's eligibility. They claimed to have been very fearful during the investigation. The student was not readmitted to the institution.

In the usual course of affairs, such cases as the loaded pistol in the glove compartment did not require or have direct involvement of the president. They were handled by the vice president for student affairs, in conjunction with input from other appropriate persons, or by a student-faculty committee. The results were reported to the presidents. In such a situation as the exam case, with direct presidential involvement, the intent of NCAA rules, and indeed the requirements of ethical and moral behavior so central to the integrity of higher education, were not invoked. Compromising educational values for the sake of winning athletic programs is a Faustian trade that can only sap the core strengths of colleges and universities.

Analysis of the two cases

The athletics director was being held responsible for managing day-to-day operations of the athletics department. He took his job seriously. It was his responsibility to insure the department complied with institutional, conference, and NCAA policies, rules, and regulations. He was disappointed to hear McPherson say he compared the concealed gun charge, which is a criminal offense, to the lying and academic fraud by the two student-athletes, which constituted unethical conduct. He further regretted hearing the president say the penalties were too harsh for the athletes committing academic fraud. At most institutions of higher learning the penalty for proven academic cheating and lying is dismissal. The A.D. believed the incidents at the institution constituted gross misconduct.

Both charges were conspicuously bad and the circumstances warranted distinct penalties that had no correlation. Based on the evidence, it appears the student-athlete gun case did not require direct presidential involvement. There already was established precedent at the institution based on the behavior of other students in previous gun possession cases on campus. They served as benchmarks within the jurisdiction of the vice president of student affairs to apply appropriate penalties, although, naturally, the president should have been appropriately notified of the cases and the results.

As the institution's chief executive officer, McPherson should not have gotten directly involved with the unethical conduct/academic fraud case. The decisions by the athletics director, with concurrence from the vice president, to dismiss the two student-athletes from the athletics program and the subsequent actions taken by their colleges to dismiss them from the institution should have been final unless those decisions were overturned on official appeal. McPherson, in acting that way, undermined the authority delegated to those in charge. Such behavior weakens the spirit and morale, as well as creating future uncertainty.

Although the decisions turned out to be final, McPherson did question the athletics director's judgment and felt an interest to get involved with an academics fraud case. The A.D. believed the president got involved to protect the eligibility of the student-athletes and he believed the coaches of the two athletes pressured the president to have them re-instated. There were rumors surfacing that the coaches wanted the athlete who took the exam to return to the squad the following year. He had an impressive first year.

The head coach had called the athletics director to inquire if there was a chance for the athlete to be reinstated. He was told no. The head coach didn't apply any pressure, knowing full well that the A.D. wouldn't bend. The A.D. believed the coaches took their case to the president so that he could exert pressure on the athletics director.

Circumvention erodes a compliance program and never should be permitted. Typically, some coaches who don't get their way with a rules interpretation from the compliance staff will go to higher authorities on campus to have pressure applied to the person making the interpretation or the decision. They want flexibility given in the rules when none exist for their situation. That kind of practice is a cardinal sin and will quickly erode the integrity of a compliance program. Presidents should never allow such circumvention either for themselves or by their coaches to shop around for the best answer in their individual situations. Only NCAA membership services staff members should be contacted by the compliance director for clarification on rule interpretations. The decision received should be final, unless there is an appeal by the institution.

Issue of institutional control

One of the most grievous NCAA violations is the lack of institutional control over the athletics department. The NCAA requires the chief executive officer to be responsible for administering the entire program in compliance with all rules and regulations of that body. Institutional control has far reaching implications, including responsibility for the actions of its trustees, staff members, student-athletes, boosters, alumni, friends, and any other individual or organization involved in activities for the promotion of the athletics interests of the university. It is a demanding responsibility that requires daily monitoring by the institution.

In addition to violations of NCAA rules and regulations, incidents of the lack of institutional control can occur both from the absence of internal institutional procedures that govern the activities of the athletics department, and from improper use of such established procedures to provide an advantage to student-athletes. The charge may also stem from the actions of external groups engaged in activities for the promotion of the athletics interests of the institution.

All institutions present the image of control. They have athletics boards or councils and faculty athletics representatives to placate the faculty. In essence, they give the semblance of control without actually having any. What the institutions really want and have is pretty much a free rein to do as they wish. They control who is on the athletics boards/councils and as long as you are "flexible" you may remain there for years and support the president's agenda. The faculty views are lost in the process.

Consider the confusing signals and lack of control in the following situation. A former student-athlete at Michigan State University made some NCAA allegations against the institution's football program. The allegations included extra benefits, improper transportation, and ethical conduct issues. After a lengthy cooperative investigation between the university, its outside consultant law firm, and members of the NCAA enforcement staff, the institution found itself in violation of a number of the allegations, plus new ones. The institution elected the option of self-imposing some stringent penalties on the football program. It was a good move to help minimize the additional stiff penalties from the NCAA committee on infractions.

The institution fired staff, isolated some athletics representatives found guilty of violating NCAA rules, reassigned the compliance director, and reduced scholarships in the sport. The NCAA committee on infractions put the university on four years of probation but didn't ban the team from post-season competition or television appearances. McPherson hired a new compliance director and soon initiated an annual compliance review to help detect any trouble spots before they became major NCAA problems.

At that first meeting the president had several members of his cabinet in attendance, along with the athletics director, the compliance staff, and the reassigned compliance director. The new compliance director gave an overview of the compliance program. He talked about the compliance educational program and identified a few potential minor issues. McPherson then said that revenue sports should get some slack on NCAA rules. The former compliance director said he was stunned by the president's bold assertion and said the institution had just gotten socked with four years of probation for secondary and major violations and here it was less than six months later and the president was instructing the new compliance staff to give the revenue sports some slack on the NCAA rules.

The former compliance director – whose knowledge of the compliance area was extensive and formulated over many years of experience — said he advised the president at that meeting that it wouldn't be right to do that. He gave him a scenario to help him better understand the potential problem.

"Let's assume the head swimming coach is a friend to an assistant football coach in the department," he said, "and they are talking one day and the swimming coach says to the football coach, 'Man, the compliance staff stays on my back. Every time I make any secondary violation they write it up and send it to the NCAA.' The assistant football coach responds, 'We don't have to worry about any of that stuff. We seldom get written up.' Now you have a situation where the swimming coach believes he is being singled out unfairly by the compliance staff. He thinks it is situational ethics and he'll surely tell the other non-revenue sports coaches."

"Now you've got an internal problem, not to mention a possible big NCAA problem. Such capricious treatment by the compliance staff would eventually render the entire program ineffective among staff. It will dissipate the trust, which is necessary in a successful compliance program and important to the integrity of the institution."

The general counsel agreed with the former compliance director and McPherson immediately changed the subject.

Slack for revenue sports?

There is great pressure within universities to build winning football and basketball programs in order to keep star athletes eligible and coaches happy and appreciated. So perhaps that is why the president said revenue sports should get some slack on NCAA rules. Maybe he was feeling pressure from the revenue sports coaches and some trustees who didn't want the NCAA probation to further harm the athletics program.

For example, I remember a staff member at a Southeastern Conference institution telling me in the 1970s that its football staff purposely recruited improperly to land blue chip athletes so that, when the NCAA caught them and the program was put on probation, they still would be left with a good football team. The program was eventually investigated by the NCAA and placed on probation.

In the first instance, maybe McPherson felt that the football program would not be under scrutiny by the NCAA with the four years probation, even though the institution is required to submit scheduled progress reports to the infractions committee. The entire budget of the athletics department depends on how successful the revenue teams perform, so the temptation to consider relaxing the rules is very great.

Based on my experience, ignoring or bending NCAA rules is extremely foolish and shortsighted. The improper practice eventually will catch up with the institution. Since the inception of intercollegiate athletics in the 19th century, the system has been plagued with three major problems: commercialism, academic issues, and integrity or ethical conduct issues. Commercialism and academic issues are being addressed partly at the NCAA level and the third one is an issue that belongs primarily at the institutional level.

- Commercialism:
Walter Camp was a successful and winning football

coach at Yale University in the 1890s. He was highly effective in taking what was considered a recreational sport and promoting football as entertainment and to generate revenue for the entire athletics department. Having observed the success at Yale, other colleges and universities rapidly adopted Camp's football philosophy. Professional coaches in football and athletics trainers were hired. Admission fees were charged and alumni made donations to their teams. I don't believe Camp and his associates could have imagined then what would come of their humble beginnings. Today college athletics is big business, with many departments having annual budgets ranging from $35 million to $60 million or more.

The athletics departments have had to resort to every conceivable strategy to generate the funds just to break even financially. Today, athletics departments have used their brand to market the department. They have expanded stadium seating, increased ticket prices, increased donor giving, sold special seating, sold naming rights to athletics facilities. They have earned revenue from broadcast rights; used the Internet to bring in more money; developed partnerships and alliances with car dealers, shoe manufacturers, clothing companies; and earned bowl revenue.

But they have just about exhausted the options to generate new revenue sources in the future. It appears that intercollegiate athletics could be near the end of their golden years. Accelerating the cost of tickets, inflation and the struggling economy over the next several years will most likely cause a drastic reduction in the sports offerings at the universities. With continuing high unemployment, struggling economy, the war on terrorists, numerous season ticket holders will scale back on their contributions to the athletics department, just as they will be required to do in other areas of their budgets.

Most Division I athletics programs sponsor a minimum of 12 men's and 12 women's sports. Don't be surprised to see that number drop to about eight each in the future. That is bound to happen because most football playing institutions already are in the hole financially, ending up in the red each year. Where will the new source of money coming from when the economy is sluggish?

- Academic issues:

There is a constant struggle at the NCAA level about what should be the academic entrance level requirements for prospects to qualify for financial aid and competition their first year on campus. Over the years the requirements have been adjusted higher many times. The real problem is the universities generally adjust their admission requirements higher annually to meet competitive needs of incoming freshmen in the overall student body.

Many talented athletes in the revenue sports and a few other sports don't have sufficient grades and test scores to become regular admissions. They are admitted at the lower range of the criteria. The NCAA standards help to serve as a minimum to insure that athletes have the basic skills for a reasonable chance to qualify for admission, stay in school and hopefully graduate. As colleges and universities continue to upgrade their admissions standards there also will be some adjustment made in the NCAA eligibility standards. Presidents should make sure it is done.

There is the issue of continuing eligibility rules once a prospect has enrolled in the institution. The NCAA prescribes the number of credits a student-athlete must earn each year of enrollment to maintain eligibility for competition and financial aid. Those requirements fall within the average standards necessary for all students to remain in good standing at the institution.

There never will be a perfect system, but overall its better now than it was 20 years ago. I have learned that the most important success factors in the graduation of student-athletes who don't meet regular admission criteria are the head coach and the leadership of a comprehensive academic support program. Leadership involves the academic professionals managing the program and the strong expectations and support of coaches to reinforce the necessity of consistent class attendance, regular study hours and effective tutoring sessions. I have assisted and witnessed many at-risk student-athletes graduate from Michigan State who, when coming out of high school, never were expected to be academically successful. But they went to their classes and worked diligently with their studies and followed procedures. Graduating at-risk athletes requires dedicated coaches, leadership and institutional commitment, which are too often lacking.

- Integrity and ethical conduct issues:
They should be the responsibility of the institutions and never become NCAA issues. It is the individual institution that should investigate and apply discipline to wrongdoers. Such inappropriate behavior as cheating in recruitment, academic fraud, lying during an investigation, athletics department staff members gambling on college sports, tampering with transcripts, giving improper money to athletes, providing extra benefits to athletes, etc., need to be dealt with at the institutional level and reported to the NCAA as a matter of course. Clearly such action would show evidence that the institution had integrity and full control of its athletics program. Such action would provide assurance to the public that the president with his/her presidential authority was in charge of the athletics department and was providing effective leadership in the compliance area.

Regrettably at most institutions ethical issues, lying, cheating, etc., are all subordinate to winning. Universities have adopted and encouraged the wrong values. Coaches are too often fired for not winning enough, such was the case with Tyrone Willingham at Notre Dame, who had a 21-15 record and was fired for not meeting the winning expectations at that institution and not because he cheated. Getting caught cheating is the sin, not cheating itself.

Compliance suggestions for the institution

A university's governing board should:
- Endorse and support comprehensive NCAA, conference, and institutional compliance programs.
- It should hire a president with proven values and practices whose philosophy is compatible with the boards' policies, principles, and plans.
- The full board of elective or appointed members should meet with the president and other appropriate university officers to develop policies that establish moral and ethical conduct principles that also encompass an institutional control plan. When the policies have been developed, the board would delegate them to the president for implementation.
- One of the standing items on each board's meeting agenda should be a "status report" of the institution's compliance program. The board should receive an annual written evaluation on the status of the compliance program.

A university's president, serving as chief executive officer, should:
- Provide the leadership to develop an effective compliance program by giving clear expectations and directions to the entire university community.
- Consider moving the compliance program outside of the athletics department and have the office report either to the president or to a vice president.
- Hire an athletics director with the character and integrity to execute the compliance plans, systems, and procedures developed by the

president for implementation in the athletics department.

- Provide regular progress reports to the board of governance regarding the compliance program.
- Meet with all university officers to explain the compliance program and seek their full cooperation by promoting the program in their units.
- Appoint representatives from the institution to serve on a compliance advisory committee.
- Require an annual comprehensive audit of the athletics department done by experts from outside the institution. That would be in addition to the NCAA requirements.
- Meet with the athletics staff annually to review standards of conduct and expectations and express support for the athletics director and the compliance director as long as they enforce the rules and regulations, as well as institutional policies.
- Meet with the board of trustees, university officers, faculty, and staff to explain what is required in their areas of responsibility as far as athletics is concerned.
- Share compliance philosophy at every talk he or she gave at the university, both internally and externally.
- Provide adequate resources to have at least six professional staffers in the office of compliance services. Some might think six is too many, but they have to look at campuses as cities with thousands of faculty, staff, students, and thousands of alumni and boosters. How secure would one feel if there were only two policemen to patrol a city and both worked the day shift? The president is responsible for the behavior of all of them if they become representatives of the athletics department.

I would assign two staffers to work exclusively with the booster and alumni groups. Education would be their main focus and some travel would be required. Two staffers would split the educational work with coaches, athletics staff, student athletes, faculty, and staff. A fifth staff member would function as a technical auditor/ monitor of all athletics department procedures involving athletics, admissions, ticket allocations, certification, recruitment, and all other institutional, conference, and NCAA procedures operating in the athletics department. And they should make sure the compliance program was functioning as planned.

The sixth person would be given the title of assistant vice president, or some title of greater esteem, and be responsible for the operation of the entire compliance program. He or she would also be responsible for working with the compliance advisory committee, developing a compliance manual, doing preliminary investigations of all allegations, and reporting findings to the president, vice president, athletics director, committee, and to the office of the general counsel.

I feel it's necessary to have the position function at the assistant vice president level or some title of greater esteem so as to give the position some respect and authority when dealing with powerful coaches, as well as other persons with political agendas on and off campus. Such a title would heighten the awareness of compliance at the university similar to the role that was created for the senior women administrators in the 1980s. That role essentially gave the women some general respect and greater visibility in the athletics department.

In addition, with proper resources, I would give the top person a five-year, roll over, contract to insulate him/ her from the political pressures that are inherent in compliance work. The assistant vice president for compliance should have a dual reporting line to the athletics director and to the office of the vice president, general counsel, or president.

- Retain final authority to review and approve the athletics department broad operating policies, procedures, and plans. They will help everyone understand where the department is going and where it is expected to end up annually. When implemented, the policies, procedures, and plans should bring about consistency in the methods of doing business in the department. That is necessary when dealing with regulatory agencies and will help folks sleep soundly at night. When the policies, procedures, and plans are fully developed and cataloged each time a new staff person is hired in the athletics department, part of the training would be to learn them dutifully.
- The president, provost, vice presidents, general counsel, alumni director, and athletics director should meet with the entire compliance staff and committee at least annually to review procedures and plan new compliance strategies. Those need to be open work sessions where ideas are shared and implemented.
- Each staff member in the athletics department, as a condition of employment, should be required to attend every planned staff compliance meeting. The meetings should be scheduled one year in advance so staff can avoid conflicts, unless there are emergencies.
- Boosters should be required to sign a standard of conduct form annually.
- Persons hired for the compliance office should have strong ethical conduct, people skills, and understand human behavior. They should be skilled, with a minimum of three years experience in NCAA legislation, and experienced at interviewing; be good listeners who can catch the drift of what is being said; have the ability to analyze situations and solve problems; be mature enough to remain calm in the worse situations;

be good with details; have integrity; and have an ability to write and speak well.

I have tried to outline, through a systematic examination of NCAA compliance at the institutional level, some of the salient issues that frequently occur on campuses of major institutions. I feel that I have just scratched the surface. It is my conclusion that what is really needed in intercollegiate athletics is a comprehensive compliance model that encompasses standards of conduct for all university affiliated personnel, as well as monitoring and effective reporting systems.

These rules would apply from the bottom up to the coaches, staff, and the president. In the final analysis, however, such a system can only function if those who staff it are ethical people of integrity and courage.

CHAPTER 7:

COACHING CAROUSEL

Saban football era successful – but brief

Michigan STATE HAD BEEN THROUGH ITS SHARE of football coaches after Duffy Daugherty's 19-year tenure and apparently it was difficult trying to get back to that level of success and stability that produced a 109-69-5 record.

George Perles had the job for 12 years and was at the end of his coaching tenure at the university after the 1994 season. His predecessors had lasted just three (Denny Stolz), four (Darryl Rogers), and three (Muddy Waters) years.

The university began a search for a new head football coach during Perles' last season with a meeting that convened at 1:30 p.m. in the office of vice president Roger Wilkinson on Friday, Oct. 21, 1994. Wilkinson wanted Athletics Director Merrily Baker and me, as the senior associate athletics director with responsibilities for the football program, to lay the ground rules for hiring a new coach. That meeting took place before the seventh game of the season as the Spartans were taking a 2-4 record into their game at Iowa.

When I arrived at 1:30, Wilkinson was in his office. Baker didn't show up until 2 p.m., saying she was waiting for a Big Ten Conference call regarding upcoming bowl games and that it was cancelled at the last minute. Wilkinson said he wanted to discuss plans for hiring the new coach to present them to President M. Peter McPherson upon the president's return from Asia. He also said he preferred that only the three of us be involved initially so he could help limit the role of Jay Morris in the process. McPherson had hired Morris from the outside as senior advisor to the president and had indicated he wanted him involved in the process.

Coach George Perles with quarterback Dave Yarema

Wilkinson acknowledged upfront that he never had been involved with the hiring of a head football coach. Baker, though, said she was part of the process at Minnesota when Lou Holtz was hired. I explained that I had served on the interviewing committees that hired Stolz in 1973 and Rogers in 1976. Wilkinson asked each of us to independently lay out our hiring strategies so that we could develop the best possible plan for the new search when we met again on Oct. 24 at 10:30 a.m. in his office. He asked that we not put anything in writing, except for maintaining our private notes.

We lost the game at Iowa City, 19-14, on Oct. 22. Baker approached me in the press box there and asked me to meet with her Sunday in her office so that we could form our strategies together, something that was contrary to Wilkinson's request. She asked me four questions at that meeting:

- At which point do we communicate with the candidates?
- What is the role of the outside consultants and did I feel it was necessary for them to be used in the process? (McPherson had hired Roy Kramer, former commissioner of the Southeast Conference, and former MSU athletics director Joe Kearney to identify possible candidates and inquire about their interest as candidates.)
- How should we meet the candidates: e.g., where should we interview them and how should we travel there?
- Who should be the candidates?

Baker wrote down my answers and together during a two-hour work session we developed a job description. I met with Perles on Monday in his office after practice and brought him up to date on the search. He mentioned that he was willing to forego his outside contractual football compensation arrangements if he was relieved of his football duties, provided he could be reassigned as the athletics director for two years. That was wishful thinking. There was no open A.D. position and Perles was trying to look at all of the options for himself. A couple days after the Iowa game, trustee Joel Ferguson, who had been communicating with McPherson about the football program, called and told me the loss at Iowa was devastating to the program, as well as to Perles' objective to meet McPherson's "outstanding season" criteria. It would be difficult, he said, to protect the coach from being fired after a 2-5 record.

261

Perles fired; successor search begins

Well, Perles was fired, Nov. 8, with two games left on the season schedule. Some questioned the motives of this timing. He was allowed to coach those two games. McPherson assembled an advisory group that month consisting of him; Baker; Wilkinson; Morris; Provost Lou Anna Simon; vice president for public relations, Terry Denbow; athletics faculty rep Michael Kasavana; and me. (Kramer and Kearney already had worked for months behind the scenes searching for viable candidates.)

The advisory group compiled a list of candidates who were recommended by various sources. It included former Spartan players, Jimmy Raye and Sherman Lewis, who were assistants with the Kansas City Chiefs and San Francisco 49ers of the National Football League, respectively; Nick Saban, defensive coordinator of the NFL's Cleveland Browns; two collegiate head coaches in Ohio, Gary Blackney of Bowling Green State, and Jim Tressel of Youngstown State; plus Fran Ganter, an assistant under Joe Paterno at Penn State.

Raye, Saban, Blackney, and Tressel were interviewed at the Marriott Hotel at Detroit Metropolitan Airport. Each did a good job in their interviews. My private ranking of them afterwards was Raye, Saban, Tressel, and Blackney. The committee met to discuss the interviewees and to identify names of other possible candidates, including Bobby Ross, coach of the NFL's San Diego Chargers; and Bill McCartney, a former Michigan assistant and ex-head coach at the University of Colorado. Some other names were suggested, but none were given serious consideration. Ganter and Saban, in that order, emerged as top candidates.

Although Raye had a good interview, I knew he didn't have much of a chance after he was asked whom he would employ as his assistant coaches. He said that Perles had some staff members who knew how to coach and he would certainly interview some of them. He had no way of knowing that it was a politically incorrect response to a president who had fired Perles and denounced any laudable image he had developed in the program.

The committee interviewed Ganter in Cowles House, the president's residence, and Mrs. McPherson sat in on that one interview. Since there were allegations relating to academic wrongdoings mentioned in the NCAA's investigation of the MSU football program, some committee members listed academic integrity among the top priorities for the new coach. Penn State had such an image under Paterno and that made Ganter a prime candidate.

Following Ganter's interview, McPherson asked me whether I thought he was ready for a head coaching position. Although he wasn't at the top of my list, I honestly believed he could be a head coach and I told the president so. To me, Ganter wasn't dynamic during his interview, but he was experienced and personable. He made a good appearance, was very nice, and I presumed he had learned coaching standards from his responsibilities at Penn State and he would know whom to hire if he were offered the position. Most assistant coaches I know keep a short list of potential candidates just in case they are offered a head job.

Tour with Ganter dulls opinion

McPherson asked me to give Ganter a tour of the Duffy Daugherty football facility at midnight when none of the coaches and staff were there. He was trying to keep the process as confidential as possible. The football program must have had its spies but there was only one car in the parking lot when we arrived. As I unlocked the exterior door and started to show Ganter the building we ran into the janitor, Preston Starks, who was routinely cleaning up. We had been there no longer than 15 minutes when Gary VanDam, administrative assistant to Perles, appeared. I introduced Fran to Gary, who appeared ruffled. It seemed unusual for anyone to arrive in the building that time of night.

As Ganter and I continued with the tour, he started asking some very basic questions, the answers to which I thought he should have known. I thought the questions were too obvious for a top assistant from a blue-chip program. He left me with the impression, rightly or wrongly, that he wasn't really interested in the job.

McPherson called the next morning to inquire about the tour. He wanted to know how it went. I mentioned the questions Ganter had asked of me. I told the president I had a different perspective about his candidacy than I had before that tour and now felt he wouldn't be a good fit for our program.

McPherson became impatient with me after I explained my second opinion of Ganter and said he would call me later. Shortly thereafter I got a call from Morris, who wanted to know what I told the president about Ganter. I shared the information with him and he told me McPherson didn't like my change of opinion. The president called in the afternoon and, in a three-way teleconference with Morris, said he wanted me to review again the reservations I had of Ganter that developed as a result of the tour of the football facility. He said, "Yesterday you said he could be our coach. Today you are suggesting to me not to hire him. What happened?"

I explained that yesterday during the interview I had made assumptions based on Ganter's affiliation with a successful football program and its legendary coach, Joe Paterno. When I was asked if Ganter was ready for a head coaching position, I said yes. I changed my views, I said, because Ganter had asked me some rather simple and mundane questions that suggested, based upon his coaching longevity and responsibilities, that he wasn't really interested in the position.

264

After all that, it was clear to me McPherson still was bent on hiring Ganter. He acted more concerned that I had changed my mind than with the opinion I was sharing with him. When we hung up, Morris called back and said I should not let Peter get me upset. He said he had known him for a long time, mentioning that he had introduced McPherson's wife to him. He further stated that McPherson once served as Jay's campaign manager for some political office.

It appeared in the *Lansing State Journal* that Ganter was offered the job and declined it and that a contract was offered to him. I wasn't involved in any of that so I can't confirm what transpired between the president and Ganter. McPherson said he never offered the job to him, but I do know the president and his wife, Joanne, were sky high on Gantner being the next head football coach after his interview. McPherson later told me, after Saban was hired, he credited Wilkinson and me for keeping him from appointing Ganter. I never knew where Wilkinson stood with Ganter. The Ganter interview took place on a Monday, Nov. 28. It was reported that he returned to the campus two days later to meet further with the president, although I can't confirm that.

Cursory interview for Lewis unfair

The full committee was not available when we interviewed Lewis at a hotel near the airport in Grand Rapids on the Friday morning after Thanksgiving Day. McPherson, Wilkinson, Kasavana were there, along with me. It was obvious from the outset, based on the pattern of questions, that it was a courtesy interview. It was the shortest session of all the candidates.

I had picked Lewis up from the Grand Rapids airport. He was full of hope and optimism. On the return trip I could not tell him how his interview had gone compared to the other candidates. I felt badly for Sherm, who had flown in from Green Bay, Wis. Normally, when an interview ended, the committee stayed in the room to discuss the candidate. That didn't happen with Lewis. As soon as he left the room, McPherson got up to leave.

I asked if we were going to discuss Lewis. He said no. As it turned out, Lewis had absolutely no chance for the position and we should never have led him to believe he had a chance. We should have been upfront with him. As soon as I got home from work Friday night, McPherson called and asked me to call both Raye and Lewis and tell them they were out of contention. He said he would make calls to the other candidates: Tressel, Blackney, Saban, and Ganter.

Sherm Lewis, during his days as MSU's defensive coordinator under Muddy Waters

Saban becomes leading candidate

McPherson called a few days later to say he was going to offer the position to Saban. He asked me to work with Nick and get him acclimated to the NCAA recruiting rules so he could pass the coaches certification exam. Since he was hired early in December during the recruiting season when prospective student-athletes were making official visits to campuses, we tried to get an exemption from the NCAA on the certification exam. All coaches who recruit off-campus must successfully pass the exam, which is based on NCAA recruiting legislation. An exemption would have allowed Saban to contact high school prospects while still working for a pro team. The NCAA denied the request, so Saban couldn't be involved until after his formal association with the Browns was terminated.

After officially getting the position and passing NCAA certification, Saban started selecting his assistants. He retained Pat Shurmur and Bobby Williams from Perles' staff. He kept Gary VanDam on a temporary basis until he hired his complement of coaches. He brought in Charlie Baggett from the Houston Oilers and Gary Tranquill from the University of Virginia. In addition, he hired, among others, Dean Pees, Mark Dantonio, Jim Bowman, and Glenn Pires.

Saban coached from December 1994 until December 1999, finishing with a 34-24-1 record. The highlight of his brief tenure was the 1999 season in which the Spartans went 9-2 and qualified for the Florida Citrus Bowl. However, he resigned prior to the bowl game to accept the head coaching position at Louisiana State University and was replaced for the bowl game by Williams, the associate head coach.

In accordance with accepted practice, Joe Dean, the athletics director at LSU, called me, in my role as interim athletics director, on Tuesday, Nov. 29, 1999, and requested permission to speak to Saban about the head football coach opening at Louisiana State. (I had become the interim A.D. in April of that year.) I consented to Dean's request and he said he already had preliminary discussions about Nick's candidacy — I didn't inquire with whom — and it was time to get serious about hiring him. I told Fred Poston, who had become the interim vice president for finance, operations, and the treasurer at Michigan State, about the call from LSU and he relayed the information to McPherson.

Poston empowered me to meet with Saban and attempt to keep him at MSU. That same day I met with Nick in his office. He was holding his dealings with LSU close to the vest. He indicated he had been contacted by Louisiana State but had no serious conversations with anyone about the position. He appeared rather nonchalant about the opportunity and I saw no need to begin a negotiation in an effort to retain him because at that point he had not expressed any interest in leaving.

Cryptic meeting suggests Saban to leave

McPherson called me that same day around 5 p.m. on Nov. 29 and said trustee Ferguson was going to Saban's home around 6:30 to meet with him and he wanted me to be in the meeting. I arrived at Saban's house close to 6:30, about the same time as Ferguson. We intruded upon Saban, who, with his mother-in-law, was babysitting his children. It was a rather awkward situation for everybody. It was dinnertime for his children and he was trying to accommodate them while talking with us. He continued to deny that he had serious involvement with LSU. We kept asking him if he had issues at Michigan State that we could address and his responses were consistently, "No." He would not comment beyond that response.

After about an hour of playing cat and mouse with him and not getting anything of substance, I suggested to Ferguson that we should leave. It had become clear to

268

me that Saban had turned sour on Michigan State and was leaning toward LSU. I got that feeling because he wouldn't provide definite responses to any of the questions we raised with him. He didn't want to talk about either institution. I felt that if he were remaining at MSU, he would have been interested in discussing the upcoming bowl game, a salary increase, his bonus payout, or something positive about the university. He gave us nothing up to that point.

Ferguson continued to question Saban. He asked him where his wife was and he said she had gone to the store. In about 10 minutes the phone rang and his mother-in-law called him to the phone. It became obvious to Ferguson and me at that point that it was a long-distance call from his wife. Nick was talking very low and primarily saying "yes" and "no" to the caller. When Saban hung up, Ferguson asked if his wife was at LSU and he acknowledged that she was. He said she went there to look over the area, but he had not agreed to anything with Louisiana State.

The next morning, Wednesday, Nov. 30, Saban met with his staff in the Duffy Daugherty Football Building and announced to them that he had taken the job with Louisiana State. He asked the entire coaching staff to join him in the transition and that he would have a private plane at the airport Sunday morning to take any of the interested coaches with him to Baton Rouge. None of the coaches accepted his offer.

Williams, at that

Nick Saban

269

time, had been upgraded in title to associate head coach after having been the running backs coach for 10 years. He was rapidly receiving a groundswell of support. Many of the football players collectively met with McPherson and advocated that Williams be named Saban's successor. The assistant coaches and other staff also expressed their support for him in visits with the president and there were gathering sentiments for Williams from others in the community, including Mrs. McPherson, who urged her husband to hire him.

The day of Saban's resignation, Williams interviewed at Eastern Michigan University and was the leading candidate for the head job there. He had coached at Eastern from 1985-89. He delayed notifying EMU of his decision pending the outcome of his candidacy for the Michigan State position.

Poston, McPherson, and I met Friday morning and agreed to name Williams the interim coach, further agreeing that he would coach the New Year's Day Florida Citrus Bowl game against the University of Florida. In the meantime, we began an immediate and aggressive search for a new head coach.

Saban explains decision

Saban called my house at 6:30 a.m. Dec. 6 from Baton Rouge and said he believed he had made a mistake in judgment by taking the LSU job. He said he was agitated with McPherson over basically two issues when he resigned:

- He believed McPherson had cheated him out of $100,000. As a means to make Saban's salary comparable to other successful Division l-A head football coaches, McPherson, as I understood it, using university funds, established an investment account in Nick's name through the university. The annual earnings in excess of a fixed university percentage belonged to Saban. It was that arrangement in which Nick felt he was shortchanged in the payout.

- His second complaint was that he believed McPherson wouldn't support him publicly if he had a losing season. He had experienced criticism from the public and media during the 1997 and 1998 seasons when his records were 7-6 and 6-6, respectively, and felt the president had demonstrated a lack of support by not speaking out favorably on his behalf during those seasons.

Saban said he wanted to come back to Michigan State but understood that he could not do so. He very much missed his family, which still was in East Lansing. I empathized with his situation and could relate to his feelings of loneliness. I, too, had changed jobs a number of times in my career and left my family behind temporarily for various reasons.

I mentioned to Nick that I would share his concerns with Poston and McPherson. I thought he had a chance of returning to his job if he made a public apology to the university relative to the way he left. He never told us he was leaving until the day he left, then he tried to recruit the coaching staff while knowing the university had qualified for a bowl game. That behavior didn't set well with some folks. Saban left a host of discontented people in East Lansing and some of them were pleased to see him go. (And I imagine after Saban left LSU to coach the Miami Dolphins of the NFL after the 2004 season it didn't set well with Tigers fans, either.)

Although Saban was sometimes difficult to work with, I found him to be intelligent, very driven, and intense about his work. I liked and respected him. He and his wife, Terry, always were warm-hearted to Noreese and me. There were some coaches and university staff members who felt he was too arrogant and too demanding, with little patience. There was a feeling that he circumvented the university administrative system too much by taking internal issues to Ferguson for resolution. I mentioned to Poston and McPherson about Saban's concerns and interest in returning to the university. McPherson appeared somewhat interested in exploring the possibility of taking him back, but some of his advisors talked him out of it.

Another search underway

The president appointed an advisory group consisting of him, Poston, Denbow, Simon, associate athletics director Greg Ianni, Kasavana, and myself. We put together a list of possible candidates. The preliminary list included Williams and, once again, Sherman Lewis, plus a bevy of others: Tyrone Willingham (Stanford), Cam Cameron (Indiana), Glen Mason (Minnesota), Sonny Lubick (Colorado State), Tommy Bowden (Clemson), Steve Logan (East Carolina), Mark Richt (Florida State), Steve Mariucci (San Francisco 49ers), Bob Pruitt (Marshall), and Tom Osborne, former Nebraska coach. McPherson wanted a thorough and quick search.

We made initial contact with Willingham, who expressed interest but later withdrew his name (he ended up becoming Notre Dame's coach in 2002 and had an outstanding first season).

We spoke with Cameron's agent and I subsequently received a call from basketball coach Bob Knight informing me that the only way Cameron would be interested would be if he were offered the job outright without an interview. Calls were made to Mariucci, who had no interest. Meanwhile, the University of Georgia hired Richt.

McPherson contacted Osborne and tried to recruit him, but he rejected an offer. Mason was left as the hottest name on the list. We interviewed him in Minneapolis on Thursday, Dec. 1 — the day after Saban announced he was leaving — and Mason was subsequently offered the position, a five-year contract worth $1 million annually. He asked us to work with his agent on the financial arrangements. Poston and I discussed the financial details with the agent by teleconference on Saturday evening, Dec. 3, in my office. Assistant athletics director for business, Peggy Brown, was in the room with us listening to the telephone conversation. So were attorney Sally Harwood, Ianni, and others.

The agent asked for an additional $200,000 annual increase in Mason's contract offer, which would have put his salary at $1.2 million. He explained that Mason was named Big Ten Coach of the Year for the 1999 season and his salary should be comparable to that of John Cooper at Ohio State. He believed Cooper to be among the highest paid coaches in the Big Ten. The agent also asked for significant increases in most of the line items in the football program's budget.

Poston and I looked at each other as the agent continued to make demands and we were thinking the same thing — that they were unreasonable and too expensive. We just let the agent continue to talk until he was finished. We didn't attempt to counter his demands or ask him any questions. We did mention that we would take his requests under advisement with the president, which we did, and concluded that we couldn't afford the coach. We notified the agent of our decision the next day.

Williams becomes best option

Poston and I decided that we needed to hire Bobby Williams. The committee had interviewed him Saturday morning, Dec. 3, in the president's conference room. Poston called McPherson, who was at the Breslin Events Center attending the MSU-Eastern Michigan basketball game. Poston asked him to come to my office in Jenison Field House after the game. When he arrived we told him about our phone conversation with Mason's agent and our recommendation to offer Williams the job. McPherson agreed with our assessment about the agent's demands. He said he needed to make some phone calls

Bobby Williams

to the MSU trustees. It was around midnight. He finished his calls close to 1 a.m. and gave us the authorization to call Williams and offer him the job.

I called Bobby at his home and asked him to come to Jenison. I didn't tell him why I was calling. Before his arrival, McPherson had contacted basketball coach Tom Izzo at Breslin and informed him of the decision. He asked him to stop by Jenison, which he and his wife, Lupe, did do on their way home from the game. We were in the Jenison conference room off the lobby area when Williams arrived. I don't believe he knew what was going on or what to expect. It was after 1 a.m. Sunday morning. The president offered him the job with a five-year contract worth $450,000 annually, plus bonuses. He was earning less than $100,000 as the associate head coach and running backs coach.

Williams accepted the offer and became the 21st head football coach at Michigan State — and the first African-American in that position. He became the fifth African-American head football coach in NCAA Division I football for the 1999 season. I believe it was historic for a black A.D. and black football coach to be employed at the same time at a major Division I institution.

Williams called his assistant coaches and scheduled a staff meeting for 8 a.m. in his office Sunday to announce his appointment. McPherson, Poston, and I attended and after the meeting I introduced Bobby to the press and supporters who had packed the standing room only auditorium of the Clara Bell Smith Center. Williams was given a rousing standing ovation. He had his family, Sheila, Nicholas, and Nataly, with him and introduced them before making his remarks. It was a great day in the enriched history of Spartan athletics. There was much excitement among the folks in the auditorium over the appointment.

Williams retained the staff Saban had assembled: Reggie Mitchell, Morris Watts, Bill Miller, Brad Lawing, Dantonio, Bill Sheridan, Pat Ruhle, Bob Casula; and he hired Don Treadwell. In addition, he retained Ken Mannie and Mike Vollmer. It was a good staff. When Dantonio, Sheridan, and Casula left for other programs,, Williams replaced them with Jeff Stoutland, Pat Perles, and Troy Douglas.

Another short tenure, then another new coach

On Monday, Nov. 4, 2002, Williams was fired by the university after compiling a 3-6 record and joined the ranks of the short-termers' fraternity of coaches at MSU. The other modern day members were Stolz (1973-75), Rogers (1976-79), Waters (1980-82), and Saban (1995-99). Williams coached fewer than three full years, having been appointed in December 1999 to take over from Saban for the Florida Citrus Bowl, and finishing up after nine games (a 3-6 record) of the 2002 season. His head coaching record was 16-17. Williams was paid a buyout of $550,000 and was hired by the Detroit Lions in January of 2003 to be their receivers coach.

By that time, Ron Mason had succeeded me as athletics director and he was the one who conducted the search for a new head coach, making a recommendation to the president. The choice was John L. Smith from the University of Louisville, who was given a six-year contract worth $9 million. He became Michigan State's 22nd head football coach on Dec. 19, 2002. I wish Smith and his staff much success during their tenure at the university.

CHAPTER 8:

NEWS MEDIA

Headline surprises become routine

FORMER BIG EIGHT CONFERENCE COMMISSIONER Chuck Neinas once remarked that the higher a person climbs the flag pole, the more exposed he becomes. That, in a nutshell, highlights my experiences with the news media.

While the media can be powerful tools for an athletics department, there are pitfalls in the relationship, namely that it is like a double-edged sword. They will praise you while you're going up the ladder and be unmercifully critical should you start down that ladder.

Criticism from news outlets, be they broadcast or print media, goes with the territory and most athletes, coaches and athletics administrators accept it and move on with a positive attitude. However, when tainted by personal bias, the reporting no longer is objective.

Bobby Williams felt the stings of media criticisms while he was Michigan State's football coach during the 2002 season. Based on the number of varsity players who returned to the team for that season, as well as the expectations from All-American wide receiver Charles Rogers, and the anticipation generated by the return of promising quarterback Jeff Smoker, the media projected a good season for the Spartans. Some even picked the team to challenge for the Big Ten title, something I felt was not realistic for a team without an experienced tailback and having mostly inexperienced linebackers who were small and with average speed.

MSU struggled in the first five games and took a record of 3-2 into the sixth game against the University of Iowa. After each game, starting with the opener, the media started questioning the performance of the very team they had built up before the regular season started. They expressed doubt about the quality of the coach, wondering if he was tough enough; if he had sufficient leadership experience to be the head coach.

Everything Williams did or said was under scrutiny by both the print and broadcast media. Some criticism was duly warranted and expected from the group of media experts, who believed they had more knowledge about the team than the coaches had. Surely, when a team loses and doesn't compete well, criticism is expected from the press in some degree. Williams perhaps made an error in judgment due to political inexperience after a devastating loss when, in response to a media question about whether he had lost control of the team, he said, "I don't know." It left him vulnerable for criticism and the media capitalized on it, big time.

The news media had become more critical after the loss, by a large margin, to a superior Iowa team that finished the season with an 11-1 record before losing to Southern Cal in the 2003 Orange Bowl game. After their loss to the Hawkeyes, the Spartans lost the next three games and then, after a lopsided loss to Michigan, Williams was fired.

I'm not suggesting the university didn't have the authority to determine who should coach its team, because it does. Nevertheless, many people in the community felt it was awkward the way Bobby was fired. Some folks felt he should have been allowed to coach through his

278

five-year contract. Instead, he was fired after coaching less than three seasons. Still others in the community felt Williams should at least have been permitted to coach the three remaining games on the 2002 schedule.

Then, there were folks who believed he should have been fired after the 2000 season (5-6) or the 2001 season (7-5) because of poor performance. And there were folks who believed he should never have been offered the job as head football coach. I spent a considerable amount of time responding to such critics.

The media's relentless criticism hastened the demise of the coach. The beat writers, broadcasters, and talk show hosts were verbally brutal to Williams personally. They continued to stir up the fans and public sentiments by criticizing everything about the program. The print media and the call-in talk show hosts relentlessly flooded their fans with negative information about the program.

When junior quarterback Smoker dropped out of the program in the middle of the season to seek medical help, and another student-athlete was later charged with a criminal offense, the media had a field day questioning the qualities of the coach and calling for his dismissal.

The media, in that case, showed its two sides: They built the coach up during the preseason and pushed him up the flagpole with much hype to create public interest in the football program and to sell their information; and just as he was getting comfortable in his position, the media steadily dropped the boom on him so he would fall and painfully exit the scene. The media can be diabolic. It earns money to stay in business by using athletics as a major vehicle to sell information to the public. I find it a challenge to work with such chameleon-like personalities.

Media training sessions needed

I believe it's critical for an athletics department to establish annual media training sessions for all its employees, including student-athletes. Some training is given, but it's not nearly as comprehensive as needed. The training sessions should be coordinated by the sports information director, whose job it is to manage media relations for the department. At Michigan State, John Lewandowski and his staff handle those functions, serving as liaisons with the beat writers and other regional and national media.

It would be natural for people in his position to design training sessions to educate staff on how to deal with the media. The sessions could benefit both the athletics department and the media. The training would establish department policy regarding how it would relate and respond to media inquiries. The program would identify who in the department would be authorized to speak to the media about internal issues.

It should also include how to deal with the media when the media requests for "off the record" information are made; how to react during interviews; how to improve the department's image; how coaches and student-athletes should respond to media questions after competition; how student-athletes and coaches should respond to questions about confidential information; and how to handle crisis situations; and what to do about misquotes.

The training would significantly improve the image of the department by minimizing leaks or staff members talking out of school. A policy should help the media know what persons they can legitimately approach in the department to obtain the necessary information they seek. The media would be able to get more accurate, frequent, and comprehensive information about issues occurring in the department from its authorized spokespersons. The current hodgepodge and backdoor way of getting inside information from some staff would be greatly reduced.

If the MSU athletics department had implemented such a program in my earlier years I might not have experienced several problems I had with the media. When

I became A.D. in 1999, I appointed Lewandowski to be the department spokesperson for the reasons I've mentioned. Even then we had some leaks, but nothing like we had in the past. We could pretty much narrow down where internal leaks were coming from and would remind the staff about the media policy. For the most part, the leaks stopped. Coaches were left alone to talk about their sports to the media, but requests for information about internal matters came from Lewandowski's office, or he coordinated such with the specialist in the particular program area.

Athletics and the media have a reciprocal relationship. They thrive off of each other. Sports are a part of our culture that has been characterized as a microcosm of American society. They reflect popular attitudes and ideas and are influenced by social and political change. The media use information about the personalities of coaches and the performances of student-athletes and other sports figures to sell information to their customers over a broad market. If the news is questionable, of a crisis nature, or if it happens to be about a minor human mistake, the print media can make a sensational headline out of the information so as to sell more papers or secure advertisements.

The media consists not only of print and broadcast elements, but also, now, the Internet. They are commercial enterprises organized to sell public information and sports represent a big and rewarding part of that product. Athletics have immense appeal in the American culture. Many Americans of all ages, ethnicity, sex, and backgrounds have a genuine interest in sports, either as spectators or participants.

On the other hand, athletics departments benefit from the positive news reported by the media. Such favorable news concerning scheduling, victories, coaches' interviews, recruiting prospects, construction of new facilities, participation in championships and post-season events, can confidently promote the department and help sell tickets. Many times the athletics departments proactively package press releases and share internal stories with the media to help promote its own image. If the department had to pay for the publicity it now receives from the media for free, the cost would be prohibitive.

Rapport with media starts to sour

I enjoyed a solid and effective relationship with sports media until 1994. I granted numerous interviews and provided appropriate information when requested; clarified NCAA and Big Ten legislation; and wrote numerous articles that appeared in newspapers locally and nationally. Yet, even today as I write this sentence, I don't know of any news medium that seemed to me to be more partisan against me than the *Lansing State Journal,* an opinion that I believe is shared by many others in the community.

George Alderton

It was not always that way. George Alderton was the paper's sports editor when I came to the athletics department in 1969. He was a very fair man who wrote the facts about sports figures and Spartan athletics. Even when he had numerous opportunities to badmouth Coach Duffy Daugherty for having six consecutive lackluster football seasons, he never did.

Ed Senyczko, Gerry Ahern, Jeff Rivers, and Steve Kline followed him. Most of the time those gentlemen reported the facts and didn't try to slant their reporting with biased opinions, nor did they try to sensationalize a

282

story. They didn't take every slip of the tongue and blow it out of context, and the opportunities were there if they had chosen to do so. The late Bob Gross; Tim Martin, a former reporter and copy editor; and former reporter Gary Miles also were impartial and worked hard to make sure a story was accurate and objective before it was printed.

For many years, sports writer Jack Ebling fit the fairness mold. Over the years I had communicated with him more than any other sports reporter about athletics issues. Prior to 1994 he called me many times to seek information and clarify facts about intercollegiate athletics issues. While I was aware he was a news reporter, I never was cautious about telling him how I really felt about certain issues because he had never taken anything out of context or used his opinions to create unnecessary controversy. He had always written his stories around facts.

That changed in 1994. He started writing about every little mistake I made. I don't know the reason for the change, but I still respect him as a person and writer. Somewhere along the way our wires got tangled and the shortage came in my direction. Rumors were afloat that MSU president M. Peter McPherson picked him to write stories about certain issues going on in the athletics department. Allegedly, he was given prime information and access before other beat writers received it. Shortly after McPherson's tenure began at MSU in 1993, he asked me what I thought of Ebling. I said he was a good writer and had a good grasp of intercollegiate athletics. We never talked about him again.

False allegations of 'cover-up' sting

Roosevelt Wagner was a former Spartan football player who dropped out of the university after the 1991 season. He used the *Lansing State Journal* to report some allegations against our football program to the NCAA in

283

1994. I first became aware that the news media had his allegations on Oct. 30 when sports editor Kline of the *State Journal* wrote a lead story about the allegations.

Roosevelt Wagner

Wagner previously reported some allegations to me by telephone on Sept. 19 and for a second time on Oct. 28. On both occasions, he said that he was calling from Cleveland, Ohio. He alleged that MSU boosters were giving student-athletes in the football program a number of extra benefits in the form of free use of cars, free rent, free merchandise in a local hotel, and use of the telephones in the football building at no cost to the young men. He also said there was leniency at the university on the payment of student-athletes' parking and traffic tickets, as well as financial arrangements between player agents and student-athletes in the program.

Ebling wrote a follow-up front-page article Oct. 31 listing the allegations Wagner made. The next day Ebling wrote another front-page story about Wagner entitled, "Perles, ex-player, both fear for safety." It claimed Wagner allegedly made some type of physical threat against George Perles and when the coach found out about it he sought a restraining order against the former player. It was further reported in the article that Wagner was carrying a pistol for personal protection in case he were confronted by someone opposed to him because of his allegations.

The saga continued when Kline wrote in the lead story of the sports page on Nov. 2, "The many faces of credibility." He questioned whom to believe about the allegations from Wagner. Was the Michigan State football program clean as Perles had claimed, or were there violations as NCAA investigations had found in other programs?

The following day, Kline wrote another lead story about the matter, headlined: "One probe down, one to go." He made reference to the conclusion of the 1993 men's basketball program investigation in which I was the lead investigator, which former student-athletes Parish Hickman and Jesse Hall had alleged that there were NCAA violations in the men's basketball program. They claimed such charges as a booster giving players money; players being paid at jobs when they did not work; players selling their university donated basketball shoes, etc. Kline reported that the NCAA had accepted the university's internal investigation and self-imposed penalties on the basketball program without additional penalties and he further mentioned the new on-going investigation into allegations about the football program.

Ebling called me at home on the evening of Nov. 5. That, I believe, showed some indication of our good relationship to that point, or else he was trying to set me up for some reason. He mentioned that the *Lansing State Journal* had obtained a tape recording from Wagner that alleged that I attempted to cover up the information he had told me by telephone, on the two occasions, about the allegations. I wasn't concerned about the charge because I hadn't done any such thing and had written proof to substantiate what I had done at the university about Wagner's calls to me. Ebling asked me to keep our conversation confidential. I was surprised when Ebling wrote a front-page story Nov. 8 about the allegations, accusing me of a cover-up relative to them.

The same day he also transcribed and reported Wagner's tape-recorded conversations with me and my responses. I didn't mind if he had merely reported the taped conversations, but when he gave his opinions favoring Wagner's allegations about a cover-up I felt it was unfair.

A day earlier I had been summoned to McPherson's office without advance notification. When I got there, already sitting in his office were Sally Harwood from the general counsel's office, and Terry Denbow, vice president for university relations. I was surprised to see them because I hadn't met with them previously in meetings with the president regarding any matter. I soon learned that Ebling was waiting for me in Denbow's office.

McPherson said he wanted me to give Ebling an interview about Wagner's tape-recorded allegations. I was caught off guard. I really didn't want to do that because I had done nothing wrong, but I felt pressured by the president to do the interview. I felt like I was judged guilty without knowing the charges. I had not heard Wagner's tape recording and already had shared the allegations of which I was aware with the president, vice president Roger Wilkinson, Athletics Director Merrily Baker, and others.

The interview was conducted in Denbow's office, with Denbow present. Ebling played the entire tape of a phone conversation between Wagner and me. Wagner had taped it without my knowledge. Ebling would play a portion, stop the tape and ask for my response. I felt extremely uncomfortable going through the process — not because I was guilty of any wrongdoing, but because I had to sit there under duress and explain each of my statements on the tape to a media person who was acting as judge and jury.

What was even more disturbing was that my own administrative colleagues were subjecting me to that terrible process, like self-appointed truth squads. I had absolutely nothing to hide. I had been totally open and honest with central administration about my two telephones calls from Wagner. I saw no justification for me to sit down with a sportswriter under mandate from the president to try and convince him of my integrity.

That interview is one of the things I still regret I permitted myself to go through. It was too demeaning and totally uncalled for.

Inappropriate 'interrogation'

I didn't work for the *Lansing State Journal* and had no responsibility to the paper and couldn't understand why McPherson was putting me through that degrading exercise. Ebling had no particular expertise in the interrogation or cross-examination, yet I felt he was playing the role of prosecutor and judge. The university put me in an awkward position. Ebling kept asking me, in front of Denbow, "What do you mean by that statement? Explain it further."

When the article was printed Nov. 8, Ebling further defamed me and cast me in a negative light. It clearly was biased reporting that gave the advantage to Wagner. It was one of the most humiliating articles ever written about me. Letters were written to the editor contesting the rationale and validity of the article. In my opinion, the interview should never have taken place. It seems to me that if the university felt I had done something wrong while carrying out my job responsibilities with the Wagner allegations, it should have discussed the issue with me as a matter of professional courtesy, rather than having Ebling and the *Lansing State Journal* do it publicly.

It was about three weeks earlier, Sept. 19, that I had gotten a phone call from Wagner alleging he had been in contact with a Detroit sports writer and a representative in the office of the NCAA about violations committed in our football program when he was a player. He was talking fast but I tried to take notes. I didn't ask him many questions or for clarification of what he was saying. I wanted to keep him on the line and not scare him away. I simply let him know that I was hearing him by repeatedly saying, "Yep; uh huh; you are right," etc. I was playing the role of a good listener. I was cordial to him, but not personally agreeing with anything he was saying because I had no information about what he was telling me. The last thing I wanted to do was turn him off by doubting him or showing disbelief.

As an experienced investigator of NCAA rules violations, there is absolutely no way I would ever accept or use an allegation given to me by telephone as fact without further investigation. I have learned over the years that it is easy for folks to say almost anything by phone and there are still folks who will look you in the eye and lie. At least, when you meet them face-to-face you can observe their demeanor and when they respond to questions you can ask for more specific details. There is a world of difference between allegations given over the phone compared with those given face-to-face. It sometimes becomes two different stories. During our conversation, I was simply letting Wagner know that I heard what he was saying, without passing judgment about the content.

Previous investigations, as well as formal training in NCAA rules and regulations, had taught me that an institutional staff member apprised of an allegation of a possible NCAA infraction has the responsibility to immediately inform his or her supervisor, the compliance coordinator, or another high level administrator of the charges. Failing to do so, the staff member may face an unethical conduct charge from the NCAA, which is a major violation.

Since I was the compliance administrator, I believed I knew better than anybody else at the university that I had the obligation to adhere to that requirement by informing Baker about Wagner's allegations on the very day he called me. I informed her verbally about two hours later because she wasn't in the office when I initially received the call from him. But in her absence I immediately told vice president Wilkinson, then I put in writing what I had done about the allegations.

VP denies interview with accuser

In addition, in a meeting on Sept. 21 involving Baker, Wilkinson, and myself, the issue of the allegations was brought up. As compliance administrator I asked the vice president for the opportunity to go to Cleveland, Ohio, to interview Wagner. Wilkinson said there would be no interviews until McPherson, who was out of town (I believe in Asia) on university business, gave his approval. Meanwhile, Wagner placed a second call to me, on Oct. 28, to ask what the university was doing about his allegations. He indicated he was also communicating with NCAA enforcement representative Les Pico. I only told him that we have the matter under review. I wasn't authorized to tell him anything else. He continued to talk in a rapid fashion for 30 minutes.

The next Saturday, September 24, McPherson was back on campus. Following the Indiana-MSU home football game he called an evening meeting at his residence to discuss the matter. I was there, along with McPherson, Wilkinson, Mike Kiley from the university general counsel's office, Baker, Provost Lou Anna Simon, and her administrative assistant, Barbara Ward. We reviewed the information we had. I presented memos I had written to Baker, as well as the one I had written for the files.

I mentioned that I had been turned down by Wilkinson to interview Wagner in Cleveland. It was agreed then that I would be co-investigator of the football probe and the university would hire outside legal counsel to also serve as co-investigator. On the recommendation of Baker and me to the president, that responsibility subsequently went to Mike Glazier of Bond, Schoeneck and King, a law firm in Kansas City. A meeting was soon held between representatives from the law firm and the university to plan for the investigation. It was decided that the investigators, including the NCAA, would first plan to meet with Wagner in Cleveland, Ohio. That was the same thing I had requested from the university but was denied.

On the morning of Oct. 31, I was in my office developing plans for the upcoming interview with Wagner when I got a totally unexpected call from the president telling me he had to remove me from the investigation because of the cover-up allegation Wagner had made against me. At that time, Ebling hadn't printed his cover-up article. McPherson's statement was shocking to me since I had told him and the many others at our meeting about how I had properly reported the allegations to both Baker and Wilkinson. I presented written documentation to verify my claim and had asked – and was denied – the opportunity to go to Cleveland to interview the former Spartan.

If there's a valid reason for removing a person from conducting an investigation due to impropriety, I can understand it. In my case, I believed I had done everything by the letter of the requirements of the university and the NCAA and I still received unfair treatment. I couldn't understand it. I felt the university should have publicly defended me against the cover-up charge. It was the right thing to do. Instead, they let the *State Journal* make me out to be a bad guy.

One of the criteria used by the NCAA during an investigation to test a possible cover-up or conspiracy is whether or not the person under review was informally alerted to the allegations before formal interviews took place with the subject. If I had been unethical or was in a cover-up situation, the most logical person I would have conspired with about Wagner's allegations would have been Perles. It was his program that was under review, but I never told him anything. And he never told me anything about what he might have known about the allegations. I was fully aware that it could have been construed as a major NCAA violation (unethical conduct) if I had tipped Perles off, thereby giving him the opportunity, if he were so inclined, to try to correct any problem prior to his formal interview with the university and the NCAA representatives.

Even when I first told Baker about the allegations and she suggested that she should tell George, I advised against her doing so. I wasn't trying to get Perles in trouble. I was trying to protect the institution and to guard against one of us facing the potential and serious unethical conduct charge with the NCAA.

Another criterion used to test a possible cover-up is how soon the allegations were reported to the appropriate authorities. I reported them immediately to Wilkinson and Baker. No fault in my behavior could be found. Looking back now on the charge of cover-up and in light of the facts, I still am perplexed as to the reason I was temporarily removed from the football investigation:

- I had properly reported the allegations to both Wilkinson and Baker.
- Wilkinson denied me the opportunity to meet with Wagner in Cleveland to interview him.
- I had presented written proof to McPherson and his committee about my role with Wagner and my follow-up action.
- McPherson acknowledged in an article written by Kline on Oct. 30 that he was aware of Wagner's allegations. He was told about them by Wilkinson on Oct. 14 and told Wilkinson to have me investigate Wagner's statements, although I never was informed.
- In a *State Journal* article written March 3 by Klein regarding the conclusion of the men's basketball investigations, which I conducted with faculty athletics representative Michael Kasavana, Denbow said, "We are very pleased that the NCAA has responded to a validation of our ability to investigate, correct, and appropriately address any violation."

- Surely I knew how to conduct an investigation and get it right.

I felt both the cover-up charge and removing me from the football investigation were affronts to my integrity. When McPherson removed me from the investigation it made headlines in an article written by Ebling on Nov. 8. Though I was very disappointed and shocked, the dilemma wasn't over. The university scheduled an interview for me with its outside legal firm relative to the cover-up accusation. The firm brought in a former FBI man who was part of the interviewing team. The NCAA had several representatives there, along with Kiley from the university.

I was interrogated for two hours about my background, my role with Wagner, and whether I had told Baker and Wilkinson about Wagner's allegations and when and how I had reported the matter to them. I was further quizzed at length as to whether I told Perles about the allegations and if he told me what he knew about them. I presented all my evidence at the meeting.

NCAA exoneration ignored

After that interrogation, the NCAA later, in written form, exonerated me. But the *Lansing State Journal* and the university never publicized that. My perceived negative image and tarnished reputation from the newspaper articles written by Ebling was left to linger publicly. Eventually, McPherson gradually and very quietly assigned various roles to me in the on-going football investigation, but I had taken an unmerciful beating in the local newspaper over the vicious and groundless charges of cover-up. And no one from the McPherson administration expressed any support for me publicly. I felt like the lonely soldier without a friend.

Ebling was co-author of basketball coach Jud Heathcote's book after Heathcote's retirement in 1995. It contained some vindictive and silly comments about me. McPherson and his wife read the book and called me, saying Heathcote had written some nasty things about me. They mentioned I was a good person and didn't deserve such derogatory comments. McPherson said he would call Ebling and have him meet with me.

I hadn't read the book, but I appreciated the president and his wife's call to me. Ebling showed up about an hour later and said Heathcote was awful in his comments toward me and Ebling said he refused to print some of them. He asked whether he could write a book when I retired and I said I'd have to think about it. Ebling no longer works for the *State Journal*.

In December 1999 at one of the home men's basketball games, our football team, with a 9-2 regular season record, was up for a bowl bid. The Florida Citrus Bowl representatives were in attendance and I welcomed them during the half-time ceremony. But during my public remarks I made a mistake, inadvertently using the name "Sun Bowl" instead of "Citrus Bowl," although I immediately corrected myself. Once again, Ebling made an issue out of it in the paper. I agree that it was a slip that never should have happened and I corrected it right away, so to my way of thinking it wasn't worth focusing on unless someone was trying to find something negative to write about me. I couldn't understand why that slip had to make the papers.

Based on such reports and other slights, when I became athletics director I was most careful about whom I talked with at the *Lansing State Journal*. In virtually every article it wrote about me the paper's reporters would call Heathcote and trustee Bob Weiss to have them contribute negative comments. The articles consistently reminded readers about my controversial memo on Heathcote and Wagner's cover-up allegations. Never did I observe any other news medium focus negatively on me as did the *Lansing State Journal*.

When McPherson shared with me in 2001 that he had received a proposal from Ebling seeking a position in the athletics department, I couldn't help but wonder whether Ebling, as I had thought earlier, had an open confidential pipeline to the president and that would be his reward.

Campus paper twists interview

In July 1999 when I was acting athletics director, Lewandowski, our sports information director, requested on several occasions that I grant an interview to a student sports reporter, Drew Chabot, at the campus newspaper, *The State News*. I didn't want to talk with the reporter because I hadn't had good success with reporters, but eventually I conceded and told Lewandowski to have the reporter call me at 7:30 a.m. in Chicago where I was attending Big Ten meetings.

The reporter called and started to explore various subjects. We began to talk about gender equity and I said it had been my experience that generally women student athletes who aren't on scholarship, unlike men, do not go out for a team as a walk-on to sit on the bench. They will participate in the sport if they have been awarded a scholarship. I said a male student-athlete would go out for a sport for the love of it and to boast to his children and grandchildren later about what a great athlete he was, even though he might have been a bench warmer.

When the article appeared in the paper it made front-page headlines, which read something like, "Underwood says women play sports for money, while men play for love." I immediately went to each of our male and female coaches in the women's program and told them what I had said to the reporter. The majority accepted my explanation without question, saying they clearly understood what I meant by the statement. Softball coach Jacquie Joseph supported me strongly in the media. However, there were one or two women coaches who understood, yet unsuccessfully tried to seize the

294

opportunity as a way to enhance funding for their sports.

I was attending the MSU Ralph Young Fund annual golf outing and dinner on campus the day the headlines appeared. The fund is the money-raising entity of the athletics department. As I was leaving the golf course at the end of the program, vice president Fred Poston, my immediate boss, and Lewandowski were waiting for me. Poston indicated that the *State Journal* had called requesting a chance to interview me about the *State News'* article and unless I did it the *Journal* would blast me the next day. I vehemently said no because it didn't matter what I told them, they would still screw me.

I really respect Poston and was aware he had my best interests at heart. So I eventually agreed to give the interview in my office, with Lewandowski present. Ebling showed up to write the story and wound up doing exactly what I said he would do: The next day's article was biased against me and, as usual, Weiss and Heathcote were called for quotes. I called Poston and Lewandowski to remind them what I had predicted the day earlier and they agreed with my assessment of the article.

List of media contributors

Despite differences from time to time, I am grateful to have dealt over the years with many media representatives and as a rule appreciated our associations. Some covered Michigan State sports extensively and others had occasion to come to our facilities to report on various events over the years. Most have been very professional in their duties and I wish them well. Among them are: Bill Jauss of the *Chicago Tribune*; Ernie Harwell and Kirk Gibson of the Detroit Tigers; George Blaha, Larry Bielat, and Will Tieman of the Spartan Network; Jimmy Smothers and Robert Watson, the *Gadsden* (Ala.) *Times*; William Rhoden, *New York Times*; Tim Staudt, formerly of the *Lansing State Journal* and currently with WILX-TV; Ron Cameron, WXYZ-

TV, several radio stations, and *Sports Fans' Journal* magazine.

Also, Bob Hammel, *Bloomington* (Ind.) *Herald-Times*; former MSU sports information directors Fred Stabley Sr. (for whom the MSU football press box was named) and his longtime assistant and eventual successor, Nick Vista; Fred Stabley Jr., formerly of the *Lansing State Journal* and *Spartacade* magazine, current SID at Central Michigan University; Malcolm Johnson and Larry Paladino of the *Associated Press*; Rich Shook of *UPI*; plus Gross, Kline, Martin, Miles, Alderton, Senyczko, Ahern, and Rivers of the *Lansing State Journal.*

Larry Lage of the *Lansing State Journal* and now with the *Associated Press*, is another I would single out, and Lynn Henning of *The Detroit News*, who got his start at the *Lansing State Journal.* There are so many others, too numerous to mention, but I commend those who were fair and balanced in their reporting.

Additionally, praise should go to Ken Hoffman, Lewandowski, Becky Olsen, and Matt Larson of MSU's SID office, as well as former assistant SID Mike Pearson, now with Sports Publishing Inc. of Champaign, Ill.

CHAPTER 9:

WOMEN'S ATHLETICS

Title IX brings attention — but not money with it

WOMEN'S ATHLETICS AND TITLE IX NEVER WERE issues with me, except for the funding.

In my opinion, since the inception of Title IX in 1972, the universities have abdicated their responsibilities to be financially accountable for women's athletics programs.

Title IX was an amendment to the federal Education Act of 1972. The preamble to the amendment states: "No person in the United States shall, on the basis of sex, be excluded from participation in, be denied the benefits of, or be subject to discrimination under any educational programs or activity receiving federal financial assistance." Nearly every educational institution is a recipient of federal funds and is required to comply with Title IX.

Significant progress has been made over the last 30 years in overcoming the limited opportunities afforded to women to participate in sports. Women's sports today are much stronger and more visible. Society has come to understand that the same human qualities that sports develop in males need to be developed in females. Research suggests that students with high athletic skills demonstrate a greater degree of personal and social adjustment than students ranking low in athletic achievement. Those with the skills possess a better self-image in areas of personal worth and freedom, self-reliance, and social adjustment.

According to the proportionality component of Title IX, the percentage of women participating in an institution's athletics program should be substantially proportional to the percentage of undergraduate women enrolled in the institution. That means that institutions must sponsor enough opportunities to accommodate the interests of the women athletes.

It has been estimated that women now account for 40 percent of all high school athletes and about 45 percent at the collegiate level. In the area of scholarships, women receive nearly 37 percent of all grant-in-aid money. The number of women coaches in college athletics is holding steady at about 50 percent in women's sports. The future of women's sports is strong, something that couldn't have been said three decades ago.

In my opinion, it is the greatest and best addition to intercollegiate athletics since its inception. Females of all ages now have the opportunity to develop their sports skills to the maximum extent for both recreational and competitive reasons. And many are taking advantage of it.

Central administrators at large Division 1 institutions across the country have tried to limit their liability for women's athletics by shifting fiscal responsibility to the athletics departments, where the source of revenue comes primarily from football and men's basketball. The majority of Division 1A athletics departments are funded largely by those two sports, but only about 15 percent show an annual profit. Many receive university support to balance the budgets.

Based on my teaching background, I have felt for a long time that women needed to participate in sports at the highest level, with the best coaches, the best administrators, the best facilities, and the best supportive environment — all requiring a great deal of funding, as it does for the men.

Women's sports options were few

I grew up in a neighborhood in which boys and girls competed together in softball and ran races in the street. Those were the only sports in which boys and girls could play together. There weren't any other co-recreational resources in the racially segregated community.

The boys also played baseball and touch football. We didn't have basketball because hoops were expensive. My high school sponsored girls' basketball, softball and track. The track team produced two superstars: Gladys Talley and Evelyn Lawler, who were outstanding sprinters in high school and college. Talley competed at Tennessee State University and Lawler, the mother of world track champion and Olympic great Carl Lewis, competed at Tuskegee Institute and ran the hurdles for the 1951 Pan-Am team. They were two of my heroes in high school.

MSU program grows

As an undergraduate student in the middle and late 1950s at Michigan State, I remember that there was an assortment of sports offerings for women through the physical education department. There was swimming, synchronized swimming, basketball, tennis, golf, gymnastics, bowling, archery, ice-skating, and volleyball. Those were funded by the university and from money provided by the intramural and recreation departments, which were under the jurisdiction of the athletics department. All those activities were not varsity sports. Some were played on a club level.

Gymnast Ernestine Russell, who was coached by men's varsity gymnastics coach George Szypula, was an Olympian in floor exercise and the balance beam and brought much fame to the university. For many years and probably in some circles today she still is recognized as one of the most celebrated women athletes in the history of Michigan State. She is a member of the university's sports hall of fame.

When I started the elementary school physical education program in 1962 in the East Lansing Public Schools, both boys and girls participated together in each of the activities and team sports. The fifth- and sixth-grade boys and

Ernestine Russell Weaver was inducted into the MSU Sports Hall of Fame in 1992.

girls had separate after-school recreational programs, which featured the same sports. There were some outstanding girl athletes in those classes.

Many of the sixth-grade girls were as tall or taller than most of the boys, which was an advantage when they played volleyball and basketball with eight-foot baskets. There were many girls with physical skills comparable to those of the boys. They could run fast, throw accurately and throw long. And, like the boys, they were taught skills in soccer, flag football, softball, gymnastics, speedball, whiffle ball, crab ball, square dancing, and other rhythmic activities.

I referred some elementary school girls with advanced gymnastics tumbling skills to an evening program for youth at Michigan State under the supervision of Szypula. I subsequently learned that some of the girls later became disgruntled with the sports offerings at the high school because it didn't sponsor the sports to meet their interests. They had learned skills in elementary and junior high physical education programs

300

that they couldn't apply in high school. One woman told me she had become depressed in high school because it didn't sponsor her favorite sports. She said the school de-emphasized certain sports because they fostered unladylike behavior.

With the advent of Title IX, the AIAW (Association of Intercollegiate Athletics for Women) program was eventually phased out and folded into the NCAA governance structure in the 1980s. Some women athletics administrators and coaches weren't content with that change. Many of them, as well as the athletes, had worked hard as pioneers, establishing and building the AIAW into a national program. It was founded on a set of principles that were different from those promoted by the NCAA. The women were disappointed to see the dismantling of the principles, ethics, successes, and championships, which were phased out as if they never existed. Only memories lingered.

Davis, Jackson pioneer program at MSU

Physical education professor Carol Davis was the first administrator to represent the women's program in the athletics department at Michigan State. Beginning in the fall of 1972 she served on the athletics director's administrative staff. She continued to work out of the women's intramural building and administer the AIAW program. The allocation from athletics was modest, but at least it was a start.

The athletics director's administrative staff was comprised of Burt Smith, the A.D.; John Laetz, the business manager; Davis; Gene Kenney, the soccer coach and assistant to the athletics director; William Beardsley, the athletics ticket manager and assistant A.D.; and me. I was the assistant director for student athletes' academics support services.

Functioning within a male environment, Davis always was very professional and was an effective advocate for the women's program. She retired after the 1972-73 academic year. Davis had worked with the women out of the women's intramural building and most of her coaches, I believe, were physical education instructors. They were part of the faculty who also coached as part of their overall responsibilities.

Dr. Nell Jackson, a black woman from the University of Illinois, was hired to replace Davis. She had been the Illini women's track coach. At MSU her title was assistant athletics director for the women's program. Jackson was hired to implement a comprehensive program for women. She worked out of Jenison Field House where all the other athletics administrators were housed. She was given a modest budget of $30,000 in 1973. Athletics scholarships weren't permitted under AIAW rules. It wasn't until the 1976-77 academic year that legislation was changed and women were permitted to receive aid for athletics, but it had to come from the office of financial aid like all other regular student aid.

Jackson instituted 10 sports over the next two years: basketball, cross-country, field hockey, gymnastics, softball, tennis, track (indoor and outdoor), swimming, and volleyball. She was a well-respected and reasonable person and was convincing in her presentations to the athletics director for additional resources. In addition to her administrative duties, she coached the track team and produced some outstanding athletes, such as Molly Brennan, Judi Brown, and Karen Dennis.

Brennan was an All-America sprinter who was a Rhodes scholar and Big Ten Sportswoman of the Year. Brennan was elected to the MSU Athletics Hall of Fame in 1993.

Brown was exceptional in track, earning All-America honors three times. She was the 1983 NCAA champion in 400-meter hurdles, was a Big Ten champion 12 times, and a member of the world record-setting sprint medley relay team. She was the MSU Sportswoman of the Year in 1983. In 1995 she was inducted into the university's athletics hall of fame and later served as head coach of the women's track program.

Dennis was an All-Big Ten sprinter who competed nationally and there were some other notable athletics accomplishments under Jackson's administration. Gloria Becksford pitched her 1976 softball team to the College World Series championship and became the first Spartan woman athlete to have her number retired. She subsequently coached softball for the Spartans and was named the Big Ten Coach of the Year in 1986.

Jane Manchester-Meyers was an excellent diver on the swim team and three times was named All-American. She was a Big Ten and national AIAW champion. She joined Becksford in 1992 as inductees into the MSU Athletics Hall of Fame.

Bonnie Lauer was a Spartans standout in golf. She was an AIAW national champion and 1976 was the Ladies Professional Golfers Association Rookie of the Year.

Jackson hired Karen Langeland as the women's head basketball coach and she was in that capacity for 19 years before resigning in 2000 to work as an assistant athletics director in the department. Another Jackson hire was Mary Fossum, a premier golf coach whose teams won several Big Ten championships.

Michael Kasavana

Dr. Michael Kasavana, a professor in the department of hotel, institution and restaurant management, was an outstanding coach of the women's gymnastics team, which won numerous Big Ten titles under Jackson. He is currently the university's faculty athletics representative.

Langeland era a long one

Karen Langeland

Langeland gave the women's basketball program a solid foundation beginning in 1976 after taking over from Dominic Marino, who has since passed away. Karen ended up with a 376-290 record, with a Big Ten championship in the 1996-97 season. Her teams appeared in five post-season tournaments and she was named Big Ten Coach of the Year several times.

After the 1999-2000 season, Langeland made an appointment with me. I was surprised by her request to be reassigned to an administrative position in the department. She said she believed she had accomplished all that she could in the women's basketball program and felt it was time to use her skills in other areas. I liked her and the way she had dedicated herself to her work over the years so I wanted to honor her request.

I met with Poston, Simon and McPherson and presented the request. After a brief discussion, I was authorized to offer Langeland a three-year contract. There was an administrative vacancy due to the recent resignation of assistant athletics director Tracy Ellis-

Ward, who had taken a position with the Women's National Basketball Association in New York.

Langeland accepted the position and I gave her the title of assistant athletics director and assigned her to be the director of the summer sports camp program, overseer of the MSU booster clubs, and administrator for 10 men's and women's sports. She also handled some special projects. She was an efficient and effective administrator during my tenure.

Who'll take over women's basketball?

Next came the task of conducting a search for a successor for the women's basketball program. I appointed associate athletics director Shelly Appelbaum, who was the administrator of the program, and former associate athletics director Kathy Lindahl, who served in the department for 19 years, to conduct the search for a successful coach. Lindahl was now the assistant vice president for finance, operations, and treasurer and had hired many coaches in her former position. The only instructions I gave them was that I wanted to see proven successful candidates. We needed a coach who could build upon the success Karen had produced.

Kathy Lindahl

Appelbaum and Lindahl put together a comprehensive strategy that had them traveling each weekend from January to March 2000 unobtrusively to an out-of-town women's basketball competition. They would do their homework in advance of the trip. They had obtained media guides and other data on the prospective candidates prior to leaving campus. The two would attend the games, observe the coaches and their management style and depart inconspicuously. I received numerous nominations from persons throughout the Midwest and passed them on to Shelly and Kathy for review and follow-up.

After screening the credentials of many prospects and narrowing the number of interviewees, the advisory committee also helped in the recruitment process. On the committee with Applebaum and Lindahl were professor Sue Carter of the college of communication and science and a member of the athletic council; Poston; and Michelle Engler, who made calls to our prime candidate, Joanne McCallie. Applebaum and I, along with Mark Hollis, associate athletics director of external relations, began the interviewing process.

We met with Melanie Balcomb of Xavier of Ohio. She was a strong candidate and presented herself well during the interview. Our next interview was with McCallie of the University of Maine, who presided over a highly successful program there. She was near the end of her pregnancy and could not travel long distances. Appelbaum and Lindahl were most impressed with her and recommended her very highly. Although I wanted to make sure we interviewed a few more candidates, I called McCallie to find out about her condition and when it would be likely for us to interview her. Since she was in the ninth month of her pregnancy, we decided to meet her in Maine.

The committee met McCallie and her husband, John, in a hotel room near the airport in Bangor. Ten minutes into the interview I was absolutely convinced that she was the person we needed at Michigan State. She spoke clearly and with conviction in response to the essential questions that I asked her. She was enthusiastic about her recruitment philosophy and her vision for the welfare of student-athletes.

I knew she was a winner, so 30 minutes into the interview, in order to openly discuss her compensation package at Maine, I asked committee members, except for Poston, to leave the room. We hired her that night. She brought a distinguished basketball career to the Spartan family and in the 2004-05 season took the Spartans all the way to the NCAA finals in Indianapolis, where they lost the championship game to Baylor, 84-62, after having upset Pat Summitt's perennial powerhouse Tennessee, 68-64 in the semifinals—after being 16 points down. The Spartans, featuring seniors Kristin Haynie and Kelli Roehrig, and junior Liz Shimek, wound up with a 33-4 record and were the talk of the state and country.

I have no doubts McCallie will further magnify her successful career at the university. Shelley and Kathy did an outstanding job searching and identifying the appropriate coach for MSU's women's basketball program.

Committee hones in on program needs

In 1978, Dr. Joe Kearney, the athletics director, appointed a committee to conduct a comprehensive review of the department's compliance with Title IX. I was the chairman and there were eight other members: Karen Escott, a student; Cheryl Flanagan, administrative assistant; Homer Hawkins, professor of racial/ethnic studies; Jackson; Annelies Knoppers, women's volleyball coach; Danny Litwhiler, baseball coach; Dr. Lou Anna Simon, institutional researcher who later became the provost and in 2005 was appointed the first woman president of Michigan State University; and Clint Thompson, head trainer.

For four months the committee met weekly. We interviewed coaches, administrators, and support personnel and conducted an extensive investigation into budgets, travel, facilities, practice and competitive

Me and Lou Anna Simon, who succeeded M. Peter McPherson as president of the university

schedules. We also compared coaches' duties and salaries, as well as coaches selection and hiring. We examined policies, procedures, and established practices.

Ed Harden, president of the university at that time, was anxious for the committee to complete its work because he wanted to discuss its recommendations at the upcoming winter meeting of the board of trustees. When the committee was scheduled to give a status report to the president on that date, I had to attend the convention of the National Association of Athletic Academic Advisors in Dallas. I appointed Simon to write the draft report, including the recommendations, and make the presentation to Harden and the board.

Simon had been a consistent participant in the meetings, showing unusual insight and understanding about the operations of the athletics department. She also brought her keen intellect and thorough working knowledge of the university to the discussions. Since she worked in the administration building and had interactions with central administration, her experience made her an excellent choice to make the presentation in my absence. She delivered the report and recommendations, gaining high praise from the president for an outstanding job. The majority of recommendations were approved with minor modification. The recommendations were:

- To allocate $50,000 worth of improvements for 1978-79 for the field hockey field, lockers and equipment area in Jenison, and to remove the softball backstop and construct a new softball fence.
- To allocate $80,000 for scholarships for 1979-80 to bring parity, at least between the men's and women's non-revenue scholarship programs.
- To provide annually over the next eight years, five full scholarships for the women's program starting with 1980-81, because the women had a higher level of competition and rate of success in terms of win/loss record over the men's non-revenue program. That would allow the women's scholarship program to reach the same percentage of maximum allowable scholarships as the men's program.
- To revamp the administrative structure to include the athletics director and three assistant directors — one assistant in charge of general administration, one for the women's program, and one for the men's program. The key rationale was to consolidate and centralize services so that men's and women's programs might be served in a manner which would be fiscally efficient and accountable on a day-by-day basis.
- To allocate $5,000 during the 1978-79 academic year for talent assessment in the women's program. (Today this means recruitment.)
- To establish an affirmative action committee as an on-going group that would monitor Title IX progress in the intercollegiate athletics program.

The overall reactions to the report and a review of the minutes of the Title IX committee indicated a number of areas that needed further review. The committee met its initial charge in terms of providing answers to the myriad of questions within Title IX compliance and developed a basis for further study.

Heretofore Jackson was functioning as the chief administrator for the women's program. She attended athletics council meetings and was responsible for hiring and firing. She negotiated resources with Kearney, but she had the autonomy to access central administrators on budgetary issues.

Kearney reduces Jackson's role

Harden became the president when Clifton Wharton resigned in 1978 to accept the chancellor's position with the State University of New York system. It was during Harden's short tenure that Jackson's job responsibilities were changed in order to have a consolidated department.

In a memo to Jackson dated March 9, 1979, Kearney wrote:

"As a follow-up to our recent conversations regarding the reorganization of the administrative structure of women's athletics, I want to re-emphasize the following:

"1. That the action effecting the change in policy was passed by the athletic council at its meeting of Feb. 16, 1979.

"2. President Harden has concurred in the policy change and instructed me to proceed accordingly.

"The policy change requires that the director deal directly with all head coaches in the men's and women's program. This will involve setting policy for a totally integrated department, planning and approving direction and scope of individual sport

310

programs, and the hiring and assignment of all personnel.

"I plan to meet with all head coaches in the near future to work on budget matters and program direction for 1979-80 and beyond. In the area of women's programs, you will be invited to the budget planning session for your input.

"In essence, the past practice of having a women's division within the department has been abolished, with the director required to be personally involved with the total program direction. Your new role will still involve your day-to-day administration of women's athletics for their regular on-going operations. The area of philosophy, policy, program, and direction will come from the director's office, with appropriate staff consultation, athletic council input, and presidential approval."

That change was similar to the role Athletics Director Merrily Baker fought hard, but unsuccessfully, to get me to assume with the revenue sports in 1993. She wanted to reduce my administrative role to that of a coordinator. The changes for Jackson broke her spirit. She had her legs cut out from under her. She told me she felt heartbroken and useless with her new liaison duties and had been stripped of her self-esteem. She was subsequently successful landing an athletic director's position in the SUNY system, where Wharton was the chancellor. She had put the MSU women's program on a solid foundation before her quiet resignation in 1980.

As it turned out, Kearney also resigned in 1980 to accept the A.D. position at Arizona State. Doug Weaver was appointed the new athletics director and held the position from 1980 until he retired in 1990.

Lindahl spends two decades in charge

Jackson initially hired Lindahl, who worked as an intern and later as a graduate assistant in the women's athletics program and for the director. Weaver recognized Lindahl's potential and named her the coordinator of the women's program. Subsequently she was promoted to assistant athletics director and senior women's athletics administrator. She had broad oversight for the non-revenue sports, Title IX, gender equity, and human resources. She held the position for 19 years during which time she was promoted to the position of associate athletics director and senior women's administrator by Baker in 1992.

Lindahl served most of her years in athletics as the assistant/associate director for 22 men's and women's non-revenue sports. Her tenure was made significant by the effective leadership she gave to enhance the overall growth of the women's program. She was instrumental in bringing the MSU women's program into the 21st century. The sport of women's crew was added under her leadership. She was smart and had the necessary foresight to identify competent coaches for employment. Those coaches had sufficient skills, knowledge and leadership to develop competitive teams in the Big Ten and nationally.

Kathy earned her law degree and resigned from the athletics department in 1998 to become the assistant vice president in the office of the vice president for finance, operations and treasurer at the university.

When Merritt Norvell was hired as athletics director in 1995, he decentralized management of the non-revenue sports, dividing them among three administrators. That was the setting in which Appelbaum was hired in 1998 as associate athletics director and senior women's administrator, to supervise eight sports, oversee Title IX, and monitor gender equity and human resources. She has proven to be an effective administrator.

With those developmental but successful beginnings in 1972, some 30 years later the women's program is among the best in the country. There still is some work to be done and improvements to make, but Michigan

State University has embraced Title IX mandates and its compliance requirements.

Vast improvements since '72

I am pleased to have had a role in the overall improvements of the status of the women's sports program at Michigan State. Women now have 11 varsity sports, with outstanding coaches and facilities comparable to those shared by the men. The following improvements were made in the overall women's program under my leadership:

- Full funding of the grant-in-aid scholarships to meet NCAA limits, except for crew, which was scheduled to reach its limit one year later by the 2002-2003 academic year.
- Construction of a $400,000 boathouse for the crew team.
- A new outdoor artificial playing field for field hockey.
- A new outdoor track, bleachers, scoreboard, and lights for the track teams.
- New locker rooms for each sport, expanded strength and conditioning room, new training and medical examination rooms, plus an enlarged practice room for the gymnastics program.
- A renovated clubhouse and offices for the golf programs.
- An addition to the Breslin basketball center that provides both the women and men coaches with state-of-the-art offices, meeting rooms, working room and a new gymnasium.

Funding problems at crisis stage

Across the country, funding for intercollegiate athletics departments continues to be a significant challenge for athletics directors. They are faced with above average inflation in the annual cost of scholarships,

313

transportation, salaries, fringe benefits, facilities, maintenance, and medical expenses. The issue is rapidly approaching the crisis stage.

For illustration, the total budget for the MSU intercollegiate athletics department in 1977-78 was approximately $3.8 million. There were about 100 staff members, 700 men and women student-athletes, and 24 sports. The women's program, with 10 of the 24 sports, received $360,000 annual funding.

For the 2001-2002 academic year, the total athletics budget was approximately $46 million. The staff had doubled to 200, but the number of athletes still was at approximately 700. The number of sports dropped by two to 22 (11 each for men and women). More than $8 million was budgeted for the women's program.

Using an annual 10 percent inflationary increase on $3.6 million over the past 23 years (from 1978 to 2001) would yield a total budget of $32,235,489. The athletics department's total operating budget exceeded that amount by nearly $14 million.

There are several reasons why the athletics budget inflation rate annually exceeds the national rate of inflation by a significant percentage:

- It must grow through successful competition or die. Failing to continuously grow the department through its revenue-producing sports would result in a non-competitive program. It's an expensive proposition to offer quality athletics entertainment to students, alumni, and fans. Devoting months to recruiting prospective student athletes from around the country and, indeed, the world, costs a great deal of money. Even the most avid supporters won't attend events as often if the team they support is not consistently successful each year.

The public wants high-class entertainment and winners. Losing means empty seats and loss of income.

Each Big Ten institution spends an average of $900,000 annually for recruitment. It is reasonable to assume that other Division 1A football playing schools' spending approaches that figure.

- Scholarships are costly. There are expenditures for tuition, fees, room and board. The athletics department can have a combined 300 men's and women's full grants-in-aid and the budget at Michigan State for them in the 2001-2002 academic year was about $6 million. When the university increases those tuition costs annually, the athletics department has to absorb the difference and generate the revenue.

- The market value of coaches' salaries constantly increases. Today, society places emphasis on immediate success — and that means winning. The fans are willing to pay the cost to be associated with a winning team at either the college or professional level. The pro teams have contributed greatly to the market value of college coaches. They are no friends to college sports and will not hesitate a second in going after a successful college coach and trying to induce him or her with a multi-million-dollar contract.

- The athletics directors are on the hot seat to try and retain their highly successful coaches and that means rewarding them with salary increases that meet market value. From a business standpoint, it is better for the athletics department to retain a superstar coach by paying an excellent salary than to start over with a new coach.

- Compliance with Title IX required funding. As I indicated earlier, I believe collegiate institutions have abdicated their responsibility in funding fairly and equitably both the men's and women's programs. Failure to comply with Title IX can put the entire university in jeopardy because it receives federal financial aid in a number of programs and that aid could be lost if there isn't compliance.

From the outset, the colleges placed the responsibility of funding the women's programs on the backs of the directors of athletics. That meant that money mostly had to come from football and men's basketball. The women were programmed from the beginning to get the short end of the stick. If the athletics department already was struggling to make ends meet or was facing a deficit with its men's sports, where was adequate funding going to come from to support the women's program?

That common scenario put athletics directors in a tough spot. They either had to generate additional revenues, cut revenue sports expenditures, or drop men's sports to support the women's needs. How much more money could an A.D. raise from gate receipts or from donors with declining attendance and declining fan interest if there are lackluster results in football and men's basketball?

The rift between men and women over the dropping of men's sports shouldn't exist. The universities should be fully responsible for funding the women's programs to accommodate the interests of the women students. It will take many years of strong public support before the women's program becomes self-sufficient. Basketball generally has already shown its potential to generate revenue, particularly at the Division 1A level. Women's sports shouldn't have to rely on revenues from football and men's basketball to grow and have the opportunities to be financially successful.

One way in which financial problems could be alleviated is for the universities to establish a fund or an endowment exclusively for women's programs. I don't see any harm in charging a student fee to help support the endowment for a specified period of time. After all, athletics is a student-oriented activity. The athletics department could be required to donate a set levy to the fund each year, along with other contributions and grants generated by the university's development fund.

In that scenario, the women's program would remain an integral part of the athletics department. Only the funding source would change. The arrangement would help make both the women's and men's programs competitively stronger. It would significantly reduce the conflict, envy, and strife that may exist between the two programs. I believe the University of Arkansas has a similar funding system in place for its women's program that works effectively.

- Facilities are expensive to construct and maintain. It is essential to provide excellent facilities for the welfare and safety of student-athletes and coaches. There is a direct relationship between commitments from blue chip prospective student-athletes and excellent athletics facilities. Athletics directors understand that nexus and stay awake at night trying to find ways to raise money to keep up with the Joneses.

  Athletics is a commercial arms race in which only the stronger programs can compete and survive to become more successful in the recruitment wars. Big time Division 1A programs are in stiff competition with each other. Coaches need to lure the blue-chippers to their institutions in order to field competitive teams and A.D.s need victories to sell out the stadiums and arenas to pay the bills.

- Cost containment is necessary. Several women's groups have vociferously suggested that one way to conserve money in the football program and reallocate it to the women's program is to reduce excessive expenditures. Certainly there needs to be a cost containment program in the athletics department, but it should be applicable to every sport and unit.

Football cutbacks not the answer

I don't believe scaling back on expenditures only in football and basketball is the answer. At most Division 1A football playing institutions, that sport accounts for about 70 percent of the total athletics revenue. That includes gate receipts, post-season games, television revenue, receipts from marketing and promotions, fund-raising, parking, concessions, and program sales. Men's basketball at Michigan State also contributes an effective amount of revenue. Ice hockey tends to earn a little above the break-even point.

Among the cost-cutting suggestions some critics have advocated for the football team are: don't stay at a hotel the night before games; use buses, rather than airplanes for travel; reduce staff by using more graduate assistants instead of full-time coaches; eliminate the training table, where players eat a special dinner as a group rather than separately in dorm cafeterias or in their off-campus apartments.

None of those suggestions have merit for the A.D. because whatever reductions could have been made already were made and more would jeopardize competitiveness, unless it was done nationally. The athletics department can't grow by focusing on reductions in men's sports. Who will buy a Cadillac at its original price if it has been trimmed down and restructured to look like a Chevy? The sensuous appeal would be lost.

So it goes in football. When you become complacent or downsize the sport and the game loses its appeal or edge to the prospects, it will become weakened and will topple. Whenever the institution no longer offers top-notch entertainment in a revenue sport due to diminished competitive advantage, the public will notice. The public wants to see athletic thrills and victories from the best athletes. If the college game can't meet the demand due to a smaller squad or some other financial constraints, the public will stay home.

The football enthusiast can observe the most competitive professional games while sitting in the best chair in his television room. It will cost him nothing. He can eat when he wants to, drink whatever he likes, has no parking and traffic hassles, and has the convenience of his own restroom. In addition, he doesn't have to be emotionally involved with either team. He simply likes the sport. Let's leave the tweaking of college football up to the specialized professionals — and not lose ground to the professional teams.

Personal reflections on women's athletics

I was a sprinter in the 220- and 440-yard dashes in high school. In 1975, at the age of 42, I was an assistant athletics director and was jogging six miles a day, seven days a week. I was in great physical shape and still had good speed for a person of my age. During the winter the women's and men's track and field teams practiced in Jenison Field House, as they do today. I consistently ran my six miles in the morning with Drs. Thomas Gunnings, William Lazer, Charles Galiano, Eugene Pernell, and others.

Frequently I also would run two miles after work with Jack Breslin, Homer Hawkins, and others in Jenison while the track teams were practicing. The women's team had a sprinter named Marjorie Grimmett, who ran the 100-yard dash in an MSU record time of 10.7 seconds. She was an All-American in the 220. My 100-yard dash time was 10.0 in high school. One day while the women's team was practicing, I felt I could beat Marjorie in the 220. I really felt strong, energetic, and motivated, so I asked Coach James Bibbs, who was the coach of both the men's and women's sprint squads, if I could challenge Marjorie when it was her turn to practice the 220.

Bibbs gave me the green light and when the time came we lined up and Bibbs shot the starter gun. We had to run two straight-aways, one on each side of the track, and make

319

two turns. On the first straightaway, Grimmett was ahead of me by about five yards. I was exactly in the position I wanted to be. My plan was to give her the lead until after the first turn, then make my move, accelerate, pass her and retain the lead until we passed the 220-yard finish line where Bibbs was standing with his timer.

As I made my move with a burst of speed on the first turn to pass her a most unusual and unexpected thing happened to me. My jock strap broke and since I was wearing running shorts I had to stop my run almost abruptly, otherwise I might have been charged with indecent exposure. I felt embarrassed, disappointed, and annoyed because I could not finish the race. I told Bibbs and a few more observers why I stopped running.

Maybe the jock strap broke for a reason, to save me from my delusions. As I think about it, I never showed the courage to challenge the women's athletes of today. They have become so skillful, talented, and competitive. Today, women's athletes are so much better than they were 30 years ago. I would not dare to challenge anyone like I did in 1975.

No matter what my age, I continued to utilize university facilities to run or otherwise exercise to stay healthy.

I never again tried to challenge a female athlete. I never had any interest in challenging Judy Brown in the hurdles, Stephanie Dueringer in the distance races, or later Sevatheda Fynes in the 100- or 220-yard dashes. They all were world-class athletes. I felt I never had a chance with them. I was much older, slower, with a bad knee by the time record-setting spring champion Fynes was on the team. Yet one day at practice I was crazy enough to challenge the defensive team in football to catch me on a punt return in 1993. I was an outstanding punt returner in high school, but that day I never had a chance. The players had too much speed. As soon as I caught the ball, six giant-sized players were staring me in the face, including big Flozell Adams, who became a starter for the Dallas Cowboys.

People ask me what is the greatest change I have seen in intercollegiate athletics over the past 30 years. There have been many. Every athlete today is bigger and better than in the past, but the most tremendous and significant change has been the growth of women's athletics. I give credit to the women athletes, the women coaches, and the women administrators for fighting for the advancement of the women's athletics program. Without their courage, dedication, and wisdom, the program would not be where it is today. They did it through sweat, practice, hard work, and commitment. Building a solid foundation for women's athletics started with the vision and hardy work of the student-athletes. They have learned, just like golf great Tiger Woods, that it takes consistent practice to improve skill levels.

When I was first employed in the athletics department I never saw a woman student-athlete, except for a few swimmers, a few track athletes, and a few gymnasts, who would work out in their sports during the summer. Today the weight rooms are filled with women student-athletes during the summer, training and refining their muscles to get greater value out of their competition.

Today's female athletes have changed the whole culture of women's sports. They are stronger, more muscular, and faster than 30 years ago. They understand the market value of sports and winning. They know that winning teams create the opportunity for more fans in the stands at their games, greater revenue for their sports, more advertisement to promote the season schedule, the opportunity for post-season competition, and the opportunity for women athletes to be drafted by the professional sports teams in basketball, volleyball, and softball, as well as receive professional opportunities in track, tennis, and golf.

In addition, there are pro opportunities for women in sports management and administrative positions today that weren't there 20 or 30 years ago, despite the fact there still are unfortunate cultural lags with Title IX issues. For example, in 1992, Carol Davis was the only woman athletics administrator at Michigan State. When I resigned as athletics director in 2002, there were: Appelbaum, associate athletics director and the senior women's administrator; Peggy Brown, assistant athletics director for business affairs; Langeland, assistant athletics director for sports management; and Jennifer Smith, assistant athletics director for compliance services.

There were other women in key athletics department supportive services roles. The Big Ten Conference office and the NCAA, as well as all of collegiate athletics, have women working in high-level management positions. The female athlete who has aspirations to enter the athletics management profession should pursue it with vigor because the door is open.

Women athletics has turned the corner. The future is very bright. It is a natural process today to see women excel in all sports areas, including boxing. They have raised the bar to a much higher level than it was in the past. I am most grateful for the opportunities I have had over 30 years to work with some outstanding young women. In general, I found them to have great character, were good students, focused on their dual academics and athletics responsibilities, and now are important ambassadors for the university and their communities.

Women get long-deserved varsity letters

One of the highlights of my athletics career was the MSU varsity letter celebration that took place on campus, Feb. 10, 2002. The university recognized and celebrated the women student-athletes who had earned, but never received, their varsity letter award from their participation in intercollegiate athletics. Approximately 200 women athletes dating back to the 1930s returned to take part in the celebration. There were many others who weren't able to return to campus and they received theirs in the mail.

Women student-athletes representing every varsity sport at the university were in attendance. For too long the women had been denied their varsity awards due to former AIAW regulation restrictions and because of university policy. With the support of McPherson, vice president Poston, and provost Simon, I, as athletics director, was pleased to approve the recommendation from the varsity letter celebration committee for the athletics department to sponsor the outstanding program. Committee members were chairwoman Appelbaum, Langeland, Sally Belloli, and Lori Schultz.

The program began Saturday evening when the women were invited to attend the women's home basketball game. There were individual introductions made at halftime, with photograph sessions. Sunday morning there was a delicious brunch, followed by planned presentations at the Kellogg Center. There were numerous speakers, including McPherson; Simon; Betty Droback, retired women's tennis coach; Kathleen Deboer, associate athletics director at the University of Kentucky; Belloli, assistant director of the MSU Intramural

Department; and myself. I had counseled many of the women athletes over the years.

The crowning moment came when each woman was introduced and walked across the stage to receive the beautiful plaque with the varsity "S" letter attached. It was a momentous occasion, one that I'll never forget.

CHAPTER 10:

MOLDING STUDENT-ATHLETES

Building a firm foundation for success

I HAVE BEEN FORTUNATE TO WORK WITH YOUNG people all of my professional life, spending 30 years with college athletes and 10 teaching in programs that dealt with young people. I've always believed in respecting students of all ages, ethnicity, and sex, being sensitive to their concerns and needs. I have found that listening to their concerns is critical to counseling them. Too often we assumed we knew the answers before their questions were asked, or would simply discount what they had to say before they said it.

At Michigan State, when I was the academics counselor and the administrator responsible for student-athletes with all kinds of problems, I practiced a shared responsibility in solving them. A student-athlete and I would discuss the problem and mutually agree upon a plan of action.

If students have input into resolving their problems and can help identify follow-up accountability measures they more than likely would clear up the issue quicker. If I directed them to strictly follow my instructions — my way of doing things — they had trouble doing so, like most people do in similar situations in society. That shared responsibility in problem solving has been the foundation in making a difference. It is an important ingredient in building the lives of student-athletes who have "stumbled" along the way.

Family vital in averting low self-esteem

Believe it or not, I found low self-esteem to be one of the more prevalent issues among some student-athletes. Although the majority had strong egos and displayed self-esteem and self-confidence in their sports and in the classroom, there were some who displayed low self-esteem academically. Those were the ones I spent a lot of time with, trying to counsel them through their problems. Some of the young men had difficulty interacting with women in a mutually respectful manner. They were dictatorial, abrasive and, at times, rude. That type of behavior concerned and intrigued me because the student-athletes were popular in their sports and had several choices of girl friends. But they had difficulty treating the ones they chose with respect.

In my search to find some answers so as to be able to counsel them in those areas I once consulted a psychologist who explained that there were many factors that contribute to low self-esteem and insecure behavior. She said, in fact, that those two issues go together and play off each other, citing as an example that issues such as constant criticism, failure at tasks, little or no positive parental support, and a host of other factors, play a role in what people feel about themselves and how they treat others. She went on to explain the importance of family in the lives of both athletes and non-athletes.

The family is the primary influence for the development of a child's academic, social, spiritual, intellectual, physical, and moral traits, she said. It's an awesome responsibility but it is the role God gave to us as procreators. Parents need to stimulate and cultivate

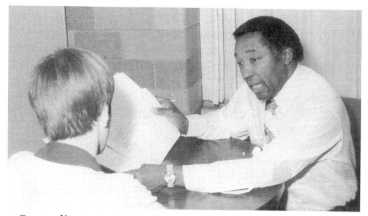
Counseling young people always has been special to me.

their children in those areas, the psychologist said, with the most important factor being the relationship with the mother. The bonding that is necessary to cultivate an effective learning relationship in a child's formative years may not always occur solidly if the mother doesn't spend constructive time with the child. Self-esteem and ego normally are developed in a child from birth to age 5, the psychologist said. If the opportunity is missed in those formative years, it takes overtime work to shape those two important traits.

Fathers, she said, deeply love their newborn daughters and often are observed hugging and kissing them on their hands, faces, and arms. They show them sustained affection and treat them like queens, all the while telling them they love them. As the female babies grow they can do no wrong in the eyes of their fathers, who constantly encourage and support them in everything they want to do. Such encouragement and support before age 5 are highly important in developing self-esteem and ego in children.

On the other hand, the father also loves his son but doesn't show him the same measure of affection, the psychologist said. As the son grows, the father demonstrates less love for the son. Most fathers are insecure or uncomfortable about hugging their sons and revealing how much love they feel for them, fearing such affection may show feminine traits. Instead, the father expects the son, by age 3, to start manifesting manly physical traits, like learning how to catch, throw, or kick a ball, how to run under control and be tough by not crying when he falls and experiences minor pain.

When the male child still is in diapers the father might go out and buy him a collegiate-sized football, basketball, net, baseball and bat, ice hockey gear, helmet, or a soccer ball. The father wants the son to be a much better athlete than he ever was. In contrast to the way he treats his daughter, the father wants the son to learn fast and grow up rapidly. If the son shows little or no interest in sports, the father's attention to him usually wanes. The father, with all his shortcomings, wants to live his life vicariously through his son's accomplishments. But that is ludicrous and is a mistake, the psychologist said.

As she explained more on the subject of development, I started to relate from my own experiences to some of the things she was saying. Many times I've seen fathers who expect their sons to accomplish things they themselves weren't able to accomplish. I have seen fathers who may or may not have excelled in a sport who wanted their sons to be superstar athletes. I've seen fathers invest a tremendous amount of time, energy, and money to try and cultivate their sons' interest in sports, but they overlook the fact that every child wasn't made to play sports. God made us all different and gave us different interests and talents. Fathers must explore their sons' interests in other areas before presumptuously narrowing them to fit their own needs.

However, the opposite occurs between mothers and their baby boys, according to the psychologist. Moms typically show more affection to their sons, even though mothers try to strike a balance between their male and female children. If a mother shows strong support and encouragement for her boy's expressed fantasies she will help develop his self-esteem and ego at an early age. He will cling to her and confide in her whenever he has an issue because he knows she will support him. Just as their daughters are so precious to their fathers, so, too, are little boys to their mothers.

Generally, though, such relationships aren't as lopsided as those examples, she said. Instead, often they overlap, with each child intrinsically exhibiting traits from both parents, either of whom can nurture the bonding process. But, she emphasized, the relationship between the mother and child is the single most important factor in the development of self-esteem and ego.

She suggested that student-athletes with low self-esteem in academics and who were manifesting abusive behavior to women probably didn't get the proper nurturing, love, and emotional support from their mothers and fathers as youngsters. And most likely they failed to receive the proper respect from their teachers. She said those young people probably could benefit from professional therapy to help them identify why they behave in such manner because they may not understand their own behavior and be bewildered by it.

They wonder why they may behave differently from their peers. The psychologist believes athletes' egos in sports skills had been developed and reinforced over the years through successes and encouragement from peers, coaches, adults, and relatives. They were living off of it, using the self-esteem to cover up their weaknesses in other areas. She advised that most humans use their developed egos to try to cover up their shortcomings.

Her advice to me was to refer the student-athletes to professional counseling and for me to work with them on positive self-talk to help change their attitudes about themselves. She suggested the athletes should build themselves up by talking privately every day about their accomplishments and by projecting high academic goals for themselves, a process, she believes, that can help build the students' self-esteem. She cautioned, however, that self-esteem is multi-faceted, being derived from balanced successes in many parts of our lives. And the athletes need to diversify their activities outside of sports.

Love is No. 1 child-raising ingredient

Perhaps the number one suggestion for parents to consider in raising their children is the most obvious — to provide love. If I had a child at home I would give that child the greatest gift on earth — love — and it's free. I would hug my children and tell them daily how much I loved them. Giving children genuine love will help them grow up loving themselves. That is important because you can't love others if you don't love yourself.

We all have to learn how to love. We must be real when we tell our children at an early age that we love them because they know when we are telling the truth. They may not be able to define the feelings or be able to express them, but they won't know how to internally process any expressions of love that may seem phony.

All humans, particularly young children, need to feel that somebody in the home loves them, preferably their parents. They need someone who believes in them; who will listen to them; who will allow them to make little mistakes without scolding them. They need to feel safe and comfortable to enable them to grow with a positive attitude.

If that love is absent, rest assured as the child grows older he or she will search for love in all the wrong places. When you don't feel loved, your self-esteem and ego become vulnerable to temptation. A child begins feeling unaccepted; starts acting out for attention; becomes emotionally unstable; and will develop problems in the classroom.

I have counseled many male athletes who told me

Me with grandsons Blake and Parker

they had displayed those behaviors at one time or another in public schools and as a result they had been placed in special education classes or singled out by their teachers in negative ways. They attributed their athletic prowess as being their saving grace, keeping them in school through graduation and providing a chance for them to get an athletics scholarship.

I recall a female student-athlete who visited my office during Christmas break one year requesting me to help her find off-campus temporary housing until university classes resumed in January. Her residence hall was closed until after the break and she didn't have a

331

place to live for three weeks. I asked why she wasn't going home for the holidays and she said she had no place to go. She hadn't lived with her mother for more than four years, starting with when she was in the 10th grade, she said. She shared with me that she didn't like her mother's male friend because he had "hit on her," meaning he had asked her to have sex with him. When she told her mother about it, her mother told her to get out of the house.

The young woman went to live with a cousin but that family was preparing to move to another state in search of better employment. Her father had left the family when she was very young and she didn't know where he was. She said she was very glad to be enrolled at Michigan State because fall semester was the first time she had a stable environment and believed somebody cared about her. She believed her coaches cared and her residence hall suitemates had encouraged her, were patient with her, and were good listeners.

She asked me if I ever felt like nobody cared for me and I said everyone has days like that. She said she had them regularly and that if she ever had a child she would love the child dearly for the rest of his or her life. I bet she will, too. I was successful in finding her a place to stay over the holidays. The point I make is that parents should never minimize the importance of believing in and giving sincere love to their children. Love is powerful and the foundation for a healthy and balanced life.

Parents need to instill discipline

The next important piece of advice for parents involves discipline, which Webster defines as training that corrects, molds, or perfects the mental faculties or moral character. To meet those objectives I would have my child become a member of some structured, organized activities where life skills and tasks are performed outside of the school day. Personal discipline can be learned in a variety of ways and is the key to a person's success. Every successful person achieved that success through personal discipline, which takes sacrifice to acquire.

Many activities, such as organized sports, music and dance lessons, reading and economic clubs, karate, photography, scouting, etc., require preparation and training. All teach discipline. I would make sure the instructor or coach was qualified and had established goals, objectives, and reasonable expectations for each child enrolled in the activity.

I would hold my child accountable for attending every practice or session and for finishing the course. Consistent attendance and completing an activity are forms of discipline in their own right. I have seen many students initially get involved in an activity then give it up when it takes more work than they expected. They missed out on the best part — learning discipline. They won't ever learn the tougher the job, the greater the reward.

Never would I permit a season to pass without my child being involved in some organized activity. Discipline is key to accomplishing anything worthwhile. Children need discipline to grow up safely. They must learn skills in reading, writing, and math, and how to get along with others in order to have a balanced perspective about life. Whenever I have a question about doing something constructive that requires a great deal of work and discipline I think of the lyrics, "On Christ the solid rock I stand, all other ground is sinking sand." Those words keep me focused on what is important in life and separates the frills from substance.

I did my doctoral dissertation on the study of values. During my investigation I did an extensive review of the literature, which described what famous collegiate football coaches in history believed the sport taught their players. Unequivocally, every one of them strongly believed, above all, it taught discipline, which is a necessary quality to help a boy grow into a man and a

Me and sons, Alvin and David, with their wives, Jackie, left, and Cheryl

girl grow into a woman and for them to become balanced adults

It's a clear indication of discipline when, as I have observed, young male and female athletes at Michigan State start their day in the conditioning and weight room at 6 a.m.; leave at 7; go to their residences; eat breakfast; attend their classes at 8 a.m.; return to their locker rooms at 2:30 p.m. to dress and prepare for a 3 o'clock practice session, which ends between 5-5:30; then shower; go to dinner; and report at 7 p.m. for a required two-hour study session.

Mentors can help parents guide children

Next on the priority list is for parents to have mentors for their children. They could be peers who are successful trusted advisors and friends who can offer guidance to the children. Parents need to identify people in the community who are trustworthy, highly respected, and who can assist their children on a continuous basis. It could be as simple as finding

334

successful students to teach the children how to do worthy projects in and out of school. A child could also learn to model his or her performance after a mentor who has achieved success.

It is wise to select a variety of successful adult mentors to help the child become aware of different aspects of their development — someone other than parents who would offer encouragement and support, provide ideas, help with homework, give advice on how to make good decisions, and explain why they had become successful.

The title of Hillary Clinton's book is, *It Takes a Village to Raise a Child*. The longer I live the more I believe that statement has a lot of merit. Parents, particularly single ones, should be pro-active in finding reputable mentors who can help their children grow academically, socially, spiritually, intellectually, morally, and in physical skills. Life is a tough journey and we all need help along the way. Life wasn't meant to be lived alone.

The community is full of good and knowledgeable people who are willing to help young people. They can have a profound effect on young life. I recall when I was in the seventh grade one of my teachers asked me on a Thursday to give a speech at a Youth Day church program that Sunday. I became filled with anxiety and couldn't think about what I might eventually say. I took a chance after school and walked to my former elementary school, arriving about 4 p.m. The new principal, whom I didn't know, was working in his office. I approached him and identified myself and told him about my assignment and asked for his help. He interrupted his work, told me to sit down, then asked a series of questions, writing down my responses.

Then he handed me his notes and said, "Here is your speech." He was so pleased to help. I became aware that learning is enhanced through shared understanding and collaboration. A person never should feel embarrassed to ask for help. All of us exist here on earth to help each other, though we sometimes forget that simple fact. I still have mentors in my life and probably will continue to have them until I leave this earth. I still help mentor children in my community and young professionals living in various parts of the country.

Among my friends is a psychologist who is a full professor at Michigan State and part owner of a successful counseling clinic. He was born in Alabama. When my friend was a young child his father was killed in a train accident. My friend wound up marrying his high school sweetheart. But long before then her mother, a school teacher, was a mentor and role model to him. She would take him to church with her family and encouraged him to participate in activities at church, where he would read Sunday school materials, act in skits, and take field trips. He credits his mother-in-law with doing more to bolster his ego and self-esteem at that early age than anything else in his life. I'm sure being around the pretty young daughter also helped a great deal to strengthen those traits in him.

Teaching integrity is imperative

Integrity is another vital ingredient for parents to teach to their children. The word isn't used too much these days, but it is most important. It connotes honesty. Most public schools don't teach that basic principle. And it is something that some of America's major corporations — Enron, Arthur Anderson, Kmart, and WorldCom, as well as the Catholic Church — have had trouble with these days. The corporations' wrongdoings have put them in bankruptcy. The church has had to face scandals involving priests who were improperly involved with their parishioners. Those problems have led to a crisis in public confidence.

Integrity is imperative in the lives of young people, whether at home, school, or in the programs that are vital to them. At Michigan State we tried to hire coaches and administrators who were trustworthy, who spoke the truth, and upon whose word athletes could rely. Upon graduation, many athletes sought my advice. They wanted any suggestions I could offer as they embarked on their careers. I told them to vigorously maintain their integrity and they would be successful.

I have seen athletes dismissed from teams and coaches and administrators lose their jobs for cheating and lying in collegiate athletics. It was my standard practice as a compliance administrator to advise athletes, coaches, and boosters upfront, whenever it was alleged they had violated an NCAA rule, to tell the whole truth to the best of their knowledge. I further advised them that it was better to tell the truth and suffer appropriate consequences than to lie and cause bigger problems for themselves, such as being charged with unethical conduct.

Young children need to get in the habit of telling the truth all the time. It will help save them from trouble later in life. Parents need to teach their children to tell the truth. It is something you have to work at all the time. It's not always easy to be honest. Sometimes folks with integrity suffer consequences for doing what's right. Take the story in the Bible of Daniel in the lion's den. He was honest and didn't compromise his integrity when the king asked him to do so. He was thrown into the den for doing the right thing.

There are times now when a person will do what's right and pay a heavy price. Think about a clean-living whistle blower at work. Then, I know of an assistant coach at another collegiate institution who was fired for not corroborating a lie with his head coach, who was under NCAA investigation. When the head coach was able to retain his job, he fired the assistant, who was in essence put in the lion's den for being honest. I would rather be honest than to live with a lying and evil conscience, or to be beholden to a devious person.

Proverbs 20:7 speaks of integrity. It says the righteous man walks in his integrity. His children are blessed after him.

Persistence pays off

Another vital piece of advice to parents is that they teach persistence to their children. Parents should sit down with their children and plan mutually agreed upon goals, short and long term ones, because they help people stay focused and serve as guidelines for becoming successful. Once a goal is determined, it should be modified if necessary, but never abandoned.

Athletes sometimes have difficulty mastering the dual role of being an athlete and student. At times, it seems, there aren't enough hours in a day to handle both adequately. The only way most student-athletes get through is if they set goals for themselves: academic, athletic, and personal ones. I often encourage student athletes to stay focused on their goals. The worst thing I have seen among student-athletes is for some to quit their teams, give up their scholarships, and drop out of the university. Then they call 10 years later asking how they can return so they can graduate and hopefully qualify for a better job.

According to NCAA rules, college athletes lose their athletic scholarships forever after six years of their original enrollment. If they are readmitted after that period they must defray their own expenses from personal funds or a work-study program. Most have families and work at marginal jobs and need to get their degrees to get better jobs. Because of the rules, there isn't much the university can do to accommodate the former student-athletes' requests, except to provide them with part-time employment to help them pay their way. With families and debts, it is difficult for them to return to the university. I advise them to seek educational opportunities in their local communities and perhaps transfer their MSU earned credits there.

Young students need to stick to worthy and constructive goals. They should never give up. They need to be consistent in going to school, doing homework, cleaning their rooms, taking out the trash, and doing other chores. By being persistent, they learn responsibility, which is a valuable lifetime attribute.

One of the reasons some young students give up on their goals is peer pressure, which can be a powerful detractor. Peer pressure can cause the students to lie, steal, cheat, use alcohol and drugs, slip outside to play when homework is due, or quit school. The best way to counter peer pressure is for parents to know the children their kids hang around with. They should have them visit their house, talk with them, learn their names and something about their parents, and find out how they are doing in school. That will give parents a pretty good fix on who is influencing their children and who might be the ones their kids need to avoid. Children are precious and need constant guidance and protection in a loving and nurturing environment.

What happens when we give up a worthy endeavor? Do we spend a lifetime wondering what might have been? If it was a worthwhile project, like finishing high school, we may start where we stopped. When we graduate and get a decent job or seek advanced education, we wonder why we ever quit school in the first place or why we wavered so long at trying again. Most athletes who sustain major injuries rehabilitate themselves and start over. Coaches who get fired for having losing seasons go to other institutions and start over. Persistence is a key ingredient to success. NEVER, NEVER give up on a good thing.

Without a doubt, teen-agers between the ages of 14 and 18 are in the most difficult and complex growth period in their lives. They become affected by a perplexed set of social, emotional, and physical issues that they don't understand. One of the biggest crises facing students in that age range is establishing an identity. They need to know who they are and what they can do, as well as what skills they have developed that will help them fit in, give them some respect and recognition with their peers.

They want to know how they compare intellectually with other students in their class. If they don't feel fairly secure about themselves during that sensitive time period, most likely they will de-emphasize the importance of school, a mindset that leads to failing grades and dropping out.

As I mentioned earlier, I have spoken with many athletes at Michigan State regarding their experiences in high school. Some young men told me they felt uncomfortable with their social skills, but because of their athletics accomplishments there were young women pursuing them. But those same young men lacked the social skills and believed they didn't have adequate self-esteem to feel comfortable with young women.

They were insecure about their academics and some, too, felt inadequate with their emotional skills. They would rather settle a conflict by fighting than talk about it. They were comfortable hanging around other athletes and said the only thing that kept them attached to school was their involvement in the athletics program. One of them said: "I was a touchdown machine and every time I scored the scoreboard would light up." He said he got a great deal of satisfaction out of hearing his name on the public address system and the fans whooping it up after he scored. Without football, he said, he would have dropped out of school by the 10th grade.

On the other hand, most of the athletes I interviewed had great experiences in high school. Some were good students, even class presidents, and they were involved in many different club activities. They drove cars to school and had a variety of friends. They were able to avoid confrontations by managing their emotions. They felt positive about their identity and had appropriate clothes to wear in any situation.

But those seemingly well-adjusted students said they were well aware of a number of others who were having various troubles coping with school and some dropped out. About a million students drop out of high school each year in America. Students who have difficulty in school start to feel alienated by the ninth grade. They continue to struggle with frustration or drop out at the first opportunity.

First, they start daydreaming in class, thinking about some outside contact or event that they believe to be more appealing and satisfying than school. The young men and women may be loners or strong-willed but lacking in discipline and persistence. They think about owning their own cars, distressing relationships in the home, and being with the opposite sex. They don't do homework because of their skill deficiencies and are embarrassed to try because they might get it wrong and be humiliated in front of their classmates and teachers. They may be labeled troublemakers who are different and have few friends.

They feel helpless and defeated in the school environment and start hanging around with students who feel as they do. They will smoke, drink alcohol, smoke pot, and find places where they can hang out together. This is a difficult age group for parents to manage. They have a big challenge just getting their growing children to recognize the importance of being respectful to them and of staying in school. It's just as difficult to know where they are day and night. Many parents lose control over their children who are in that age group.

That is the time when it is good to have a host of mentors involved in trying to help channel the students in the right direction. It is an emergency situation and parents must do everything in their power to get their children to continue in school.

Since 1995, MSU has had a mentoring program for athletes. It consists of faculty and staff members who render invaluable services. They help the student-athletes focus on academics and goal setting in their personal lives, allowing them to better handle crisis situations. I have learned from my experiences that it is just not the economically deprived or academically at-risk student who needs mentoring. All students need guidance and some need personal mentors. I wish MSU had such a program in place in the 1970s. Maybe an experienced faculty or staff member may have saved a young athlete who had a drug problem.

I remember a student-athlete from a southern state who in high school was an all-state football player and an academics honors student. His middle class parents (a high school teacher and a postal services employee) were concerned about their son's welfare because he was so far from home, so each Monday they sent him $100 for personal expenses. His football scholarship paid all of his educational expenses. I had learned of the excessive spending from advising him during the fall term. I suggested that he tell his parents to reduce the amount, but he didn't do it.

During his freshman year, I started receiving reports from his professors that he was skipping classes. I called him into my office one morning to discuss his class attendance. He was sitting in a chair across from me. To reinforce the necessity of consistent class attendance, I stood up over him and was giving him a harsh chewing out about his inadequate excuses for missing classes. When I looked at him closer I was astonished to see he had fallen asleep. He was strung out on drugs.

I became frightened because I never had seen a person high on drugs before. I immediately summoned help from a professional counselor, who continued to work with the athlete for the rest of his academic enrollment at the university, with assistance from a physician. Despite aggressive professional intervention, the athlete's behavior never changed and he eventually flunked out of school. I often have wondered if an experienced mentor could have detected his problems earlier and made a difference with the athlete.

Education is vital for success

The lack of a high school education will grossly impair the lives of children for generations to come. They won't be prepared to take advantage of opportunities that exist in a society rife with growing information technology. They'll find themselves at a major disadvantage and won't have the necessary skills to cope financially, socially and educationally. That, most likely, will leave them broke and regulated to the underclass. It is a troubling economic thought for families and our communities.

Children need to graduate from high school — and college. They need to compete and succeed in an environment that is increasingly competitive and fast changing. Societal expectations for children today are much different than they were 20 years ago. Faced with the lack of manufacturing jobs, grade-based exams, electronic communications, diversity, global realities, the need for lifelong education, and career development, are among the forces compelling educators to re-shape how society thinks about our children's future.

It is essential for every school-aged child to own a computer in order to compete in a fast-paced and knowledge-driven global economy. It is imperative that we understand clearly that our future as a society depends upon the children of today who will be the leaders of tomorrow. We must have our children understand the power of their minds and the benefits that come with applying themselves. If our children spend as much time studying math and science as they do listening to music, watching television, and hanging out, they would be geniuses. There is an old saying that, "A mind is a terrible thing to waste."

When I was the athletics director at Michigan State I received a call from an alumnus who was a medical doctor whose son had applied for admission to the university and was awaiting a favorable reply. The doctor asked if I could assist in getting a quick decision for his son. I said I didn't have any influence with the office of admissions and he would just have to wait his turn. The doctor said it was extremely important that his son get admitted to Michigan State so he could acquire a quality education.

The doctor said something that has stayed with me: He was willing to cash out his retirement account to finance his son's education. I praised him for his commitment and foresight, but wondered how many other parents would be willing to use their retirement funds for their children's education. That was a wise and noble commitment on his part.

Children's educational needs must be at the forefront of everything parents do in planning for the future. Quality education has to be the key because only the educated are free and have the wisdom and courage to weather the turbulent future. We must assume a new leadership role with our children because yesterday's success is no assurance of success today.

The question becomes, what are you doing to prepare your children and grandchildren for the future? In my profession, we have coaches who won national championships and were fired three years later. The world is hungry for instant and continued success. Yesterday's records are history. Opportune circumstances present themselves and we must help our children take advantage of them.

Finally, it doesn't always take money to teach children about the importance of education. I have a sociology professor friend at MSU who was born in the industrial city of Flint, Mich. His father worked in a factory. I asked him who inspired him and his brother (also a Ph.D. and who is an executive at Disney World) about the need for an education. He responded that every Saturday morning their mother would take them to the city library and encouraged them to spend the day reading. My friend said his mother didn't tell them what to read as long as they were reading something. They read newspapers, magazines and books. After a while, reading became fun and the brothers looked forward to spending the day at the library. He credited that early exposure to reading, plus his parents' love, as the keys to his educational success and his brother's.

Accepting responsibility for our actions

Accountability is the ability to accept responsibility and consequences for decisions, whatever those consequences might be. It further means not blaming others for the problems encountered in life. Most coaches are experts in teaching athletes to be accountable. For example, we had a good football team in 1990. The team finished the season with an 8-3-1 record. One of the losses was to Notre Dame in East Lansing, 20-19. We led 19-13 with less than a minute left and Notre Dame had the ball on our 30-yard line with third down and 10 yards to go. On the next play, the quarterback passed to one of his receivers in our end zone. The ball hit one of our senior defensive backs squarely in the chest, bounced off and landed in the hands of an Irish receiver for a touchdown.

It was a very important game for us, played before a sold-out crowd and millions watching on television. People became very emotional, blaming the athlete for the loss. The radio talk shows tried to castigate him, but his teammates and coaches didn't blame him because they understood the meaning of accountability. Surely the coaches and players were disappointed in the loss, but the player never blamed anybody but himself. He walked with his head up all week to his classes and continued to play his position to the best of his ability for the rest of the season.

Teen-agers often blame others for their mistakes. It is so easy and convenient to blame parents, other family members, teachers, administrators, and friends for their problems. Comedian Flip Wilson used to say on his television show, "The devil made me do it." Teens must be taught to take responsibility for their actions. Blaming others for their mistakes is a copout. It can be a devastating approach that won't help someone learn life's positive values and become successful.

I heard an excellent sermon on accountability. The minister was preaching on the subject of the "second sin." He said the first sin, recorded in the Bible's Book of Genesis, was when Eve ate fruit from the Tree of Knowledge in the Garden of Eden and tempted Adam to eat the fruit against the will of God. But the minister said the second sin may be worse than the first, saying it was bad to eat the fruit after the Lord told them not to, but it was worse that neither Eve nor Adam accepted responsibility for their mistake.

When the Lord asked Adam if he had eaten from the tree, which he was commanded not to do, Adam responded, "The woman whom thou gavest to be with me, she gave me fruit of the tree, and I ate it." God then said to the woman, "What is this that you have done?" The woman said, "The serpent deceived me and I ate." The two had cast the blame on someone else. Adam blamed Eve and she blamed it on the snake. They tried to placate the almighty God by failing to confess to their own weaknesses.

Here are some distressing statistics involving teen-agers in the United States:
- Four and a half million girls are sexually active and about a million become pregnant each year.
- Three million teens use illicit drugs and two million drink alcohol.
- Five million smoke cigarettes and chew tobacco.
- A million drop out of school every year.

Our teen-agers long ago cried out for help and we

didn't deliver the proper services to them. We were too busy working on our own problems, doing our own things, and didn't allow adequate time for our children to speak to us. We all must now pay the price because those problems have a devastating impact on all levels of our society. The students continue to speak to us today, but are we listening to them? They are crying out for help. It doesn't matter about class, race, gender, or socioeconomic backgrounds. The problems are prevalent in all segments of our society and put tremendous strain on the human and financial resources of our country. They erode family values and the future strength of our country.

Many teen-agers don't have goals. They don't know where they're headed or where they might end up. They simply float with the crowd, which can and often does lead them to no place of benefit. They don't have control over their lives. As parents and coaches of young people, we need to give them direction, which they don't think they need until it's too late.

They all want freedom and independence from authority figures, but there is a heavy price to pay for both. You have to earn freedom from control through discipline, integrity, persistence, listening to mentors, graduating from high school and college, and being accountable for your actions and decisions. There is an old West African saying that goes like this: "If you wait for tomorrow, tomorrow comes. If you don't wait for tomorrow, tomorrow comes." The implication is clear: Tomorrow is coming, my friends, ready or not. So we may as well prepare our children for it. It is coming after all of us, ready or not, and it all starts with accountability.

Izzo among many MSU role models

Among some excellent examples of role models and mentors is Michigan State Basketball Coach Tom Izzo. He's the kind of person it takes to lead teen-agers to success today. He grew up in the small town of Iron

Mountain in Michigan's Upper Peninsula. He was an All-America basketball player at Northern Michigan University and has received more honors than time and space will allow me to list.

Izzo was an assistant coach at MSU before becoming head coach in 1995. He hasn't had a losing season and is rated among the best coaches in the country. In his first eight years his teams posted a 189-77 record. The 1999-2000 team won the NCAA championship. His teams have captured four regular-season Big Ten titles, two conference tournament championships, have participated in the NCAA tourney Final Four on four occasions, and he has won three national coach of the year awards.

His 2002-03 team filled with underclassmen seemed at one point like it wouldn't make it to the NCAA tournament, but it did and wound up in the Elite Eight. And the 2004-05 team went to the Final Four, upsetting Kentucky and Duke along the way before losing to North Carolina, 87-71, to close out the season with a 26-7 record. That put his 10-year MSU record at 233-97 (.706) and 117-47 (.713) in Big Ten play. He is the second winningest basketball coach in MSU history behind Jud Heathcote (340). Those are impressive achievements and there is a real person behind them all.

Izzo is one of the most down-to-earth persons you'll ever want to meet. He relates exceedingly well with all types of people. He is honest, intelligent and treats folks with dignity and respect. He has an outstanding family and I have never seen anyone work as hard as he does.

I remember his first season as head coach when he ended up with a 16-16 record, losing some tough Saturday afternoon games along the way. He was a young man with a young staff and I felt he needed some consoling. I called his home four or five times that season after tough losses to tell him his young team played well, even though it hadn't won the game.

The calls were made around 9:30 p.m. and each time his wife, Lupe, told me he was still at the office working. Sure enough, I would call his office and talk to his assistant, Tom Crean, who now is the head coach at Marquette University (a Final Four NCAA team in 2003). They would work very late into the night and early mornings reviewing game films and planning for the next game. He demonstrated the same level of commitment in recruitment. Izzo becomes professionally focused and works unlimited hours making contacts with prospects and their parents when he recruits.

Relaxing with basketball coach Tom Izzo

Is it any wonder why so many universities have sought out Izzo's assistants to become head coaches of their programs? Besides Crean, Izzo has lost the following assistants to head coaching jobs elsewhere: Mike Garland, Cleveland State; Brian Gregory, Dayton University; Stan Heath, Arkansas; Stan Joplin, Toledo.

Izzo is an amazing, successful person who expects excellence from his players in all aspects of their lives. And, believe me, the man means business. He works individually and in group sessions with his players. He holds them accountable and wants them going to their classes consistently.

Izzo expects his assistant coaches, office staff, trainers, doctors, managers, and the tutors and mentors of the players, to be all business and experts in the services they provide. Missing classes and earning poor grades will mean the player may not start or play in a game or games. He treats the players as if each one was his own son. He wants the very best for them. He wants them to be goal-oriented, to demonstrate good citizenship and service to the community, to show respect for themselves and others, to manage their lives responsibly, and to graduate.

Players who finish his program leave as talented, confident, and dedicated winners. They leave as leaders. If I had a son who was a basketball player and was capable of playing big-time college basketball, I would persuade him to play for Izzo. I know that he would be a pacesetter as he finishes the program and heads into his professional career.

Slobodnick demands excellence

Another fine role model and mentor is Stacey Slobodnick, the Spartans' women's golf coach. She was a former student-athlete at MSU and an assistant coach before becoming head coach in 1997. She is a winner and has done an outstanding job developing the young women in her program into champions. In five seasons, her teams have made four consecutive NCAA regional tournament appearances, three championship appearances, and earned one Big Ten championship.

She works hard and demands excellence from her players in the academics and athletics areas, as well as in their personal lives. Like all MSU coaches, she wants her players to strive for lofty goals and reach them without making excuses. She has an outstanding graduation success rate with her players.

Mason tough, but understanding

Ron Mason, the former ice hockey coach who was my successor as athletics director, also is a top role model and mentor. He was a hockey coach for 36 years and is the winningest coach in collegiate hockey history with 924 victories. There is absolutely no way that any coach in any sport could have been so successful without providing effective leadership to his players.

Mason was outstanding at identifying the type of players to recruit and understanding their mentalities and personalities. He set high goals for them, molding them into a team. He expected the very best from them in all phases of their lives. Similar to Izzo and Slobodnik, Mason required his players to attend classes and graduate. He required them to demonstrate responsible behavior on campus and in the community. He expected them to show pride for the program and respect themselves, others, and the university.

Ron Mason

Mason demonstrated an appropriate blend of toughness and understanding. He has had numerous athletes who went into the professional ranks with confidence, leadership qualities, and as winners. They all are fortunate to have played for Ron, the legend.

Bryans won't let her crew cruise

Next on my fine role model-mentor list is Bebe Bryans, head coach of the women's crew team at MSU. She was hired from Georgetown when the sport was added to the varsity ranks in 1997. She has coached her teams to five NCAA appearances, with three top-10 finishes. MSU has finished third in the Big Ten championships and she has earned two coach-of-the-year honors.

Bebe Bryans

About a hundred students try out for the crew squad each year and about half end up making it. Crew is a tough endurance sport. I learned in a kinesiology class as an undergraduate that the one sport requiring the most endurance is rowing. The crew squad works out on campus nine months of the year. Bebe accepts no excuses for mediocrity, demanding exceptional performance academically, athletically, and in her players' personal lives.

Bryans gets exactly what she wants — winners. Her student-athletes rise to the level of expectations with hard work and pride. For the first time in their lives, some of them learn the feeling of being victorious in big-time competition. It's an exhilarating emotion. She exhibits

352

the same level of demeanor as other successful coaches: that is, the players in practice and competition have to be focused, work hard, and be all business. She turns out some amazing young women who leave the university with demonstrated leadership qualities and successful academic backgrounds.

Stintzi a top motivator

Jim Stintzi, MSU's cross-country coach, is another excellent role model and mentor. Cut from the same cloth as the other previously described coaches, he is an expert in knowing how to motivate students and get the last burst of energy from them during distance running. He has been the men's cross-country coach for 19 years and the dual coach of both the men's and women's squads for three years. Both teams are recognized as being among the most competitive in the nation.

Stintzi has produced many All-Americans and Big Ten champions and has been recognized as coach of the year many times. He is a no nonsense coach who has high expectations for his athletes. He is knowledgeable, intelligent, and well respected by his players and knows how to mold them into winners. His athletes graduate in very high percentages. Jim was a seven-time All-American himself as a cross-country runner at the University of Wisconsin.

Mannie a 'strong' mentor

Also a fine role model and mentor is Ken Mannie, Michigan State's strength and conditioning coach. He has been at the university since 1994 and is a certified strength and conditioning specialist with the National Strength and Conditioning Association. He is a highly respected authority in his field, embodying all the positive qualities we want young men and women to emulate.

He is intelligent, compassionate, knowledgeable, in

Ken Mannie

great physical shape, confident, honest, has an admirable work ethic, communicates very well, has vision, and is responsible. Those are traits he displays daily in his work. However, when an athlete fails to abide by expectations in the conditioning room, Mannie becomes a different person — the meanest, baddest, toughest guy you'd ever want to meet.

He acts that way to help teach accountability. Athletes know he won't tolerate their sloppiness and expects no less than their best efforts. He teaches them that there are no shortcuts in life. Everyone must earn their way to excellence.

Mannie has established a few simple rules he expects an athlete to follow in the conditioning room: report on time, be in proper uniform and look tidy, enter prepared to give the best effort for the full hour, display a cooperative and willing attitude regardless of the difficulty of the task at hand.

He is a professional and expert educator who knows how to condition athletes and build their strength, something that requires persistence and hard work. He is proficient in teaching physical fitness, speed and endurance exercises, and knows what the individual training sessions will deliver based on the athlete's sport and position.

One conditioning and strength coach told me that Mannie is among the top five experts in his field nationally. He knows how to motivate young students and they truly respect him, even when he gives them a strong verbal reminder when they goof up. I wish every young athlete had the opportunity to train under Ken. He has an excellent quote on his wall taken from the Bible: "Just as iron sharpens iron, one man must sharpen another."

There are other MSU coaches, current and former, who also devote themselves to making winners out of athletes in all aspects of their lives. Some of those who have the same passions for teaching, competency, responsibility, persistence, and commitment as those I've previously mentioned include: Chuck Erbe (volleyball), Bobby Williams (football), Joanne McCallie (women's basketball), Jacquie Joseph (softball), Kathie Klages (women's gymnastics), Tom Minkel (wrestling), Mark Hankins (men's golf), Darroll Gatson (men's track and field), Joe Baum (men's soccer), Tim Bauer (women's tennis), Angie Goodman (women's track and field), Tom Saxton (women's soccer), Gene Orlando (men's tennis), Michelle Madison (field hockey), Ted Mahan (baseball), and Jim Lutz (men's and women's swimming and diving).

Tips to high school athletes

Here are some tips, based on a lifetime of experiences, which I would give to high school athletes who aspire to participate in college athletics:

- Maintain your integrity. Don't do stupid stuff like stealing; lying to your teachers, coaches, and parents; cheating on exams. If you are doing them – STOP NOW OR YOU WILL BE CAUGHT. You are old enough to know right from wrong. Such negative behaviors will catch up with you and cause you much embarrassment and hurt. If you don't believe me, read the newspapers. Choose any section.
- Earn the very best grades in all your subjects.

Don't avoid the tough courses. Start taking math, science, social studies, English, and foreign language courses in the ninth grade. Currently, you need to pass 13 of those courses to qualify for practice, competition, and an athletic scholarship in your freshman year in college. College professors are very demanding academically. They expect you to be a student first and an athlete second. You need to do well in your high school courses in order to meet the academic challenges in college.

- Take care of your mind and your body. You are gifted with special talent. Don't mess it up by the destructive use of alcohol, tobacco, and illegal drugs. There are state laws against the use of tobacco and alcohol by minors and it is illegal to possess marijuana, cocaine, and other harmful substances.

- Learn all you can from your coaches and other experts in your sport. Ask them for suggestions on how you can improve your skills. Participate in sports camps. Refine your skills and build upon them. You will be trying out against some of the best athletes in college. Competition to make the team is fierce. The better your skills and the more knowledge you have will give you a greater chance of success.

- If you are not already doing so, START TODAY writing down goals for yourself. They will serve as a road map for your life. If you don't know where you are going, you don't know where you will end up. Write each goal based on what you want to accomplish when you complete the goal. For example, you might plan to earn a 3.0 grade-point-average in Algebra 102. Now write directly under that goal several strategies showing how you intend to reach it. Develop goals covering your personal, academic, social, and athletic priorities in that way. Developing goals is crucial when you need to manage your time to excel in academics, sports, and in your personal lives.

- Take responsibility for your choices. You never will grow into the leader you can be unless you start taking credit for your successes and mistakes. It's important that you discuss tough decisions with your parents, teachers, or other trusted persons before acting on them.
- Learn to respect yourself, your parents, siblings, and people of all persuasions. Talk decently, be helpful, be patient, and treat all the people the same way you want them to treat you. Make many friends and learn from them.
- Learn perseverance. Life is a tough race, just like it is in competitive sports. Learn to live one day at a time and give it your best. In sports, you take one competition at a time and not the whole schedule at once. When things are bleak, don't despair. Tough times only last for a short time. Keep the faith because perseverance is the accomplishment of a series of short races, one by one. Stay positive.
- Start thinking long term about academic majors. What do you want to be doing when you are 25? Talk to different professionals about their jobs. Sort out two or three majors before you go to college. Don't wait until you get to college to start thinking about that important area. Doing so early will save time, money, and energy.
- Graduate from college. You may never be recognized positively in life without a college degree. You may never find your identity. You may never earn a great salary. I can tell you about many student-athletes who finished their collegiate eligibility without graduating, tried out with pro teams, or played for a few years, got cut from the team, and had no degree to fall back on

and no marketable skills. What you do is who you are in society. There is life after sports and that's when the real challenge begins. A college education will help you to grow through the challenges.

Tips for athletics administrators

Here are some suggestions, now, for athletics administrators, who are on the firing line every day.

- Focus on the big picture. You'll never attain tremendous success if you lose sight of the grand vision of what you want to get done for the department. One of the inadvertent errors athletics administrators make is to worry and struggle with the small stuff and not to stay focused on the worthy short- and long-term goals. They spend too much time worrying about their ability to advance the department and balance the budget each year, whether their revenue sport coaches can win consistently, whether the compliance program is functioning effectively. They worry about their athletics competitors and whether they can keep up with them in revenue generating and facilities improvement. All of those functions are most important but should be built into the grand strategic plan and worked on.

Worry doesn't translate to positive results. It's a lot of wasted energy and time for the athletics director. One of the reasons our attention gets drawn away from our objectives is that we set them too low. Most of us can achieve much more than the goals we set for ourselves. We can accomplish much higher results that will grow the department by restructuring the goals to a higher level. Go for it. Don't be afraid. Step outside the box.

- Start operating your department with systematic written policies and not in a reactive mode so you can predict the outcomes. I once worked for an athletics director who had no written plans for the department. He reacted to whatever the department encountered from day to day. I had a training background and was successful in getting him to initiate a system of written policies and procedures. Staff training in the development of written procedures and policies will significantly improve the operations of the department, enhance communication, raise morale, and reduce cost. A system of coordinated and functional policies will improve efficiency tenfold.

  I observed an office recently in which five staff members were sitting around playing solitary cards on their computers. If they had work to do it was not being done. That wouldn't happen in a formalized office where training has occurred and the procedures, policies, systems, plans, and standards of conduct have been established and clearly communicated to the staff. And particularly it wouldn't happen if staff members were involved formulating the policies, procedures, plans, and systems because they'll all be on the page and helping each other do good work. They'll have an ownership attitude.

- Be careful about who you hire because few presidents will support a losing coach, even though the coach operates an ethical program free of numerous NCAA violations and has a high graduation rate. Most presidents lack the courage to buck the alumni. An exception to that attitude, in Division 1A, is the administration at Ohio University, where Dean Pees, who is a great person, outstanding coach, and friend, is the head football coach and has properly survived despite a losing record.

- Strategic partnerships can be a successful tool for athletics departments, as already has been proven in the broadcast areas. Partnerships should be reviewed as program expansion opportunities similar to what has happened at AOL-Time-Warner, Fifth-Third Bank, and many more companies. It is the business way of tomorrow for athletics departments with scarce resources. It can be difficult and expensive to try to improve upon functions if the department lacks the resources to handle them.

  The question that should be addressed is, do you have adequate staff to get the job done quicker, with quality, and less expensive in compliance, marketing and promotions, fund-raising, sports camps, academic support services, facilities operations, etc.? If the answer is no, then looking for outside partnerships may be the solution. Strategic partnership is an area with many options, such as outsourcing and joint marketing and strategic alliances, which are designed to promote growth in the department. It provides greater access to more qualified experts in broader enterprises.

- As the economy continues to struggle, how about meeting with your sponsors and a few major donors, folks who have given loyal financial support to your department, to share your visions. It also gives you the opportunity to see what's on their minds and what they are doing in their businesses. You can find out about how they envision new developments in their areas that may help you. How about meeting with a few successful non-competitors, institutions that are accomplished and in fields you'll probably never compete against, companies such as General Motors, General Mills, and IBM. Look at their strategies and plans and examine their minds on various practices and procedures. Sharing visions is one of the most effective ways to learn new techniques and new insights for doing things better.

- (Those of you who know me and read this will probably want to run me out of town, even out of the country, but I want you to think seriously about it.) Mostly everything I purchase with my hard-earned money, whether in the service or retail industry, with the exception of the entertainment sector, offers a guarantee. If you are dissatisfied, they will do it over to your satisfaction. If you don't like the item you purchased, simply return it with your receipt and get an exchange, a refund, or a credit. That is a regular practice in the retail industry.

Somehow, athletics has not figured out a way to provide some type of guarantee to its customers. I don't have the answers and I'm not advocating providing a money refund, but there must be a way in which athletics can shift some of the chance away from its customers. As it currently stands, customers buy the tickets and assume all the risk if the event doesn't meet their satisfaction. The issue is athletics departments need to promote real quality teams and make quality high priority for its donors, alumni, students, and fans. The ticket purchasers, not the athletics department, need to determine what quality is to them.

There needs to be some form of recompense to customers who feel the quality of competition didn't meet their expectations. Customers who support athletics events have to come first in the pecking order, at the very top, and staff must be trained to recognize that concept. The first institution that can figure a way to shift the risk or offer a guarantee in some degree for their customers will be 10 shoulders above its toughest

361

opponents. Think about it. Is it a problem or an opportunity worth pursuing? Major league baseball's financial problems are just the tip of the iceberg of what can happen with the entertainment dollar in a struggling economy and when customers aren't satisfied with the product.

- Athletics administration, with all of its demands and long working hours, can be stressful as well as sometimes frustrating. The athletics director always is on center stage in front of a house full of people expecting perfection in the athletics department. I can't overemphasize the importance of the A.D. maintaining good health.

It's important to establish a regular exercise program that can be done both at home and away. There needs to be regular medical checkups and good nutrition. Family vacations are important and should be scheduled and taken. You need to do everything you can to stay healthy for the benefit of yourself, your family, and your institution. Don't put off what you know you should be doing — reducing the amount of alcoholic beverages you drink, stopping yourself from eating the wrong foods, and by quitting smoking. Your health is your most important asset.

- Generally, athletics administrators don't rely on former research studies as a learning tool. We have a tendency to borrow or copy ideas and strategies from other successful athletics programs. Copying is done in coaching, compliance, facilities, marketing, academic support services, staffing, and almost in every component of the athletics department. We do that to keep up with the Joneses. That isn't a bad thing because most major corporations have become successful by emulating other successful organizations. We must keep in mind that copying is not our own thinking.

Athletics departments have to keep pace with innovations and changes in the market place and administrators must continually grow intellectually or become unenlightened. Considering the lack of time athletics directors have for continuing education, let me suggest a strategy. There are a number of new relevant books and tapes that appear on the market each year that have concepts and principles that are applicable to the operations of an intercollegiate athletics department.

Why not hire a graduate assistant or another person available in the community who has the skills to summarize the materials that meet your objectives? You need to select someone who has the ability to listen carefully, follow direction, and write a clearly understood and condensed summary that will serve your needs. The information will keep you updated on the latest business and educational trends. Your alumni and boosters also would be impressed when you use a quote from one of the popular books during your presentations with them. Share the materials with your staff for discussion and training purposes.

- The traditional way of managing employees has gone out of the window. Employees don't respond well today in a department in which the authority and information is shared only with a few. Staff members still want structure in an organization, but they also want the opportunity to have some input in the operations.

Open communications today is essential in a successful department. When an athletics director's staff understands what's going on and works in a system in which input can be given without reprisal, it makes for a much better department. It improves morale, builds loyalty, and produces more efficiency in all units. In order to set the stage for such an environment, the A.D. must be the type of leader who has integrity, is secure, trustworthy, can engender team spirit, and has a keen sense of fairness.

Believe me, staff knows if you are strong in each of those areas. If they detect a weakness, the word spreads like wildfire in the informal grouping. Then you must be able to communicate effectively and be a good listener. You must respect your staff and get to know their families. You've got to make them feel they are an intimate part of the athletics family.

You must understand that you are the main source of their financial well-being and their security. You must recognize that they depend on you to allow them to earn and save money in order to buy a house, a car, and pay for their children's education. You must appreciate what they, including the janitor, do on a daily basis. You must respect them as equals and make sure everybody else in the department treats each other as equals in the work place. If you establish that kind of culture in your department, the results will be amazing.

- Finally, a word to the athletics directors who have trouble delegating responsibilities to their staff. It is impossible for the best A.D. to have the time and knowledge to adequately perform all of the tasks associated with operating an athletics department. There are just too many things to do in a timely and efficient manner.

The A.D. needs to be involved in strategic planning in order that the department can move progressively forward. He or she should delegate to experts who can do functions significantly better than the A.D. expects. By so doing, it frees up the athletics director to focus on the big picture.

The A.D. needs to write down and keep track, by priority, the things the university is paying him or her to do and to do them very well. Do the things you are an expert in and delegate everything else to staff. Keep your eyes on the big picture and develop the real plans and strategies that will make a significant difference in the department. And stop worrying. Good luck, my friends.

CHAPTER 11:

OVERCOMING HEALTH PROBLEMS

Fighting off diseases
that run in the family

M**Y NO. 1 GOAL, ESPECIALLY NOW THAT I'M** retired, is to maintain my health, principally through daily exercise and diet. Since early elementary school I have regularly engaged in some form of physical fitness activities. As an adult my exercises consisted mostly of jogging, walking, and weightlifting, until I reached age 63. I jogged six miles a day, seven days a week. Then my old football-injured knee became more aggravated.

I first injured it in high school and over the years the pain had become more intensified. One morning in 1999, while working out with Fred Poston in the Duffy Daugherty Building weight room, I re-injured my knee while walking on the treadmill at a 6-mile-an-hour pace. I felt excruciating pain and the knee felt loose in the joint. I made an appointment with Dr. Herb Ross, the Michigan State team physician. He indicated I had torn cartilage in the knee joint that had also atrophied to the point that surgery was necessary.

Dr. Ross performed arthroscopy to remove the

damaged cartilage and advised me that my knee no longer could support jogging. He suggested I start a walking program, which I implemented. Now I walk between 30 and 60 minutes each day, depending on my schedule.

My other choice to further aid in my goal of maintaining good health has been to watch what I eat. I have reduced the amount of carbohydrates and fats I consume. In addition, I try to get adequate sleep and have an annual medical examination. The routine has become an integral part of my lifestyle because I very much wanted to ward off diabetes and prostate cancer, two life-threatening diseases that long have been prevalent in my family's history. I realize there are many more factors that contribute to a person contracting those deleterious diseases, including heredity. I believe it is my responsibility to control whatever I can relative to the attainment of my personal health goal.

My paternal grandmother and grandfather both died from diabetes complications and my grandfather's autopsy showed he also had prostate cancer. My mother struggled with diabetes for many years. Both of her legs were amputated below the knees due to poor circulation. She died from a heart attack in 1986 at the age of 75. My father died in 1979 at the age of 70, the result of a stroke. His autopsy showed he, too, had diabetes and prostate cancer. If he was aware of that I don't believe he ever told anyone about it.

My mother kept her children informed about issues at their home and she never told us about daddy's health problem. She did call to tell us about his stroke. It wasn't common 30 years ago for men from economically disadvantaged backgrounds to have their prostate checked annually by a medical doctor. Even today, when the economic and social conditions have improved significantly in America, many men 40 and older still ignore the advice of the American Urological Society and the American Cancer Society to have an annual rectal examination and a PSA (Prostate Specific Antigen) test. Those are two screening procedures for prostate cancer.

Advice that probably saved my life

I returned to Michigan State in August 1990 from the Big Ten Conference office in suburban Chicago. My MSU office was in Jenison Field House, where many staff members and persons from the community used the indoor track to jog and walk at noontime. That practice has been a tradition since the early 1970s. I routinely do my exercises early in the mornings before the normal working hour.

One day in September 1992 I was leaving Jenison for lunch and long-time East Lansing resident Bill Sharp, a great person and member of the East Lansing City Council, was approaching to do his noontime walk. We exchanged greetings and he voluntarily told me he was a prostate cancer survivor, mentioning that he recently had a radical prostatectomy. He explained that his cancer wasn't detected through the rectal exam and PSA tests but was determined from an ultrasound exam.

Sharp asked when was the last time I had my prostate checked and I replied it was done recently, within the past 90 days, through a rectal exam and PSA, test and the results were negative. He then said I should have a follow-up test with the ultrasound. He also mentioned a biopsy procedure in which samples of prostate tissue are extracted for microscopy analysis to test for a malignant prostate. Bill insisted that I make an appointment soon with my urologist to have the ultrasound test because it was more reliable. I could see he was a strong advocate of advising men to have their prostates checked annually through that procedure.

Bill motivated me and I became convinced to call my urologist. Sharp scared me to the point where I called and made an appointment that very day. In the back of my mind were thoughts that both my grandfather and father had been detected with prostate cancer upon their deaths and neither one was aware he was stricken with the terrible disease. At the time I was 60 and in great physical shape and hoping I'd never contract the disease.

When I made the appointment I asked the urologist's secretary to schedule me for both the ultrasound and biopsy exams. I had no known symptoms but was full of anxiety and wanted to make sure I didn't have the disease. The secretary said I would have to make my requests known to the urologist when I visited with him. In his office, the urologist asked for a urine sample and gave me a rectal exam. In addition, he wrote a prescription for me to have my blood drawn. He agreed to schedule, on separate days, the two exams I had requested.

The first exam was the ultrasound, which was done by a female technician at Sparrow Hospital. She used a computerized procedure to take many pictures of my prostate while I was lying on a gurney. That was an easy test that lasted about 30 minutes.

The biopsy, meanwhile, was performed a few days later by the urologist and his nurse in a medical surgery facility. His exam was more pervasive. Samples of tissue were removed from the prostate and sent to the lab to be microscopically analyzed for cancer. The procedure wasn't painful, but each time the doctor skillfully inserted the instrument through my rectum to extract a sample, I anticipated pain — but never felt any. The doctor called me two days later to inform me the results were negative. I was greatly relieved and he encouraged me to continue to follow my exercise and diet routines. We agreed that I should have the same procedures performed the following year.

Re-tests show cancer

In March 1993 I went through similar procedures with the same urologist. I became a bit nervous and suspicious when he called a few days later requesting me to make an appointment with him to receive the results. I didn't know what to expect. I thought that he only called me on the phone to give the results as he had done a year earlier. But now he wanted me in his office. During the visit he told me I had malignant prostate cancer. I couldn't believe what I was hearing. I became light-headed, a feeling I hadn't experienced since I was in Basic Training in the Army and one day received a series of medical shots and later fainted while standing in 100-degree heat.

I didn't feel good about what I was hearing from my urologist. Had he made a mistake? I understood that I wasn't infallible, but the news was horrifying to me. I tried to remain composed as the doctor described the cancer and showed me pictures from the ultrasound test and also explained the results of the biopsy. At the time I didn't know too much about prostate cancer, except that it could metastasize to other parts of the body and cause death. I was concerned and afraid about what would happen next.

The urologist told me he believed the cancer was localized and hadn't spread to the lymph nodes, but he couldn't be certain until he had done additional testing. He asked me to bring my wife to the next appointment so together we could discuss the situation and decide what the appropriate treatment should be. I started to think that maybe there was more to my situation than I had been told.

Naturally, I had planned to tell Noreese the distressing news as soon as I arrived home, but now I also had to ask her to accompany me on my next visit to the doctor's office. That was unknown territory for both of us and I didn't want to put her through undue stress. She accepted the news calmly and asked several questions to which I didn't know the answers. We agreed to write down our questions and present them to the doctor upon my next visit.

At the next appointment the doctor again explained the results of my diagnosis and the location of the cancer.

371

We asked him many questions that he answered patiently. One of my important questions was, what causes prostate cancer? The doctor responded that the evidence to date was inconclusive and he didn't want to speculate about possible relationships. He did say that there was some evidence suggesting that the incidence of prostate cancer among African-American men was higher than in the majority male population.

The doctor explained that the reason for his second appointment was to discuss possible treatment. He indicated he wanted Noreese in attendance so she could understand the cancer and its treatments. He described three types of treatments:

- Radical prostatectomy: surgically removing the prostate. He said since he believed the cancer was in its infancy and hadn't spread, that procedure would remove the cancer from my body. He said the risk factors associated with the procedure are impotence and incontinence. He indicated he would be as careful as possible during surgery to spare the sex nerve to not cause impotence. He said I'd be hospitalized three or four days and would be home for about six weeks for recuperation. The doctor recommended the procedure.

- Radiation: using a machine to administer radiation to the cancerous prostate. The doctor said the procedure requires daily treatment over a period of about six weeks. The side effects were incontinence and impotence. He said if the radiation didn't remove the cancer and the disease spread, surgery would be almost useless.

- Cryosurgery: a freezing technique used to destroy cancer cells. He said that technique was in the experimental stage and he wouldn't recommend it.

The doctor gave us some literature to read. He asked us to discuss the three alternative treatments and call him in a day or two with our decision.

Getting a second opinion

Noreese and I did discuss the treatments and had tentatively settled on the radical prostatectomy. We believed it was the surest method for removing the cancer from my body. But we also concurred that we should seek a second opinion. I called the doctor and told him we were leaning toward surgery but wanted a second opinion. He recommended that we make an appointment with a female urologist at Sparrow who was an expert in radiation treatment.

She was a very nice person and recommended I take no action at that time. She said since it appeared the cancer was localized and in its infancy, I should simply monitor it annually with my urologist. She said the type of cancer I had was slow growing and whenever it showed evidence of new growth I should make a decision about some form of treatment. She said if I lived in Europe my insurance company wouldn't pay medical coverage for treatment because the cancer was in the early stage of development. We appreciated her advice and I felt somewhat relieved to know that, based on the evaluation, my cancer didn't seem to be as perilous as I had believed.

Advice from survivors

I began to receive unanticipated helpful advice from friends and others who I was totally unaware were prostate cancer survivors. Neither did I know they were aware of my situation. What I found interesting was that each of them agreed with the treatment option Noreese and I had already chosen. I then called the male urologist to schedule my surgery at Sparrow Hospital. It was set for the next Wednesday. On Monday of that week I had lunch with a friend who was a cancer survivor. He told me he was disappointed with the results of his surgery, which he had in a different city. He explained that his surgeon had assured him prior to the operation that he would be able to spare the sex nerve. He learned, however, in the post-operative recovery room, that the surgeon was unsuccessful in sparing the nerve.

The friend mentioned the work of Dr. Patrick Walsh of Johns Hopkins University in Baltimore, Md. He was a pioneer in discovering the nerve-sparing radical prostatectomy, a surgical procedure that reduces injury to the sex nerve. The friend suggested that I should call Dr. Walsh's office and try to make an appointment, although it might be difficult seeing him because he had an international reputation and was a very busy man. However, he said, it was worth the chance. I later learned that Walsh was the long-time chairman of the Brady Urological Institute at Johns Hopkins.

I called Walsh's office on Monday afternoon, three days before my scheduled surgery. I identified myself to his secretary and asked if he was available to speak with me. I was surprised when she connected me directly to him. I introduced myself and explained my situation. Walsh asked me for some biographical data and inquired about the medical procedures I had undertaken to detect the prostate cancer. After hearing the results, Walsh said, "Mr. Underwood, you are a lucky man because I will do your surgery."

"Normally I'm not in the office," he said. "I'm either involved in surgery, research, or speaking engagements. You caught me on a day when I was in the office and have a surgical opening. He said if I could come to Johns Hopkins on Thursday afternoon he would do the surgery on Friday. I said I'd be there. He asked me to bring my medical charts and have the American Red Cross send two pints of blood that I already had given in preparation for my scheduled surgery at Sparrow Hospital.

I arrived at Johns Hopkins that Thursday and was admitted after meeting Walsh in his office. He was soft spoken but to the point. He appeared highly confident and patient. He reviewed the charts and gave me a physical exam. He wrote orders for a series of tests and had several doctors, nurses, technicians, and the anesthesiologist visiting and attending to me throughout the evening. He explained that the operation would take about two hours and he didn't anticipate any complications. He indicated that Johns Hopkins was a teaching hospital and there would be a team of doctors and fellows in the surgical room with him.

The operation

At 6:30 a.m. Friday morning two nurses entered my room and injected a needle into my arm to start an intravenous procedure. A technician came in a half hour later with a gurney and asked me to lie on it. He rolled me into the operating room where Walsh and his team were already assembled, wearing green uniforms and masks over their mouths. It was my first experience in an operating room and the temperature was cool. I remember changing from one gurney to another one that was directly under some huge ceiling lights. I recall the anesthesiologist asking me to sit up so he could give me a spinal shot. The last thing I remember was Walsh asking me to count to 10. I started counting but don't know if I got that far.

When I woke up I was in the recovery room. Noreese was there. She had arrived that morning. Walsh came in and said the surgery was successful and the cancer hadn't spread to other parts of my body. I was moved to my room where I was hospitalized for seven days. Each morning Walsh and his team of doctors and fellows would visit with me to check on my condition. I walked the corridors several times a day with the aid of a walker. After a week I was discharged and given the following instructions:

- No lifting for six weeks of any object weighing more than five pounds.
- Practice squeezing my sphincter muscles several times a day for six weeks.

- No sex for six weeks.
- Keep the monthly telephone interviews scheduled with Walsh to discuss my progress.
- Take daily walks.
- Return to his office within six months for a check-up.

After my second check-up with Walsh, he suggested that I could continue to visit him for my annual check-up or he could refer me to a colleague, Dr. Ananias Diokno, a urologist, in Royal Oak, Mich. I chose Dr. Diokno because it was more convenient and less expensive. I still receive a letter from Dr. Walsh annually requesting the results of my PSA.

I also have seen Dr. Leonard Zuckerman, a Lansing urologist. I would recommend Drs. Walsh, Diokno, and Zuckerman highly to any man needing a prostate exam. I also am very pleased with my family doctors, Rafael Javier and Mary Sharp. I was Mary's elementary school physical education teacher at Glencairn in East Lansing and now she does an outstanding job teaching me about healthy living.

Gratitude magnified after insurance info

I feel indebted to Bill Sharp (not related to Mary Sharp) for giving me the awareness of the ultrasound and biopsy as two effective procedures in the detection of prostate cancer. I have learned that the disease, which is the most widespread cancer among American men and second leading cancer killer among them, isn't easily detectable through a rectal exam and a PSA. Bill gave me the inspiration and motivation to request the ultrasound and biopsy procedures from my urologist in a timely fashion.

Without his unselfishness and strong encouragement, I may not be alive today. The reason I make that assertion is based on some new information I learned about my cancer from an insurance company in 1996. I applied for some additional life insurance. After several weeks, I was approved with a rate more costly than I expected. I called the insurance actuary to find out the reason for the expensive rate and told him I probably was in better health than he was. The actuary responded that I was correct and the company knew that, but the reason for the high cost was that my prostate cancer was the fastest growing cancer.

I hadn't heard that before and mentioned the advice given to me by the female urologist who said I shouldn't take any action, but rather monitor the cancer annually with my urologist, because the cancer was slow growing. The actuary repeated that the medical results his company had received from Dr. Walsh showed I had the fastest growing type of cancer. I called Dr. Walsh and he confirmed the validity of what the actuary told me. I felt frightened all over again and felt so grateful to Bill Sharp for his thoughtfulness and caring advice.

Recommendations

Here are some recommendations I make in view of what I've been through:
- Every man 40 and older should have an annual prostate exam, preferably including tests through an ultrasound, biopsy, or both.
- If prostate cancer is detected, the man should get a second opinion and meet with cancer survivors to learn about their experiences.
- Read as much as you can about prostate cancer to learn what it's all about. Dr. Patrick Walsh has just written a book for the layman that tells everything he knows about the disease.
- If you aren't already doing so, start an exercise program and reduce your fat intake. Although the cause of prostate cancer is unknown, there is evidence suggesting it is higher in countries that have diets high in animal fats.

Another diagnosis brings bad news

I was diagnosed with Type II diabetes in the spring of 2000. I joined 10 of my family members known to have been afflicted with the disease for many years. Similar to prostate cancer, diabetes is a most serious disease and there is no cure. Yet it can be controlled. It is a disease in which, in layman's terms, the body doesn't properly use glucose (sugar) for energy. Yet if the sugar level remains too high, over a period of time it can cause blindness, high blood pressure, heart attack, stroke, amputation of limbs, and death. It is a devastating disease.

It has been estimated that approximately 17 million Americans have diabetes. But out of that number about six million don't know they have it. Diabetes is an insidious and subtle disease that has many symptoms, but a person may be afflicted without knowing it and without having any of the related symptoms of blurred vision, poor circulation, frequent urination, slow healing cuts and bruises, bladder infections, and numbness in the hands and feet.

I had no obvious symptoms when my diabetes was detected. Since I was keenly aware that diabetes was prevalent in my family, I requested my doctor to check for it as part of my annual medical examination. In addition, I used Diastix, an over the counter test for glucose in the urine. All of the tests were negative until that Saturday morning in June 2000 when several tests from the Diastix showed the glucose level was higher than normal.

My doctor's office was closed so I took a chance and called the dietician at Sparrow Hospital, who was kind and gracious to talk with me. She advised me to see my doctor as soon as possible. I asked her about what foods to eat and she gave me a tentative meal plan until I could see the doctor. She was a wonderful person and freely reached out to me when I was full of anxiety.

I saw my doctor, internist Rafael Javier, who examined me, gave me a urine test, and wrote a prescription for a blood test at a lab. A blood test is the most accurate method of testing for diabetes. He later told me that although I was a borderline Type II diabetic, with medical assistance I could control the disease. He referred me to a diabetes class, gave me some medication, and referred me to a dietician for immediate help with my meal planning. Dr. Javier also encouraged me to walk a minimum of 30 minutes a day and to adhere to my diet.

I do everything the doctor asked me to do because diabetes is nothing to play around with. More than 2 million people die each year in America from diabetes complications, making it the fifth leading cause of deaths in the United States. There is not any conclusive evidence about the cause of the disease, but some medical professionals believe there is a relationship between diet, being overweight, and heredity in the incidence of diabetes.

I agree with Dr. Javier that diabetes can be controlled through daily care and personal attention. I have made the following practices a part of my daily life:

- Eat a healthy diet in order to control the sugar I ingest. I eat lowfat foods and count the carbohydrates listed on containers.
- I seldom eat sweets and if I do it's a small piece and I trade it for something else.
- I walk at least 30 minutes each day.
- I try to eat breakfast, lunch, and dinner at a regular time each day.
- I use a glucose monitor and test my blood sugar two and three times daily.
- I visit my doctor as much as I need to in order to have things checked.

I would strongly advise any person with diabetes to adhere to their doctor's instructions. If a person is aware of a history of diabetes being in their family I would urge him or her to get an annual blood test as a preventative measure.

CHAPTER 12:

FRONT-ROW SEAT FOR GREAT GRID, CAGE MOMENTS

Half-century of exciting teams, coaches

MICHIGAN STATE HAS HAD SOME GREAT FOOTball and basketball teams and players in its history and I was fortunate enough to be around to see many of them.

Of course, there were some glory years long before I arrived on the scene as a student and walk-on football athlete in the mid-'50s and there are sure to be many more in the years to come.

It would be a privilege to have been able to see some of the earlier teams, such as football squads during the Charles Bachman and Clarence "Biggie" Munn football coaching eras and basketball squads under the leadership of such coaches as Chester Brewer and Ben VanAlstyne.

Brewer was athletics director and head football coach from 1903-1910, 1917, and 1919. He finished with a record of 58-23-7. His successor, John Macklin, had a fine record also, 29-5, from 1911-1915. Jim Crowley, a member of the fabled Four Horsemen backfield at Notre Dame, had a 22-8-2 record over the next four years, and left in 1933 to take a coaching job at Fordham, where he became architect of the famous "Seven Blocks of Granite" front line. The Bachman era followed, he piled up a 70-34-10 mark through 1946.

Those records are impressive, but things really became special when Munn took over and his teams were 9-0 and won national championships in 1951 and 1952. In 1953 the team suffered its only loss, 6-0 to Purdue in West Lafayette, Ind., breaking the Spartans' 28-game winning streak. But it was the Spartans who, as Big Ten co-champion, represented the conference in the Rose Bowl game in Pasadena, Calif., beating UCLA, 28-20. That was the game I watched on television when I was in the Army at Fort Bragg, N.C., and which, as I said earlier, was instrumental in my ultimate decision to enroll at Michigan State.

Bachman and Munn's teams were filled with outstanding athletes, including: Jack Breslin, George Guerre, Lynn Chandnois, Sonny Grandelius, Tom Yewcic, Robert Carey, Ellis Duckett, Jim Ellis, Don Coleman, LeRoy Bolden, Billie Wells, Henry Bullough, Larry Fowler, and Bill Quinlan. They played before my arrival and it would have been a real thrill for me to see them.

Some of the All-Americans who played for Munn were: guards Ed Bagdon, Frank Kush, and Don Mason; halfbacks Bolden, Chandnois, Grandelius, and Don McAuliffe; ends Duckett, Carey, Don Dohoney, and Dorne Dibble; tackles Coleman and Larry Fowler; quarterback Al Dorow; defensive back Ellis; and center Dick Tamburo. Munn, who was coach of the year in 1952, was elected to the College Football Hall of Fame in 1959.

Daugherty era lasted 19 years

Duffy Daugherty became the coach in 1954 and by the time he stepped down after the 1972 season his teams had posted a 109-69-5 record in 19 seasons. He was coach of the year in 1955 and 1965 and, in 1984 was elected to the College Football Hall of Fame.

His 1955 team was one of the best in Spartans history.

The 9-1 squad beat UCLA 17-14 in the 1956 Rose Bowl game on "Golden Toe" Dave Kaiser's field goal with seven seconds remaining. The Spartans were named national champion that season, outscoring opponents 236-69. The only loss came on the road in Ann Arbor, 14-7, to a Michigan team filled with standouts that included All-America end Ron Kramer. The 14 points were the most scored against MSU that season.

I was a freshman then and, since I wasn't recruited, I was a walk-on with the 175-member freshman team. The only time I could watch the varsity was during its games on Saturday. Freshmen practiced on what are now the soccer fields. The varsity practiced in the same general area where its works out today, adjacent to the Duffy Daugherty Building. Mason was coach of the freshman squad and he had two assistants. Only the 30 scholarship players from the huge roster received attention from the coaches, with the rest of us trying somehow to get noticed.

Watching the varsity play was an exciting experience that I'll never forget. It was my first time seeing a major collegiate football game in person. While in high school I attended the annual Thanksgiving Day game between Alabama State and Tuskegee, two traditional black colleges at the Division II level. Michigan State was strong on both sides of the ball. Clarence Peaks was a powerful senior left halfback. He is the only running back I ever saw at the college ranks who was a triple threat from the left halfback position. He could run, pass, and punt. He was given the ball frequently on critical third- and fourth-down situations — and he made a first down most of the time.

Despite the fact that both he and Earl Morrall were effective passers and punters, there were some gutsy calls and tense moments when Peaks was handed the ball on third or fourth down and seven yards to go. He would run an end sweep behind several outstanding blockers. It was a sight to see and the crowd went wild every time he made the first down.

Morrall, also a senior, was the quarterback. He was an accurate passer and ran on occasion. His greatest strength was faking the ball to his backs in the multiple offense. His wizardry opened up the pass routes for sure-handed players like Kaiser, Peaks, John Lewis, Jimmy Hinesly, and Don Zysk. Other great players on that team were captain and senior guard Buck Nystrom; senior offensive tackle Norm Masters; sophomore right halfback Walt Kowalczyk; and senior fullback Gerry Planutis.

Planutis was one of the most surprising and effective runners. He weighed just 165 pounds, yet served mostly as a blocking back. He was seldom given the ball but usually got good yardage. He was a tough dude. The center was senior Joe Badaczewski and senior Leo Haidys was the right guard. It was a senior-oriented team. The players had skill, unity, pride, and made few mistakes.

For some reason, maybe because it was my first year at Michigan State, I remember that season and the outcomes. You couldn't tell by the first two games how good we would become. We beat Indiana 20-13 in the opener then lost to Michigan. After that came victories over Stanford (38-14), Notre Dame (21-7), Illinois (22-7), Wisconsin (27-0), Purdue (27-0), Minnesota (42-14), and Marquette (33-0), before the classic triumph over UCLA in the Rose Bowl. Daugherty's six teams in the '50s overall were 35-19-1.

I watched one of the most glory-filled and energizing periods in Spartans football history from 1955-65. The Spartans were one of the most popular and nationally ranked teams annually in NCAA football. Daugherty and his staff were excellent recruiters. They took advantage of the segregated South by recruiting outstanding black prospects who couldn't attend white institutions in the South. Michigan State fans expected their team to win and they weren't often disappointed. I'll never forget that successful decade. It is embedded in my memory bank forever.

Daugherty's teams won national championships

in 1955, 1957, 1965, and 1966. His record in the '60s was 59-34-3. In his first two decades, through 1969, the Spartans were 10-4-2 against Michigan and 10-4-1 against Notre Dame, with the tie being the infamous 10-10 game. I wasn't able to see the two championship teams much in person in the '60s, only when they played away games on television. I was working in game program sales in 1965 and when we finished our work the games were nearly over. Since I worked at Northern Michigan University in 1966, I wound up missing most of the two greatest back-to-back football seasons in university history.

Daugherty coached some exceptional All-Americans, many of whom played in the National Football League and some of whom are now in the College Football Hall of Fame: tailback Eric Allen; fullbacks Planutis, Bob Apisa, and George Saimes; guards Dave Behrman, Earl Lattimer, Carl Nystrom, Ron Saul, and Joe DeLamielleure; defensive backs Allen Brenner

Bubba Smith is a giant next to me.

and Bill Simpson; offensive tackles Masters, Jerry West, and Ed Budde; defensive tackle Ron Curl; center Dan Currie; tight end Billie Joe Dupree; linebacker Ron Goovert; halfbacks Kowalczyk, Clint Jones, and Sherm Lewis; quarterbacks Morrall, Steve Juday, and Dean Look; middle guard Harold Lucas; defensive end Charles "Bubba" Smith; wide receiver Gene Washington; safety Brad Van Pelt; roverback George Webster; and end Sam Williams.

There were a number of players who didn't receive All-America recognition but were most important to their teams' overall success and recognized by the fans as stars. Many played in the pros for 10 years or more. Such standouts include:

- Herb Adderley, a running back and defensive back at MSU from 1957-60. He was drafted by the Green Bay Packers in 1961 and played 12 years with them and Dallas. He played in three Super Bowls and was on three championship teams. He was inducted into the Pro Football Hall of Fame in 1980 and joined there in 2003 by DeLamielleure.

- Morten Andersen, an outstanding place-kicker from Denmark who graduated from a high school in Indianapolis. He was drafted by New Orleans in 1982 and played 13 years with that club. He also played for Atlanta and the New York Giants and remains a standout. He is a possible future pro hall of famer.

- Gary Ballman, a right-halfback who was drafted by Pittsburgh in 1962. He played with the Steelers for five years, then with Philadelphia, the New York Giants, and Minnesota for six more years.

- Carl Banks, a hard-nosed linebacker drafted in 1984 by the Giants. He played there until 1992, then was in the league three more years, playing with Washington and Cleveland. He was one of the most studious players I ever met.

- Daniel Bass played linebacker for the Spartans. He started out in the Canadian Football League in 1980 with Toronto and also played for Calgary and Edmonton, spending 10 years in the CFL. He was the only player who ever told me outright he didn't want a college degree. He felt he didn't need one. He had a sense for the ball and always was one of the leading tacklers every game.
- Al Dorow was a quarterback in the early '50s. He was drafted by Washington in 1954 and played there three years. He played six more years in the pros: with Philadelphia, CFL teams British Columbia and Toronto, plus the New York Jets and Buffalo.
- Elison Kelly was a guard in the '50s. He was drafted by the Giants in 1959 and played 14 years in the pros, including with Hamilton and Toronto of the CFL.
- Greg Montgomery was a punter in the late '80s. He was drafted by Houston in 1988 and played there until 1993 before spending three more years in the NFL, for Detroit and Baltimore.
- Jim Ninowski was Morrall's successor at quarterback. He was drafted by the Cleveland Browns in 1958 and played 12 years in the league, including with Detroit, Washington, and New Orleans.
- Bill Quinlan played end in the early '50s. He played for the Hamilton TigerCats of the CFL, plus with Cleveland, Green Bay, Philadelphia, Detroit, and Washington of the NFL in a 10-year pro career.
- Andre Rison played wide receiver under George Perles. He was drafted by Indianapolis in 1989 and later played with Atlanta, Cleveland, Jacksonville, Green Bay, Kansas City, and Oakland in a 12-year career.
- George Saimes, a fullback for Daugherty, was

drafted by Buffalo in 1963 and played with the Bills for seven years, then three years with Denver.

- Rick Saul, a linebacker and defensive end for Daugherty, played for the Los Angeles Rams from 1970 to 1981.
- Ron Saul played offensive tackle and guard for Daugherty. He was drafted by Houston and played with the Oilers from 1970-75. He closed out his career at Washington, playing there from 1976-81.
- Lonnie Young, a cornerback, played for the Cardinals in St. Louis and Phoenix from 1985-91, then five years total with the New York Jets and San Diego.

Basketball program starts slow

The basketball program, meanwhile, had an inauspicious start. The program began in 1899 without a coach, but the sport had only been developed eight years earlier by Dr. James Naismith, an instructor at the Training School of the International YMCA College in Springfield, Mass. The 1899 Spartans lost the only two games they played. Charles W. Bemis coached the 1900-1901 team that won five and lost two. George Denman coached from 1901-03, compiling a distinguished 11-0 record. His team beat Alma College 102-3. He also doubled as the MSU head football coach during his two-year tenure.

Brewer became the jack-of-all-trades in 1904, coaching the football and basketball teams, as well as being athletics director. His football record was 58-23-7. In basketball he retains the best winning percentage in Spartans history, .736, with a 70-25 record, from 1904-10.

VanAlstyne coached from 1926-49 and posted a career mark of 231-163 (.586). He had become the golf coach when I enrolled in 1955. Forrest "Forddy" Anderson was the basketball coach then and it was during his tenure the Spartans captured their first Big Ten championship. In fact, they put together back-to-back title seasons, in 1956-57 and 1957-58. Both teams played in the NCAA tournament and the '57 squad reached the Final Four. He coached some notable athletes, as did his successors, John Bennington (1965-69) and Gus Ganakas (1969-75).

Memorable 19-year string for Heathcote

Jud Heathcote succeeded Ganakas in 1976 and coached for 19 years. His 1978-79 team was one of the most sensational I have ever seen. Led by Earvin "Magic" Johnson, the most dominant player I ever saw, and smooth Gregory Kelser, plus sure-shooter Jay Vincent, the team was awesome and dazzling. Besides winning the league championship, it won the school's first NCAA crown, defeating the Larry Bird-led Indiana State team.

MSU lost six regular season games that year — by a total of 26 points. Five of the losses were by a point or two and the largest margin was 18 by Northwestern. Every game was exciting and watching Magic bring the ball up the court was stimulating. And his fakes and sharp and sometimes no-look passes roused the crowd, especially his alley-oops to Kelser, who'd slam the ball home. Mike Brkovich, Terry Donnelly, Vincent, and Ron Charles were an effective supporting cast, scoring from short- and long-range.

I can't forget the four games our team played in the 1979 NCAA tournament. The first was in Murfreesboro, Tenn. against Lamar University of Beaumont, Texas. The media promoted the height of the Lamar players and their team's overall success. Their players were whooping it up in the media as if they already had won the tournament. I know many MSU alumni and boosters who believed the media and felt our team was at a height disadvantage. Once the ball was tipped, Magic and company took over. We won the game 95-64.

The second game was against a good Notre Dame team. It was close all the way and reviewing the film it would show Kelly Tripucka bumping Magic Johnson down to the floor on a time-out call. It appeared to be intimidation similar to a sucker punch. I'm sure he thought Magic would retaliate in some way and get penalized but, being the classy guy he is, Johnson simply got up and never displayed any emotion. He continued to score and Michigan State won 80-68.

The third game was against the University of Pennsylvania of the Ivy League and it was a blowout all the way. The Spartans won easily, 101-67. The fourth game was the title game, which the media built up as if it were a heavyweight championship boxing match that featured superstars Johnson in one corner and Bird in the other. With all the fan excitement, the sharp shooting of the two and their supporting casts, plus the intenseness throughout, it wasn't a place for a person with a weak heart. Our team prevailed in one of the greatest games I ever have seen at any level, winning 75-64. Magic and Larry were truly All-Americans in every aspect of the game. They were fierce competitors.

'Magic' excitement started in junior high

Seven years earlier, Athletics Director Burt Smith mentioned to me that there was a remarkable junior high school basketball player in Lansing by the name of Earvin Johnson. I believe Burt's daughter was a teacher then at Johnson's school, or at least within the Lansing school system. Smith asked me on a couple Friday nights to accompany him to watch Johnson play.

I had worked 60 hours or more during the week and had a family waiting for me to come home for dinner. Since Noreese and I both worked, Friday was a big family night at our home, so I declined the invitations. I thought to myself, no one in junior high could be that great to entice the interest of the MSU athletics director. I further thought Burt was going there primarily to appease his daughter.

In a few years, Earvin entered Everett High School. I kept hearing from different people and reading the sports pages about his basketball feats but I wasn't ready to give up a night during a busy week to go watch a high school basketball game. Besides, that was the role of Ganakas and his staff.

When Johnson was a high school senior, Everett played at East Lansing on a Friday night. My son, David, who was a junior at East Lansing High, bought two tickets for the sold-out game and I was his guest. During the first five minutes I had difficulty believing what I was seeing. From the opening tip, Johnson — who got the nickname "Magic" hung on him by *Lansing State Journal* sports writer Fred Stabley Jr. — controlled the game. He would dribble down the court and when he reached the top of the key he'd shoot and the ball would hit nothing but net. Or he would look left, fake, and pass to a teammate on the right side near the basket. Or he'd fake to someone on the left and drive to the basket for an easy lay-up.

He was an amazing athlete and his basketball skills were far above those of others his age. It was a lopsided game at halftime in favor of Everett, so much so that Coach George Fox benched Johnson after the second-half tip. Earvin must have scored 20 points already. You would have thought he'd relax on the bench and enjoy the game, but instead he was trying to help Fox coach the rest of the way. He was up and down the bench, yelling instructions to his teammates. It was a sight to see.

The best description that came to my mind that night was that Johnson's ball-handling skills resembled those of Goose Tatum of the Harlem Globetrotters. He was a wizard with the ball and made his teammates better because they had to be alert all the time he had the ball. He never telegraphed his passes, which were quick and crisp. If a player wasn't alert, likely he might have been embarrassed with a passed ball that hit him in the face or another part of his body. Tatum was such a dominant and intelligent player and so was Johnson.

I was the assistant athletics director in charge of the student-athlete support services when Johnson enrolled at Michigan State in the fall of 1977. I was responsible for monitoring athletes' academic progress and all freshmen were required to enroll in my one credit orientation course. Earvin had a pleasant personality, attended his classes, and kept academic appointments with his professors and me.

During his two years at MSU, I don't ever recall receiving any complaints about his lack of class attendance or other off the court mischief. If he had such problems, they never came to my attention and one of my chief responsibilities was over student-athletes welfare issues.

I was amazed at the number of faculty members in various academic disciplines who asked me to have Johnson enroll in their classes. I never did inquire about their motives because I had no intentions of passing the information on to him. I wanted him to follow the plan outlined by his academic advisor so he would take the courses necessary for progress toward his degree, which was a Big Ten requirement.

Johnson left Michigan State after his sophomore year, making himself eligible for the National Basketball Association draft. He signed with the Los Angeles Lakers, where he carried the same level of enthusiasm, flair, and excitement that he had demonstrated as an amateur. He was a high-profile player whose successful style brought a renewed interest among fans of the pro game.

Johnson is a special individual, as demonstrated by his past, current and future presence in the social, financial, sports, and political arenas internationally. He is the highest profile athlete ever to enroll at MSU. He was among the first basketball players in the country to

Magic Johnson hugs Terry Donnelly after a regional
tournament victory over Notre Dame in 1979.

leave school early for the pros. He was instrumental in projecting a positive international image for the university.

Every place I visit, if folks find out I'm from Michigan State the first person they ask about is Earvin "Magic" Johnson. They get very excited when I say I know him and once served as his athletics academic advisor. He is the most recognizable Spartan in the world.

The second person I'm often asked about is Steve Smith, the two-time All-America basketball guard at the university. Besides being an outstanding person, great player in all phases of the game at both the collegiate and professional levels, he is a philanthropist. He donated the lead gift to Michigan State, $2.5 million, to help build the $7.5 million Clara Bell Smith Student-Athlete Academic Center. Steve's gift was the largest to an institution of higher learning ever given by a professional athlete. The center was named in honor of Smith's mother, Clara Bell. It houses a state of the art support center that provides tutoring services, study rooms, academic advice, computer labs, and meeting rooms. Smith visits the campus annually and always generously supports MSU with his appearances.

Izzo's star quickly rises to the top

Based on reactions I have gotten from people everywhere I have visited over the years, I would say that besides Magic and Steve Smith, those who have done much more than anyone else to project a positive image for the university around the world are Bubba Smith and Dr. John Hannah. And now basketball coach Tom Izzo is quickly moving up to the top of the class. He currently is the hottest name among our alumni and friends.

I don't think anyone could envision the success Izzo would experience after he was appointed to his job for the 1995-96 season, except perhaps Izzo himself. Many people asked for my opinion as to whether I thought he was ready for the position and if he could win. Was the institution making a mistake by not doing a national search? I was up front with everyone who asked me such questions. I said I believed Izzo was the right person for the job and would be a successful coach.

In 1992 Heathcote supported me for the athletics director position on the condition that I would name Izzo his replacement if I, in fact, became the new A.D. But that job went to Merrily Baker. Heathcote pushed for Izzo over the next three years before resigning in 1995. Credit for hiring Izzo really goes to Heathcote, trustee Joel Ferguson, and President Gordon Guyer. They made it happen. I knew three things about Izzo that convinced me to believe in him as a coach: He was an excellent recruiter; he worked hard and long hours; and he cared about athletes. Those are three essential qualities for any successful coach. In his third year his Spartans won the Big Ten championship. He had arrived.

Izzo had some incredible teams from 1997-98 through 2000-2001, but the 1999-2000 squad was by far the best, winning both the Big Ten and NCAA tournament championships. That team had superior talent and a blue-collar work ethic. It was led by iron-man point guard Mateen Cleaves, a durable competitor; plus sharp-shooting forward Morris Peterson; guards Charlie Bell and leaping Jason Richardson; plus forwards A.J. Granger and Andre Hutson. The Spartans had a 32-7 record.

It was beautiful to see them score off the fast break. With Cleaves as the master ball-handler, bringing the ball up the court and passing to Peterson, Granger, Bell, or David Thomas for either a three-point shot, dunk, lay-up, or jumper, that was a fun team to watch.

I traveled with the team for a few away games each season. One of them was against Indiana in Bloomington, Ind., on Feb. 26, 2000, when the team's record was 21-6. The coaches and players were aware that they needed to win the remaining four regular

Tom Izzo

season games to get a high seed in the NCAA tourney. It was a tight game against a well-coached and proficient squad typical of Bobby Knight-coached Hoosier teams. The lead changed many times in a sea of red-shirted fans.

The game was tied at the end of regulation and continued to be close in overtime. Indiana scored a basket near the end of the overtime to go up by two points. The Spartans had the last shot but missed at the buzzer, losing 81-79. It was pandemonium in the stands and on the floor. The Hoosiers had beaten the favored Spartans.

In the Michigan State locker room there were tears, obvious expressions of pain, disappointment and frustration demonstrated by both players and coaches. As I tried to console them I never heard a word of criticism. There was no blame. It was more like a family coming together during a crisis. There was a genuine feeling of love and unity. In between the tears, the players and coaches supported and tried to comfort each other with hugs, pats on the back, and words of encouragement.

The determined leadership from the coaches and captains set the tone for a quick recovery because Minnesota was next in just four days. Observing the level of unity, strength and loyalty, I knew that was a very special team. It didn't lose another game that season, winning 11 in a row against some formidable opponents, including the championship game in Indianapolis on April 3.

In the NCAA tournament I thought the game

against Iowa State at the Palace of Auburn Hills north of Detroit on March 25 was the most difficult. Iowa State had a good team, featuring three outstanding shooters in Marcus Fizer, Jamaal Tinsley, and Michael Nurse. The Spartans countered with Hutson, Peterson, Granger, Cleaves, and Bell. Iowa State led 34-31 at the half then the teams traded baskets until late in the second half when the Spartans gradually showed their superiority and won 75-64. It was exciting and the fans surely got their money's worth.

Prior to defeating Syracuse 75-58 and Iowa State at Auburn Hills, MSU blew past Valparaiso 65-38 then beat Utah 73-61 in the first round of games, played in Cleveland, Ohio. In the Final Four in Indianapolis, MSU defeated Big Ten rival Wisconsin in a tough physical game, 53-41. But the best and most exciting contest of the entire NCAA tourney was the championship match-up against a highly-skilled and efficient University of

I was proud to welcome all-time boxing great Muhammad Ali at a Spartan basketball game.

Florida team. The Spartans prevailed in a thrilling and energetically played game, 89-76. The game was undecided until the waning minutes when the proficient play of Cleaves, who got hurt in a collision near halftime, came back in the second half to lead his team to victory.

The game reminded me of the Magic Johnson years. Cleaves wasn't alone in his adroitness, though. The three-point sharp-shooting of Peterson, Granger, and Bell was exciting and effective. Hutson, Richardson, and David Thomas played important roles in all phases of the game. Other contributors were Mike Chappell, Adam Ballinger, Aloysius Anagonye, Steve Cherry, Mat Ishbia, and Brandon Smith. The talent and chemistry that comprised that championship unit were exceptional and I'm pleased to have been part of that moment as the A.D.

Izzo's 2004-05 team was another that went to the Final Four, winding up with a 26-7 record. That squad included standout seniors Alan Anderson, Chris Hill, and Kelvin Torbert.

Many big-name Spartan cagers

Michigan State's first basketball All-American was Chester Aubuchon in 1940, coached by VanAlstyne. Forddy Anderson had four All-Americans, Julius McCoy in 1956, Jack Quiggle in 1957, Johnny Green in 1959, and Horace Walker in 1960. There wasn't another All-American until Ganakas' Ralph Simpson received the recognition in 1970 and, later, Michael Robinson in 1974 and Terry Furlow in 1976.

There were a bevy of All-America honors during Heathcote's tenure. Magic Johnson was an All-American in 1978 and 1979; Kelser in 1979; Sam Vincent in 1985; Scott Skiles in 1986; Steve Smith in 1990 and 1991; and Shawn Respert in 1994 and 1995. Although Izzo has only been the coach since 1995-96, Cleaves received All-America honors three times (1998-2000), followed by Peterson (2000), Bell (2001), and Richardson (2002).

Scoring averages don't make All-Americans but they usually are a prime consideration. Here are players who averaged at least 15 points a game without getting any All-America recognition: Bob Brannum (1948); Al Ferrari (1953); Bob Anderegg (1959); Lance Olson (1960); Dick Hall (1961); Ted Williams (1963); Larry Hedden (1958); Art Schwarm (1961); Pete Gent (1963).

Also, Fred Thomann (1964); Stan Washington, Bill Curtis, Marcus Sanders, and Matthew Aitch (1967); Lee Lafayette (1968); Rudy Benjamin (1971); Bill Kilgore (1973); Lindsay Hairston (1974); Bob Chapman (1977); Jay Vincent (1980); Kevin Smith (1982); Darryl Johnson (1986); Kirk Manns (1990); and Quinton Brooks (1996).

There have been, of course, countless other Michigan State athletes who have been accorded All-America status over the past century in sports other than football or basketball. But they are too numerous to mention here — that is, for the men. Since the men had a 75-year head start on varsity collegiate athletics I have decided to forego mentioning the great athletes in the non-revenue men's sports. The women, on the other hand, have only had about a quarter of a century to make their mark and rarely get much recognition, so I want to highlight some of them.

Great women's basketball teams, players

Before 1971, the women's athletics program was operated within the intramural sports program. In 1971, women's athletics came under the rules and regulations of the Association of Intercollegiate Athletics for Women (AIAW). At that time the NCAA didn't offer any sports or championships for women's teams. The first AIAW women's basketball national championship was conducted in 1972. There were some outstanding teams and student-athletes in all sports prior to and after the inception of AIAW.

Both the NCAA and AIAW separately sponsored and

hosted the women's national basketball championships in 1981-82. The NCAA voted to sponsor the women's tournament and other sports after that year and it officially began sponsoring championships for most women's programs in 1982. Its membership voted for that, but strong supporters of the AIAW spoke vociferously at the NCAA convention challenging the proposals.

The issue was a huge national debate. The AIAW felt it had more of a 'purist' student-athlete approach and didn't want the women's athletics program to conform to that of men's athletics, where there always have been some unethical issues. Additionally, the AIAW knew that if the wealthy NCAA voted to have championships it would be the demise of the AIAW.

The first MSU women's varsity AIAW basketball team was in 1972 and was coached by Mikki Baile, whose teams compiled a record of 32-12 over her three years. Dominic Marino succeeded her and coached the 1975-76 team to a record of 6-16. Karen Langeland became the next coach and held the position for 24 years, compiling a 376-290 mark. Coach Joann McCallie was hired in 2000 as her replacement and quickly made the transition a positive one.

Baile's 1973-74 team participated in three post-season games at the State of Michigan AIAW tournament, winning two and losing one. It also qualified for the Midwest AIAW tournament, where it lost both its games. The following year the team played four games in the SMAIAW tourney and went 3-1, good for third place. Marino finished fourth in the 1976 state tourney and that year his team was the first MSU team to participate in the unofficial Big Ten women's tournament.

The Big Ten didn't have women involved in its conference championships package until 1982. Everything was unofficial up to then. Langeland had an impressive first year as her Spartans went 23-6 in 1976-

77 and won both the SMAIAW and MAIAW tournaments before losing to the University of Tennessee in the national AIAW championship game. Her teams appeared in the state AIAW tournament five times, winning twice and being second three times. Later, her squads competed in the NCAA women's tournament for three seasons, each time reaching the second round. Her teams also competed in two post-season Women's National Invitation Tournaments, reaching the quarterfinals each time. McCallie's 2001-02 squad got to the WNIT semifinals.

Langeland's 1996-97 team tied for first place in the Big Ten with a 12-4 mark and was 22-8 overall. There were some outstanding athletes on that team, led by senior tri-captain Paula Sanders, along with Cheri Euler and Tamika Matlock. Sanders showed tremendous leadership and was the team's top scorer with 12.6 points a game and was the top rebounder, snaring an average of nine rebounds a game. Langeland said Sanders was the single biggest reason the team won the championship. She was vocal and inspirational.

Other prominent players on the team were point guard Matlock, who ran the team on the floor, and Euler, who quietly led by example on and off the court. There also were two talented freshmen who contributed a lot, Maxanne Reese and Kristen Rasmussen, who went on to play for the Miami Sol of the Women's National Basketball Association. Also part of that team's success were Bella Engen, Jamie Wesley, and Nicole Cushing.

Then, of course, as mentioned in an earlier chapter there was the great 2004-005 team of McCallie that reached the championship game of the NCAA tournament and wound up with a 33-4 record.

Women's basketball has produced some other outstanding athletes. Among them were: Kathy DeBoer (1977-78), who later became an associate athletics director at the University of Kentucky; All-American Kris Emerson (1984), Kim Archer (1984), and Kisha Kelly

Paula Sanders

(1994), all coached by Langeland. In addition, all-region honors were bestowed upon Mary Kay Intyre (1978 and 1980), Nanette Gibson (1980), and Kelley (1995) during Langeland's tenure.

Many standouts in softball program

The 1974 MSU women's softball team under the direction of Coach Dianne Ulibarri finished ninth in the AIAW College World Series. Her 1975 and 1977 teams finished third and the 1981 squad was seventh. Ulibarri's team won it all in 1976 and had a 24-4 record, led by All-America pitcher Gloria Becksford, who was a remarkable athlete both as a pitcher and hitter. She won 17 and lost one that season and appeared in 24 of the 28 games. Becksford had a .370 batting average. In 1980 she became head coach and continued in that role until 1993. She was inducted into the MSU Athletics Hall of Fame and remains one of my close friends today. Another great player under Ulibarri was Kathy Strahan. She won a gold medal at the 1979 Pan American Games.

Deanne Moore was the first All-American in the softball program. She was first and second team All-American in 1983 and 1984, respectively. She won a silver medal at the 1979 Pan-Am Games, a gold medal in the USA team International Softball Federation World Championship in 1986, and participated in the U.S. Olympic Sports Festival in 1983 and 1985. She was inducted into the MSU hall of fame in 1996. Tracy Beadlescomb was on the USA team that played in the South Pacific Classic in 1985. She and Moore played for Beckford.

Jacquie Joseph became head coach of the Spartans softball team in 1994. She coached her 1997 and 1999 teams to the NCAA regional tournament. She also coached the bronze medal team at the 1997 USA Softball National Festival and the gold medal-winning squad in the 1997 Pan-Am Games. She is a hard worker, committed to student-athletes, and a great person. By the end of the 2001 season she had accumulated a 223-221 record.

Among her star athletes was Keri LeMaster, 1996 All-American, who was a gold medal winner in the 1997 USA Softball National Team Festival and was a participant on the 1997 USA Superball Team. Others included Patti Raduenz, 1996 second team All-American; Stacey Phillips, 1998 third team All-American; Shealee Dunavan, participant in the 1999 USA Softball National Team Festival; and Tiffany Thomas, 1999 USA Junior National Team silver medal winner.

Exceptional women's track and field athletes

Karen Dennis was the 1975 AIAW champion in the 220-yard dash with a time of 24.90 seconds and also was on the winning 440-yard relay team. She was hired as an assistant track coach at Michigan State and later became head coach before accepting the women's head coaching track and field position at the University of Las Vegas. She now is the head coach at Ohio State.

Judi Brown was a tremendous track athlete, earning All-America honors in distance medley relay in 1981 at the NCAA Indoor Championships. In 1983 she became an All-American in both the 4x400-meter relay and the 400-meter hurdles. Brown competed in the 1983 summer Olympics in the 400 meters, with a time of 56.44 seconds, winning a silver medal. She later was appointed head coach of the women's track and field program for the Spartans and was inducted into the university's athletics hall of fame. Her achievements earned her the honor of MSU Sportswoman of the Year in 1983.

Sevatheda Fynes earned All-America designation in three events during the 1997 season by posting a 60-meter indoor time of 6.65 seconds, a 100-meter outdoor dash time of 11.04 seconds, a 200-meter outdoor time of 22.61

In 1979, this quartet of MSU sprinters set a world's best indoor time in the medley relay: from left, Judi Brown, Pam Sedwick, Diane Williams, Molly Brennan.

seconds, and a 220-meter indoor time of 23.24 seconds during the NCAA Track and Field Championships.

Stephanie Dueringer became an All-American at the 1997 NCAA championships in both the 5,000-meter run and the 10,000-meter run. And Anne Pew earned the designation in the distance medley in 1981 and in the 3,000 meters at the 1982 NCAA championships.

Other athletes awarded All-America status in the track program were: Chandra Burns (1996 and 1997) in indoor 200 meters, and (1996) in outdoor 400 meters; Susan Francis (1994), 200 meters; Odessa Smalls (1986), 100 and 200 meters, plus (1987), 55 meters; Cheryl Gilliam (1981), 60 meters; Pam Sedwick (1981), 600 meters and distance medley relay; Kelly Spatz (1981), distance medley relay; Jamie Krzyminski (2002), 10,000 meters; Lynlee Phillips (2002), javelin; Ann Somerville (2002), 3,000-meter steeplechase; Sherita Williams (2002), triple jump.

Also, Jen Denkins (2000), 10,000 meters; Sara Reichert (1992), 1,500 meters; Mary Shea (1987), 10,000 meters; Karen Campbell (1984), 10,000 meters; Marcell Kendall (1984) 400 meters and 400 meter relay; Connie Burnett (1984), 400-meter relay; Joanna Childress (1984), 400-meter relay; Julie Boerman (1983), 4x400-meter relay; Jill Washburn (1982), 10,000 meters; Candy Burkett (1983), 4.400-meter relay; Sue Latter (1977), 800 meters; Marjorie Grimmett (1975), 220-yard dash and 440-yard relay; Laurel Vietzke (1975), 440-yard relay and long jump; Jacqui Sedwick (1983), 4x400-meter relay.

Women swimming stars also abound

Many All-Americans have been developed in Michigan State's women's swimming program. Most have been repeat honorees, such as: Jane Manchester in one-meter and three-meter diving (1973, 1974); Barbara Harding, one-meter and three-meter diving (1974, 1975); Martha Perez, one-meter diving (1974); Laura Seibold, three-meter diving (1974); Kathy Barrett, Suzy Brevitz, Lynn Hughes, and Vicki Reibeling, 400-yard medley relay (1975); Nancy Beel (1982), Jeanie Mikie (1977), and Sue Prior (1982, 1984), in one-meter diving.

Julie Farrell is the first women swimmer to earn six All-America honors in diving. She was awarded them for one- and three-meter diving (1989, 1990, 1991). In addition, she was MSU's Sportswoman of the Year in 1990 and Big Ten Athlete of the Year in 1991. She also was an NCAA champion in three-meter diving in 1991. Carly Weiden, meanwhile, was a three-time All-American (in one- and three-meter diving in 2000 and one-meter in 2002. Summer Mitchell was an All-American in 2001 in one- and three-meter diving.

Fossum leads way in women's golf

Mary Fossum was the first women's golf coach at the university, coaching from 1972 until 1997. Her teams won five consecutive Big Ten titles from 1974-78 and her squads competed in six straight AIAW national championships (1973-78). Her 1982 team again won the Big Ten championship. The 1987 team was second in the conference. Her teams participated in the 1982 and 1984 NCAA championships.

Stacy Slobodnik was appointed as her successor for the 1997 season after six years as Fossum's assistant. Slobodnik's squad won the conference title in 2001. Her teams qualified for the NCAA regionals for four consecutive years and were in the championships three successive years. Fossum has produced many All-Americans: Bonnie Lauer (1973), Sue Ertl (1978), Syd Wells (1982, 1983), Barb Mucha (1984), and Lisa Marino (1985). Emily Bastel (2002) was an All-American under Slobodnik.

Seven field hockey coaches

Michigan State's field hockey program has gone through seven coaches since its inception in 1972 under the AIAW. Mikki Baile was the first one and during her three-year span her teams had a 14-4-8 record. Diane Ulibarri coached the teams in 1975 and 1976, winning 18, losing four and tying one. Next came Samnoa Kajornsin, 1977-79, who was 39-15-8. Then Nance Reed, 1980-81, also had a winning record, 24-17-2.

The fifth head coach in the program was Rich Kimball, 1982-88, and he wasn't able to keep things above .500, posting a 43-81-16 mark. His successor, Martha

Ludwig, 1989-92, was 20-57-5. Michele Madison took over the program in 1993 and continued into the new millennium, posting an 85-96-2 record through the 2001 season — which was a particularly good year since the Spartans won the Big Ten championship and participated in the NCAA tourney, reaching the Elite Eight. It was MSU's first-ever field hockey appearance in the tournament. All-Americans over the years were: Maggie Lezzi (1991); Rayna Hiscox and Terry Pacheco (1995); Hiscox and Jill Lusher (1996, 1997); Melissa Pryor (1998); Marleen Tui (1999); and Bridget Cooper (2001).

Erbe has volleyball program at peak

Volleyball became a varsity sport for women in 1972 under AIAW rules and regulations, with Carol Davis being the inaugural coach and holding the post for two seasons, the teams compiling a 6-11 record. Annelies Knoppers was her successor and ran the program through 1984, posting a fine 250-197-18 record. Ginger Mason's teams from 1985-92 were 67-181, then Chuck Erbe became coach in 1993 and became the most successful coach in the program's history, leading his teams to 10 NCAA tournament appearances in 12 years. He was named national coach of the year in 1995. Erbe retired on Dec. 2, 2004, and Cathy George, who spent 11 highly-successful seasons at Western Michigan, was hired Dec. 9 as his replacement. All-Americans in the program through 2001 were: Dana Cooke and Val Sterk (1995, 1996), Courtney DeBolt (1995), Jenna Wrobel (1995, 1998), and Erin Hartley (2001).

Chapter 13:

THE DEFERRED DREAM

One step forward, two steps back

DESPITE THE RECENT PUBLIC AWARENESS initiatives, the problem collegiate institutions have hiring and retaining black head football coaches was more revealing in 2005 than it was in 2002. When the football season commenced in 2002 there were four black head football coaches leading Division 1A teams. At the end of the 2004 season, after a series of firings, hirings, and a resignation, there were three black head coaches. Bobby Williams was fired at Michigan State during the 2002 season.

Fritz Hill resigned at San Jose State at the close of the 2004 season after suffering four consecutive losing autumns. Tony Samuels was fired a few days later at New Mexico State and Notre Dame fired Tyrone Willingham on November 30, 2004 (Willingham was later rehired as head coach by the University of Washington in December 2004).

Also, Karl Dorrell was hired December 2002 at UCLA and Sylvester Croom at Mississippi State University in December 2003. But November 2004 will be remembered as a devastating month for the three black head coaches and their departures sent discouraging signals to all the other black assistant coaches who have aspirations of heading Division 1A football programs somewhere, someday. Their dreams have been deferred and some have been shattered based on the treatment of those coaches.

Williams was hired as MSU's head football coach in December 1999 after the resignation of Nick Saban, who left for Louisiana State at the end of the regular season. Williams had served nine years as an assistant and associate head coach at the university when he was elevated to the top position. He inherited a program that had gone 34-24-1 over the past five years, including 9-2 during the 1999 regular season, and he coached the team to a victory over Florida in the 2000 Citrus Bowl. He was fired during the 2002 season with a record of 16-17, with less than three full seasons as head coach.

Samuels, having spent many years as an assistant at Nebraska, was hired as New Mexico State's head coach in December 1996. He compiled a record of 34 wins and 57 losses over eight seasons before he was fired in November 2004. Historically, the football program had only four winning seasons over 35 years and Samuels' record included two of them. He was dismissed despite being the coach with the third most victories in the school's football history. Athletics Director Brian Faison said: " I think Tony had a chance. I think resources are an issue. We have got to go out and we've got to do a better job of providing resources for our coaches.

Fritz Hill earned his Ph.D. in higher education in 1997 while serving as an assistant coach at the University of Arkansas. He was appointed to lead the San Jose State football program in December 2000. He resigned in November 2004 after four frustrating seasons. Hill stepped into a program that initially provided only 60 football scholarships when 85 were permitted in NCAA Division 1A. The remaining 25 were gradually phased-in over five years so that the full allotment would be offered for the 2005 season.

Competing in football without a full complement of scholarship athletes is a great handicap. It is like fighting in a boxing match with one hand tied behind your back. The biggest drawback is the lack of depth. One of the primary reasons 85 scholarships are allowed in Division 1A football is the high rate of injuries. Another factor is attrition, combined with coaches recruiting mistakes. A few athletes run into academic difficulty or quit the team each year, while a few others lack the talent or the intestinal fortitude to compete at the collegiate level. Under such circumstances, a coach with significantly fewer athletes than the maximum permitted has a limited chance of winning anywhere. Hill never was given the opportunity to be successful and ended up with a record of 14-33.

Hill is a skilled researcher and national authority on the hiring of black coaches at the collegiate level. In 2002 he released data that showed, since 1982, black head coaches have been selected for 18 of the 348 football head coaching vacancies — 5 percent. Of the 109 vacancies in the last six years, African Americans filled six. Those are troubling statistics in a sport where approximately 50 percent of the athletes are black.

Rug pulled out from Willingham

Willingham and I first met in the fall of 1973 when he enrolled at Michigan State as a walk-on football player. He eventually earned a football scholarship and, despite his size (5-foot-7, 135 pounds), lettered three years at quarterback and wide receiver. I was then the assistant athletics director for student-athletes academic support services. Out of all the hundreds of male and female student-athletes I counseled in that position for 11 years to help them make progress towards their academic degrees, graduate, and demonstrate appropriate behavior on and off the playing surface, Willingham stands with a few others at the top of the list. He was a role model. I

Tyrone Willingham in his days as an assistant coach at MSU

never had to call him into my office or reprimand him for anything improper like I did with many other athletes. Whenever we met it was to proactively make plans for an academic assignment or to constructively discuss some other aspect of his student life. I could tell back then that he would become prominent in his chosen profession of physical education and coaching.

Notre Dame received international acclaim when, on Dec. 31, 2001, it hired Willingham as head football coach, the first African American head coach at the institution. Prior to going there, Willingham had nearly 25 years of progressive and successful coaching experience at both the collegiate and professional levels. The highlight of his career then was the seven years he spent as head coach of the University of Stanford Cardinal, a member of the Pac Ten Conference. Willingham amassed a 44-36 record, including appearances in the 1995 Liberty Bowl, 1996 Sun Bowl, the 1999 Rose Bowl, and the 2001 Seattle Bowl. He was honored as coach of the year for his outstanding performance in the 1999 season. Over the previous five years before he was hired there, Stanford had a record of 30-27-1.

Willingham compiled a record of 21-15 at Notre Dame before receiving the axe on Nov. 30, 2004. He was permitted to coach only three years of a five-year contract. I was in the MSU office of admissions where I am employed, talking with senior associate admissions director Jim Cotter when I received the news. Maureen Shagonaby, an admissions counselor, shared the distressing news with us. I felt very disappointed to hear about Willingham's firing and my two colleagues expressed their sadness. I thought Willingham had a promising 2004 season with a 6-5 record, playing perhaps the most difficult schedule at the Division 1A level with a relative young team. I had watched many of Notre Dame games on television and felt the young team would be more successful in 2005. I had hoped that Notre Dame, with all of its resources and international prestige, would have allowed Willingham to coach the five years in his contract.

Willingham represented Notre Dame with class and productivity in all phases of his responsibilities in a high profile position. Such behavior was typical of him. He has acted that way since I've known him. Notre Dame athletics director Kevin White praised Willingham for having performed commendable in his position. He said, "From Sunday through Friday our football program has exceeded all expectations, in every way, but on Saturday we struggled. We have been up and down and sideways a little bit". White further justified the firing by saying, "We simply have not made the progress on the field that we need to make. Nor have we been able to create the positive momentum necessary in our efforts to return the Notre Dame program to the elite level of the college football world."

Willingham was the first black head football coach to be fired and rehired in another collegiate head coaching position at the Division 1A level. The University of Washington hired Willingham on Dec. 13, 2004. That is encouraging to black assistant and former black head coaches who have hopes of becoming a Division 1 head coach.

Dorrell was hired at UCLA, his alma mater, in

413

December 2002. He had previously coached at both the collegiate and professional levels. He took over a program that struggled over the previous five years with an overall record of 34 wins and 24 losses. In his first two seasons his teams had a 12-13 record.

Croom was an assistant with the Green Bay Packers when Mississippi State hired him Dec. 2, 2003. He became the first African-American head football coach in the Southeastern Conference. He inherited a program that had only won eight games over the past three seasons and was under NCAA investigation for rules violations occurring from 1998 to 2002. He finished with a 2-10 record in 2004.

Racism? Or business decision?

There appears to be no valid reason for the very dismal number of black coaches heading Division 1A programs going into the 2005 season. There were three black head coaches out of 117 positions. Since the early 1970s, most Division 1A grid programs have fiercely recruited black athletes. It is common for half of the football squads to consist of black athletes. Some go on to become graduate assistants, high school coaches, or play in the professional ranks. Today there exists an abundance of black assistant coaches with a wealth of experience at every level of the game and they want and deserve a chance to be a collegiate coach somewhere. Several more black head coaches may get hired over the next 10 years, but it will not be an easy road to travel. They will be confronted with a culture of resistance and precious time will not be on their side. The black coaches will be expected to win immediately, consistently, and win big or expect to get fired. Some persons will classify the firings as racism; others will say they were business decisions.

As director of athletics at Michigan State, I recall receiving many letters and even a petition from white

Bobby Williams and I ring in the New Year.

fans demanding that Williams, who was hired in December 1999 as the first head black football coach at the university, be fired. Those letters started coming in his first day on the job and they continued during my three-year tenure. Most of them came from alumni and fans in the state of Michigan, but some were written from as far away as California. The critics observed his every move at home games or from watching television. Nothing he did could satisfy those disgruntled fans. They criticized everything. Those folks simply did not want to give Bobby a chance.

I made a point of answering each letter without the coach's knowledge. I defended him, something that every director of athletics must do. I'm not saying all of the letter writers were racist, even though I know racism exists everywhere in American society, including intercollegiate football. I did not know enough about them to decipher their motives and make judgments. But I will say that I never recalled another A.D. at Michigan State receiving such nasty letters about white football coaches, even when they experienced mediocre seasons.

And I worked very closely with other A.D.s for 20 years, with duties that included responding to their mail. It taught me that white fans are less tolerant of black coaches than they are of white coaches.

Former MSU football coach Duffy Daugherty was one of the early pioneers in recruiting black athletes from all over the country. From the mid-1950s until his retirement in 1969, he started numerous black players in games on both offense and defense. He was among the first coaches at predominately white institutions to start a black quarterback when it was not fashionable to do so. After one game in the 1960s when he started seven blacks, he was asked the question, "How many blacks should start in a game"? Duffy responded, "If I'm winning, I can play 11 but if I'm losing, one is too many." He was responding to the perceptions of white alumni and fans that show little patience or tolerance for blacks in athletics unless they win most of the time.

Revenue and hiring decisions

Most athletics departments at the Division 1A level are financially self-sufficient, which means they must generate the revenue they spend. The largest portion of the budgeted revenue is derived from gate receipts, money that comes from the sale of game tickets to alumni, boosters, and other fans. Another portion comes from broadcast sources, such as television, radio, and the Internet. It also is essential to solicit funds annually from donors to help balance the budget.

Various levels of fund-raising categories have been established at the institution to accommodate interests of donors making financial contributions to the athletics department. Some donors feel their contributions give them the right to make suggestions about the hiring and firing of coaches. Any institution which allows donors to have influence into personnel issues in the athletics department is headed for big trouble with the NCAA and could be accused of leadership vulnerability. The NCAA could cite an institution with a major violation for losing control of its athletics program.

When a new coach inherits a football program with a record of fewer victories than losses over the previous five years, or the fans have determined that the program has become mediocre, the new coach is in a quick-fix situation. Fans are expecting a miracle worker. They want to see instant success from the new coach. The fans are hungry for their team to participate in a sequence of annual postseason bowl games, the bigger the better. If the new coach also continues to struggle with the program and there is no appreciable improvement in the victory column over a three- to four-year period, the administration gets very nervous.

Because fans support in the stands and their donations start dropping, ticket sales decrease and the broadcast revenue may be slashed because of low ratings. All of these factors will negatively impact the amount of revenue for the athletics department. Just as in the case of any other business, when the annual expenditures begin to exceed revenue, major decisions must be made. In athletics, that may mean finding another source of revenue, which is often difficult. It could mean very strict cost containment measures or downsizing the department by cutting programs and laying off staff. Those are most difficult decisions brought on because of a mediocre football program.

Given this situation, let's assume you were the administrator at the institution responsible for making immediate changes in the football program. Would you fire the current coach and hire another new coach? What kind of coach should be hired in that situation? Should it be an established head coach with a winning record from another program that the alumni and fans would immediately accept? Would you bring in a coach from a program that has a series of losing seasons? How about hiring a black assistant coach from a winning program at another institution, either college or the pros? Then there may be the opportunity to promote an assistant coach already at the institution. What kind of coach would energize the interests of fickle alumni and fans to the extent they would immediately return to the stands and renew their donations to the athletics program?

I believe each institution must decide the type of coach best suited for its football program. Two requirements should always be standard for all public institutions when openings occur at the head football coaching position: a black tenured faculty member should serve on the search committee, or there should be another equivalent black staff member with the freedom to advocate for black candidates. That is not to guarantee that a black candidate would even be interviewed for the position, but to insure that such candidates be notified of the opening in a timely manner and have a chance to get a fair assessment of their credentials.

The search process

Institutions of higher learning usually use two methods to search for head football coaches:

The First Method:

- The Search Committee: The president of the institution usually serves as chair and appoints a committee to serve as advisory to him/her during the search for football candidates. The committee often consists of about five to seven people, including the president, some of his officers, the athletics director, and maybe a currently enrolled student-athlete. It is customary for the president to convene the group, spell out the purpose, define the qualification criteria, and request the group to provide names of prospective candidates.

  The president may give assignments to committee members to call certain prospective candidates to find out about their interest in the position. Whatever information is gleaned from the telephone calls is shared with the president either at the next meeting of the committee or to him or her directly prior to the committee meeting. Usually, additional names are given at the second meeting. Some of the original candidates are deleted for various reasons, either a candidate isn't interested or the committee feels the candidate would not be a good fit for the institution. Committee members are then given the assignment to check the references of those candidates who have submitted their resumes and appear to the committee to be likely candidates. A few of the candidates have agents to represent their interest in the position to the committee. Those initial contacts by agents usually are made with the president or the athletics director. Then the president may hire a headhunter to further recommend candidates to him.

- The Interviewing Process: The president, with advice from the committee, decides, which of the candidates will be given an in-person interview. That is a crucial step for black candidates because most committee members are white and often are unfamiliar with actual accomplishments of black assistant coaches working at collegiate or professional levels. Usually, most whites don't know the names of any black assistant coaches at those levels, except for one or two employed at their institutions. Black assistants seldom get the prominence from the media they rightfully earn from their job performance. They are hidden in the background. It is important that a well-informed, non-intimidated black professional be appointed to the committee to serve as an advocate for black candidates otherwise, those candidates may go unnoticed because most resumés look alike.

In the absence of a strong black committee member, some liberal person on the committee may push hard suggesting that one black be interviewed to protect the institution from the allegation of the lack of affirmative action efforts during the search. Although such a statement usually isn't stated so directly, it often is made as a charade to strictly protect the institution and it's not in the best interest of the black candidate.

When the list of candidates has been narrowed down for in-person interviews, arrangements are made to either conduct the interviews on or off the campus. The institution tries to be as private as possible to protect the search process, the candidate, and the institution. Depending on the number of candidates involved, that phase of the process may take anywhere from three to five days.

- The Selection Process: Once all scheduled interviews have been conducted, the president may ask for input from the committee relative to its rankings of the top three candidates. The president will listen to members' suggestions and make the selection either at the meeting or privately with his or her officers and the athletics director. The president has the discretion of choosing any one of the three recommended candidates or the president may decide to search further.

The Second Method:
- The athletics director meets with the president and the A.D. is delegated the responsibility of searching for coaching candidates. That is a quick way to fill the vacancy and both public and private institutions use it a lot when hiring a football

coach, claiming the first method takes too long. There may or may not be a loosely formed search committee. If so, it would mainly consist of three to five members from the president's staff who would hear reports from the A.D. regarding updates of his search. In that method, black candidates are most vulnerable to being overlooked. Unless the athletics director knows someone who knows of a good black candidate, blacks would not normally be included in the pool except at the last minute, upon someone's suggestion, to cover somebody's tail.

In that case, one of the currently employed black assistant coaches may be asked to interview for the position. Sometimes the interview could take place with a weak-credentialed black assistant coach employed someplace else. The black assistant coach knows as well as the athletics director and president that he doesn't have a chance of getting the job. That process is nothing but subterfuge. The other way that a black may be included as a legitimate finalist, but it's a long shot, is if the institution hired a headhunter and was told upfront to include a black for affirmative action purposes. All of the former athletes who played their hearts and souls out to help enhance the image of the institution and now coaching elsewhere may be forgotten in the process.

- The athletics director makes a recommendation to the president and it usually is accepted. The president notifies the board and the person is hired.

Is change on the way?

There may be change in the air, which could impact the future hiring of head football coaches at collegiate institutions to give black coaches more consideration in the hiring process. Three different black groups expressed dissatisfaction with the way coaching changes occurred at their institutions at the close of the 2004 season.

- The Black Alumni Association of the University of Notre Dame, comprising almost 2,000 graduates, disagreed with the firing of Tyrone Willingham and made its position known to the administration and the trustees. Their statement made clear that the firing might negatively effect the recruitment and the retention of black students and faculty. They called the decision to fire Willingham both premature and unprecedented. It disregarded Willingham's outstanding contribution to the university.

- The Black Coaches Association located in Indianapolis, Ind., has a system in place to assist universities with their search for black head football coaches when vacancies occur. They have a Hiring Report Card, which is used to rate institutions that do or do not use their services.

  In December 2004, the University of South Carolina hired Steve Spurrier without the assistance of the services of the BCA. The association sent its volunteer guidelines to the university before the coach was hired, but the institution ignored them. The association in turn requested black prospective student-athletes and black assistant coaches to stay away from the institution. However, Ron Cooper who is black and former head coach at both Eastern Michigan University and the University of Louisville and currently employed as an assistant coach at South Carolina, said he was contacted about the position but chose not to pursue it when he was told that Spurrier was interested.

- At the University of Illinois, approximately 62 black former football players sent a letter to the administration questioning the process used to hire football coach Ron Zook. The letter was sent Nov. 22, 2004, requesting the institution to include African-Americans and other minority candidates in the process. A list of candidates was enclosed with their letter. The group of former athletes was disappointed when they learned that Zook's appointment was made less than 24 hours after the 5 p.m. deadline on December 6. They believed the process was not open to all qualified candidates. The interim chancellor made a statement saying, "I know who was in the final five, there was clear representation of black coaches, and we wound up with the best person.

What will we see in the years ahead in this regard? There should have been more progress by now. I'd like to be optimistic, but as can be seen by the examples I've outlined, pessimism is closer to reality.

Chapter 14:

ROAD TO ATHLETICS DIRECTOR JOB

Diligence, integrity among keys

Young professionals and college students often ask me how a person becomes a director of athletics. There are different roads to every job and athletics isn't any different. I will reiterate some of the information I've already mentioned in detail and outline some additional details about the road I took and perhaps anyone else with similar ambitions will get insight that may help them.

I'm assuming that the aspiring candidate knows that at least one college degree is absolutely necessary to get a professional foot into the athletics department door at a college or university. The aspiring candidate may want to satisfy the degree requirement by graduating from an athletics administration program, or in any other academic major found at many colleges and universities. Athletics directors have academic degrees in most disciplines from a host of different accredited institutions. Many of them have multi degrees.

I believe I became aware of my interest in athletics when I was in the sixth grade at West Gadsden Elementary School in Alabama. We had to write an essay on what we thought our future vocations might be. I recall writing that I wanted to have a career in sports. At the time, with the exception of coaching high school football, I didn't know enough about professional opportunities. There was no television at home when I was in the sixth grade in 1946.

And accomplishments of blacks were not featured in textbooks. Our local role models were the people we knew and national boxing heroes like Joe Louis, Ezzard Charles, Jersey Joe Wolcott, and Sugar Ray Robinson. I listened to their boxing matches on the radio. Playing sports was easy and fun for me. I had an inspiring role model in Mr. J. T. Williams, the principal, who was my sixth-grade teacher and after-school recreational leader.

Although my interest shifted to educational administrative functions at various times early in my professional life, little did I know that I was preparing myself to become a collegiate athletics director, a position I never anticipated attaining until quite late in my career. Generally, my earlier jobs were in programs that dealt with a diverse population of young adults. I already focused on most of the issues from those programs.

I was 36 when I was first hired in 1969 at the Michigan State Athletics Department as an assistant ticket manager. It was a brief stay, but three years later I returned. Since I had a broad educational background I was able to immediately be effective as an assistant athletics director for academic support services, aiding student-athletes in that regard. Inherent from my background was a habit of devoting more time to a job than the employer required, doing quality work with integrity, and being respectful and honest to my superiors and colleagues. Those attributes were necessary in my assistant A.D. position.

The office provided centralized services and had a limited staff that encompassed a number of extensive and critical responsibilities. It was like a one-stop shop for both athletes and coaches needing services in areas of academics: monitoring eligibility, personal advice, certification, interpretations of Big Ten and NCAA rules and regulations, book loan procedures, financial aid, and human resources issues. Today there are many specialists employed to handle those critical areas in the athletics department and many of the procedures I implemented early on still are in existence today.

Burt Smith initially was hired for the position in 1965, primarily to counsel and monitor the academic affairs of football players. His role was later expanded to include men's basketball and ice hockey players. In addition, he handled certification, book loans, eligibility, and the grant-in-aid budget for 14 men's sports. The women's program wasn't part of the department until 1972.

Early jobs ideal training for future

When I succeeded Burt, I assumed his previous duties, integrated the women's components into my office, and initiated additional ones. For example, we didn't have a liaison to the human resources office. Each athletics office basically was doing its own thing with searches and hiring people. Because of my previous background from working in the personnel office of the Michigan Department of Education, I was aware that a liaison role would help the department become more efficient. With more than 100 union and non-union employees, we needed a centralized office to coordinate those responsibilities. That would bring about improvement internally, as well as consistency between the athletics department and university personnel procedures.

I worked an inordinate number of hours, seven days a week, to stay abreast of my responsibilities, often getting phone calls from student-athletes very late at night or in the early morning hours to address personal problems they had encountered, or from a coach asking about a university procedure, as well as interpretations of Big Ten and NCAA rules and regulations.

427

I don't want to give the impression that I worked autonomously or my job was without scrutiny. Smith was my boss and there was second-guessing from some faculty members and administrators, as well as some coaches who felt I was interfering with their duties. Some of the non-revenue sports coaches never had the luxury of Smith monitoring their athletes or developing and processing procedures in a number of areas that affected their sports. But now I was in charge and had all sports as part of my administrative responsibilities.

A few faculty members failed to understand the need for an athletics academic office. They believed athletes should follow the same system of receiving academic advice and support services as regular students. They failed to understand that the athletes were participating in their sports up to 30 hours a week to represent the institution appropriately. Then, too, some of the athletes were academically at risk with poor study habits and without the services provided by my office they would have flunked out.

There were a few campus administrators who questioned every insignificant clerical error found on any paper processed through my office to theirs. How did I handle those complaints? What worked for me was meeting with my critics so as to better understand their concerns and to address each one directly and honestly. I would document the discussion, meet with my staff to correct the error, and send a follow-up memo to the complainant. If the issue were trivial, I would simply call the complainant to show appreciation for the matter brought to my attention. I never shied away from substantive complaints or ignored minor ones. I always was searching for ways to improve the services of my office.

I enjoyed meeting with student-athletes and dealt with them in a straightforward manner. If they missed a class, a study session, an appointment, or weren't meeting academic requirements, I called them in for a face-to-face interview to reinforce expectations. I gave advice to student-athletes who found themselves confronted with disciplinary problems at the university and criminal problems in the court system. Most of the coaches would routinely refer those student-athletes to me for assistance. Some student-athletes were proactive and would contact me first on their own. I wanted each of them to talk through why the mistake occurred and what was necessary to resolve it. If there were problems I couldn't help them with, I referred the student-athletes to specialized professional assistance on campus. I encountered some real tough issues with some of them and tried to provide the best guidance and psychological support to help resolve their issues. In most cases, we resolved the problems without fanfare and in all cases with integrity.

As a professional, I attended university, community, and Big Ten Conference meetings. I served on many university committees and community service groups, not just as an appointed member but also as a volunteer, and was elected as an officer in many groups. Among them was being elected secretary of the East Lansing Rotary Club, a board member of the Boarshead Theatre and

Speaking at a Lansing Rotary Club meeting

also of the Parkwood YMCA, to university bargaining committees for union positions, coordinator of Title IX, the university's affirmative action advisory committee, and secretary to Alpha Chi Boule of Sigma Pi Phi fraternity. I represented the university at Big Ten meetings with the athletics academic advisors. I was a fill-in for each of the A.D.s whenever they couldn't attend university and conference meetings.

The point I make is that I learned an aspiring athletics director must devote some time on campus and in the community networking as well as serving in a voluntary capacity. I attended NCAA and National Association of Collegiate Directors of Athletics annual conventions and participated in every session that I could. I wrote many articles for the print media related to my work, was interviewed many times on radio, and featured on television locally and nationally.

In 1976 I organized the first national conference on academically advising the student-athlete and was co-founder and later president of the National Association of Athletic Academic Advisors, serving as its president in 1978 and 1979. Also, I wrote, *The Student-Athlete: Eligibility and Academic Integrity*, the first book of its kind in the nation.

Job feelers from universities abound

My name certainly was becoming broad in athletics circles and was augmented at the national level by my appointment in November 1983 to the position of assistant commissioner of the Big Ten. I received many inquiries regarding my availability from such universities as Stanford, Illinois State, and Indiana. Additionally, I received general inquiries from institutions asking that I recommend black candidates for different jobs in the athletics departments. I did recommend a number of qualified candidates but found out that only a few were interviewed, so I became cautious in my referrals.

I never wanted to be part of a scheme for referring blacks to openings merely so the school could satisfy, on paper, affirmative action plans. So I started asking the representatives whether they were merely calling me for that purpose or were they seriously searching for minority candidates to be interviewed for job openings. One or two said they were searching for names for both reasons and if they found an outstanding black candidate they would give that person fair consideration for the position. One black candidate, I believe, got an interview after I specified my concern to the representatives.

I went through six live interviews: five for director of athletics positions — at the University of Houston, Indiana University, North Carolina A&T State University, and twice at Michigan State — and one for a commissioner's job with the Southern Intercollegiate Athletics Conference. I also went through a telephone interview for the athletics director position at Illinois State. I withdrew my candidacy from two of the jobs, turned one down, and wasn't offered the others.

The first interview at MSU was in 1991 but the job was awarded to Merrily Dean Baker, who then was employed by the NCAA. She resigned the Michigan State job in 1994 and in 1995 I was given my second interview. But that time the A.D. job went to Merritt Norvell, who had worked for IBM and served on the athletics council at the University of Wisconsin.

The first time I was a candidate at MSU I was privileged to have much internal and external support from individuals and groups, including written support from most of the coaches and athletics administrators at the university. Also, many athletics leaders from around the country wrote recommendations on my behalf. Some I requested and others were unsolicited efforts to help me.

The MSU Black Faculty and Administrators Association gave me its strong support in 1991. Dr. Gloria Smith, Dr. Thomas Gunnings, and others from the association made a sterling presentation to the board of trustees recommending me for the post. I had verbal support from trustees Joel Ferguson and Bob Weiss. And alumni and friends from around the country wrote unsolicited letters and made phone calls on my behalf.

There were four other finalists then for the position: Baker, Debby Yow, Gene Smith, and Max Urick. Central administrators, athletics department staff members, the search committee, and President John DiBiaggio interviewed each of us. The president asked me questions about my loyalty to George Perles, who was both the football coach and athletics director. I didn't deny that George was my supervisor and friend. I was committed to helping him be the very best in his two roles.

DiBiaggio said he believed I could be fair and he would appoint me to the position if the search committee sent my name to him. I accepted his words at face value. However, two weeks earlier I had heard from a vice president on campus who told me I was a viable candidate but the position would be given to the woman from the NCAA (Baker). And that's precisely what happened.

In 1995, prior to my becoming a candidate for the second time and after the announced resignation of Baker, I made an appointment to see President M. Peter McPherson. I wanted to know if he would appoint me A.D. if I emerged as the top candidate. I was senior associate athletics director at that time and assistant to the provost, Dr. Lou Anna Simon. I attended her weekly staff meetings and her weekly council of deans meetings.

During one of the council of deans meetings McPherson left early. As he was leaving, he stopped briefly to chat with Dr. Lee June, the vice president of student services who was in attendance. June left the meeting with McPherson. When June returned about 20 minutes later, he told me the president wanted to see me. I immediately went to the office of McPherson, who I had called at his office a few days earlier for an appointment to discuss my candidacy for the vacant A.D. position. He was not responding to my request.

I told him of my interest in becoming the athletics director and asked if he would appoint me if I successfully went through the interviewing process. I mentioned that I had been an unsuccessful candidate when Baker was

Noreese and I with President M. Peter McPherson in 2002

appointed, but made it clear I was satisfied with my senior associate athletics director job and didn't want to go through the process again and not be appointed and wind up being vulnerable to whoever was named A.D.

McPherson told me he thought I would be a good candidate and that I was a good man. He mentioned that he was only going through the search process to find out what an athletics director's responsibilities were. He said he didn't know what they do. He said I had been effective assisting him with some tough athletics issues. He also said he liked my wife, Noreese. He asked me to visit each of the members on the A.D. advisory search committee and tell them about my interest in the job. He explained the advisory search committee would be just like the search committee he formed to interview the head football coach position candidates. It would serve strictly in an advisory capacity. I said I would become a candidate and thanked him for his time, support and advice. I assured him that I would start talking individually with members of the advisory committee.

Search committee kept in dark

Names of the committee members appeared in the campus newspaper on May 8, 1995. I soon found out some of them hadn't been formally notified of their appointments and the committee hadn't even met, things of which I wasn't aware as I tried to carry out the president's advice to talk to each committee member. I was eager to follow McPherson's suggestion and I made four appointments with committee members, the first with Denise Anderton, director of the human resources department. When I entered her office, she was astonished to find out why I was there and was unaware she had been appointed to the search committee. Anyhow, I told her about my candidacy and Denise, who is a nice person, listened but appeared uncomfortable because she was caught off guard. I cancelled the other appointments but did speak informally with another committee member, Maxie Jackson, who also wasn't aware of his appointment.

The committee, chaired by McPherson, interviewed me for 90 minutes and I left feeling I had fared well. I spent time explaining various athletics concepts and practices. Norvell, though, got the job. I later approached McPherson in his office to find out what happened relative to my candidacy and he said simply that the appointment had been made and it was now time to move forward. I accepted that and continued to focus on my job while trying to help the new A.D.

When Baker was the athletics director, McPherson called me frequently to discuss many different issues. His calls were less frequent when Norvell became director. Usually when he called during Norvell's tenure he would ask how things were going in the department. He'd sometimes ask me to talk about the specific performance of each administrative staff member. I stayed positive. I had committed myself to providing the best possible support to Baker and Norvell, continuing to work at the highest level of ethics and integrity with everyone inside and outside the department. But it was hard and I felt awkward giving McPherson my secret assessments of the administrators, including the athletics director.

He would ask me to go down the alphabetical list of names and tell him about the work performance of each administrator and anything else I chose to tell him. Of course, he never wanted to know about me. I believe he trusted me and felt he had gotten to know me fairly well. We had many conversations over the telephone, at Cowles House, and at social functions. Whenever we would happen to be in attendance at the same function, he would seek me out to discuss some aspect of the university, particularly matters in the athletics department.

When Baker was the A.D., McPherson would call me three and four times each day. The calls would come both to my campus office and my home. He wouldn't hesitate to call me at 11 p.m. at my home. My wife became upset a couple of times when he called after she had gone to bed and gone to sleep. Once he called me at 2:30 a.m. in Madison, Wis., on the eve of a football game to remind me to tell Nick Saban that an MSU athlete couldn't play in the game because he was ineligible. We had already discussed the issue with McPherson, Wilkinson, and Saban before we departed campus for the game.

The 2:30 phone call was very scary because normally at that time of morning when the phone rings it signals bad news in the family. Noreese and I both were afraid something had gone wrong with one of our children or another member of the family. We were upset but felt relieved when McPherson gave us the reason for his call. I don't believe either of us could return to sleep.

Under Baker's tenure, McPherson would call to seek

information about some issue that had surfaced in the department, or he would call to fish for information. Often, he wanted to know how the administrative staff was performing, how the athletics director was doing, and what I thought the issues were in the department. He would frequently make inquiries about one of the coaches and a few times he asked me to do some confidential research on a topic for him.

Then there were times he called on what I privately labeled his "fishing expeditions". He would call to chat without disclosing a specific subject. He would start out by saying, "Hello, Clarence. What do you know?" Those were difficult calls for me because I was trying to anticipate ahead of him by guessing where he might take the conversation. Sometimes there would be brief pauses of silence. At other times I would mention something that perked his interest and after discussing it he would say, "This is some interesting stuff. You take care."

Whenever things were not going well in the department under Baker, McPherson would make inquiries about the issues and then listen carefully to the information I shared with him. He would ask a series of questions trying to pinpoint who was responsible for the problem. On the other hand, when he called about issues under the leadership of Norvell, he appeared not to want to hear problems involving him. He was more interested in how the administrative staff was supporting him. And if I happened to respond in a manner contrary to what he wanted to hear, he would end the conversation by saying, "OK, my friend, I'll talk to you later". It was quite clear to me that since McPherson hired Norvell, he wanted him to succeed and didn't want to hear missing links in Norvell's management style.

He didn't demonstrate to me the same level of compassion for Baker. For example, I recall when she administered the development of a strategic plan process for the athletics department with the help of her administrative staff for the 1993-94 academic year. It was a good plan, but like so many other strategic plans, unless it is implemented and enforced year-round by one of the senior staff members, it is a lot of time wasted. It was well written and made sense for the future of our department, but it didn't go anywhere and nobody seemed to care.

On the other hand, Norvell for the 1995-96 year secured a team of experts from campus who were adept at helping organizations develop strategic plans. The team met with our entire staff over several weeks to draw out information from us for consideration of the various strategies. When the brochure was complete, it was politically distributed to members of McPherson's cabinet, athletics administrators, athletic council members, and others—just like Baker had previously done.

McPherson called me one day after the project was complete to ask my opinion of it. I told him Norvell's strategic plan was limited in scope. It was on fancy paper but I didn't think it was comprehensive enough to meet the future pressing issues of our department. I explained I felt the strategies were basic starting points and we would have to add to it and fill in the blanks as a department. McPherson didn't want to hear my critique. He took a deep breath and abruptly said he had to go and would talk with me later.

I suppose most folks would have been flattered to have such a relationship and access to the president. Surely there were times when I felt comfortable about my role with McPherson. But at other times I felt like I was being exploited. I surely didn't like giving personal assessments of our administrative staff when they didn't report to me. Further, I felt McPherson needed someone other than trustee Ferguson to help educate him about athletics matters and he chose me. I always felt uncomfortable talking to Baker and Norvell after McPherson had asked me privately to talk about their strengths and weaknesses.

McPherson put me in a position where it was difficult to be honest with them. I could never talk to them about issues McPherson and I had privately discussed. So I did the best I could by avoiding some issues and simply commenting briefly on others. It was a tough way to earn a living, particularly since they were my bosses and we worked so closely together.

I am human, with pain and faults like everyone else. There were times when I got angry and was disappointed over situations over which I had no control. I felt McPherson had misled me concerning my chances to become the A.D. and I felt strongly during and after the Jud Heathcote memo leak that McPherson had used and exploited me. He obtained information from me, which he didn't feel comfortable getting from anyone else. I really don't believe he wanted the board of trustees and members of his cabinet to know what a steep learning curve he had about intercollegiate athletics. So he used me to help educate him.

He started to call me less and was tentative about talking with me in a room full of people at social events after the Heathcote memo. It was no longer politically correct for him to do so in front of some of Heathcote's supporters. I felt better if I stayed away from him at those functions. In that way he wouldn't be playing his games with me. Although I could deal with the situation, it didn't make sense to put myself in a position that would prompt the university president to try to diplomatically dodge me.

Whenever I felt I'd been kicked in the pants, I took the high road. It is something I had learned much earlier in my career. I have seen good people get emotionally upset and vindictive because they thought someone did them wrong. Either somebody lied to them, said something nasty behind their backs, disclosed personal or confidential information, or did other insensitive things. I'm not advocating that a wrongdoer shouldn't be confronted, but if that is the case it shouldn't be in a fighting mood.

Persons who lower themselves to the level of a

438

wrongdoer never will be successful. Too much valuable time will be wasted trying to get even, and we never do. When I find myself in a negative situation that I believe to be unfair, I try to remember what the Lord says in Deuteronomy 32:35: "It is mine to avenge; I will repay. In due time their foot will slip; their day of disaster is near and their doom rushes upon them." Dr. Martin Luther King also advocated that effective philosophy in his non-violent civil rights movement.

Occupational necessity: biting your lip

If you try to manage your emotions at a high level you'll win people over. They'll admire and trust you. Your belief and commitment to the forgiveness philosophy has to be real and unbending, otherwise the system, its vast resources, and its inequities will most likely overcome you. As an aspiring professional, be prepared to face disappointments and be tested often, for adversity will surely come your way when you least expect it. But don't lose sight of your integrity in the process.

The other important factor in maintaining your attitude equilibrium is by having short- and long-term goals. They will help you see exactly where you want to go, although goals are useless if you don't put the process and effort in place to reach them. That can best be done in writing. When you take one step toward your goal, mark it off. If you started with 25 steps, you now have 24 to go. When you finish 24, you have 23 steps left. That is a great way to stay focused and not be sidetracked by emotional trivia.

Another criterion is to try to find a mentor, someone who will give you straight advice and career guidance. It could be someone in your area of expertise who works outside of your institution. Hang with like-minded people who will hold you accountable and to high standards so you will grow both personally and professionally.

Flurry of interviews

Hayden Murray, faculty athletics representative at Indiana University and a friend, invited me to become a candidate for the athletics director position there. The job had become available due to the death of Ralph Floyd, who was a good friend of mine. Murray assured me that I had his support and that of basketball coach Bobby Knight and football coach Bill Mallory. I visited the campus for an interview with the search committee in early March 1991. It was a two-hour session that I felt went exceedingly well. The committee recommended two candidates to President Thomas Erlich: Clarence Doniger, a lawyer and an Indiana alumnus; and myself.

My second interview was on March 29 with the president at a hotel in Washington, D.C. He called a couple days later to tell me he was having difficulty making a decision. He wished I had a broader financial background and said that was the only weakness he found in my candidacy. At that point I knew I probably wouldn't get the position and so I withdrew and the job went to Doniger, who served in that role for about 10 years. I feel most grateful to Murray, the search committee, coaches Knight and Mallory, and to Erlich for giving me the opportunity to become a serious candidate for the position at their institution.

For the North Carolina A&T opening I met with a search committee and Chancellor Herschel Fort. Subsequently, a call from the president and my letter of withdrawal intersected in the mail. I determined I did not want the job because, although it would have been an athletics director position, it would have been a professional step down. It would have meant going from Division 1A to Division 1AA. I appreciate the opportunity I was given to interview for that position.

I met with the University of Houston's vice president for finance, Jim Hale, at a hotel in Chicago near O'Hare Airport. I thought the interview was going well until the subject of at-risk student-athletes was introduced. The vice president asked my opinion on the recruitment of such students for the athletics programs and I said every major university with a football and basketball program had at-risk student-athletes and Houston would have to do the same to become competitive in those sports.

The main focus in recruiting those students, I said, was a comprehensive support services program, along with commitments from coaches to ensure athletes comply with academic expectations. I didn't know it at the time, but it was the wrong response for Hale. He said there needed to be a reduction in the number of at-risk athletes because they were too costly to the university. Then his demeanor changed and he asked one or two more questions and terminated the interview.

It was quite clear he didn't appreciate my response. We ate dinner at the same time in the hotel's restaurant, at different tables. He didn't speak with me again and I didn't look his way. It was a very strange ending to the interview. He did send me my reimbursement expense check and I'm still grateful for the time he spent with me.

Illinois State University handled its interview with me by phone. That is the worst type of interview. It is a cheap way to screen candidates. But I'm thankful for being considered because the interview helped prepare me for subsequent interviews. The vice president interviewed me and we got involved in philosophical discussions over my lack of fund-raising experience. Later, as I suspected, I received a rejection letter.

As for the commissioner opening with the 14-member Southern Intercollegiate Athletics Association, I met with the group's council of presidents at Morris Brown College in Atlanta. They offered me the position and if I accepted I would have had an office at Morris Brown. It was a challenging opportunity but there were some unresolved issues regarding salary and fringe benefits that I don't believe could have been settled to my satisfaction. The job was offered at a time when Perles was asking me to come back to Michigan State, which is what I did. I have the deepest respect for and appreciation of the presidents I met at that interview and at the follow-up discussions and I appreciate their confidence in me.

Third MSU candidacy brings redemption

Finally, the third opportunity for me to become athletics director at Michigan State, my alma mater, occurred in 1999. Norvell announced his resignation on April 15, 1999, and stayed in office until June 30. He was paid for the balance of his five-year contract, which had a year remaining, and also received a $100,000 consultation fee for another year.

I was aware Norvell was about to resign because McPherson called a few days earlier to tell me about it, asking whether I had any thoughts about what he should do about the A.D.'s position on an interim basis. He said a search would start soon and the new permanent athletics director needed to be someone who could function in the position for 10 years. I told him if he didn't have confidence in a current athletics department staff member, he should find someone outside the department for the interim role. Once the search for the new A.D. would have commenced, he could even allow the department to function without a temporary leader, I suggested, and that he needed to find the very best candidates because our department had suffered enough from leadership gaps over many years.

McPherson asked if I was interested in the interim role and I said I would be if I were given authority to move the department forward. It had been without effective leadership for a long time, I said, and there were pertinent issues I wanted to address. He said all I needed to do as interim was talk to staff and be a good listener.

It was evident by his response that he was either unaware what the real issues were in the department, or he felt there wouldn't be adequate time in my interim role to address them. For example, morale was at rock bottom. Staff had to work around the athletics director and go to central administration to get answers to issues and there was a communication problem between the A.D. and head football coach. The non-revenue sports coaches couldn't get answers regarding funding levels affecting their sports and there was an urgent need to construct new facilities and renovate others for gender equity and competitive reasons.

McPherson didn't elaborate further relative to my authority request. He asked me to talk his offer over with my wife and he and I would talk the next day. When he called the next day, I said I'd accept the interim position. Once again I requested the authority to make appropriate decisions and he reiterated that I should talk with staff and be a good listener. He mentioned that as interim A.D. I shouldn't become a candidate for the permanent position. Since he was asking for a 10-year appointment and I was 65, I agreed I wouldn't be a candidate.

(Ironically, perhaps, McPherson found himself with his own title of "interim" in 2003 when, in April, as the United States' war in Iraq continued, he was selected to run the financial aspects of reconstructing that country on an interim basis. He would serve as a liaison between the U.S. Treasury Secretary John Snow and military officials in charge of the rebuilding effort. He returned to the university in the fall and subsequently retired at the end of the 2004 calendar year.)

With my new position as interim athletics director, I immediately started to meet with individual staff members, professional and clerical associates, and the rest of the department. We developed a strategic plan, sorted out top priorities, and established fund-raising goals. I met with alumni and booster groups, as well.

I had a highly capable administrative staff that met as a cabinet, plus a smaller group of those administrators who met with me weekly in an executive session. The total group consisted of six associate athletics directors, seven assistant athletics directors, and four others. Associate A.D.s on the staff were: Shelly Appelbaum, senior women's administrator and liaison for human resources, sports management, Title IX and gender equity; Greg Ianni, sports management and facilities; Mark Hollis, external relations; Roger Grooters, and then Demetrius Marlowe, student-athlete support services; and Christopher Ritrievi, development. (Ritrievi was named associate athletics director in 2001.)

The assistant A.D.s were: Peggy Brown, business affairs; Karen Langeland, sports management and summer sports camps; Jeff Monroe, sports medicine and athletics training; John Lewandowski, media relations; Judy VanHorn, then Jennifer Smith, compliance services; and Mike Vollmer, director of football operations. The others were: Terry Braverman, the Ralph Young Fund major gifts director; Don Loding, and then Chris Besanceney, the athletics ticket managers; and Richard Bader, administrative assistant to basketball coach Tom Izzo.

When I first was appointed interim A.D. I met with the athletics administrators over a three-day period to review every inch of the department searching for issues and potential issues. We evaluated every staff position and I established a host of other important strategies, including cost containment, possibilities for increasing revenue, and ways to improve our internal and public image. I commended and rewarded employees for noteworthy accomplishments and emphasized a positive, cooperative and supportive working environment for both student-athletes and staff members. I further emphasized open and honest communication between staff members.

We never compromised our integrity and within a relatively short time, positive and harmonious attitudes began to surface within the department. The spirit flowed from within, out to our faculty, alumni, and friends. Things were moving forward in a positive way. There was progress being made in all facets of the department.

Secretaries and other staff told me the athletics department was then a good place to work. We were moving harmoniously in the right direction.

Surprise, surprise — job criterion changes

I announced to the media during my press conference with them on April 16, 1999, that I was awarded the position on an interim basis and that I wouldn't apply for the permanent position. I had relied upon McPherson's statement to me that he was looking for an A.D. to serve for 10 years. But my feelings changed when I later read, in the *Lansing State Journal* on April 29, an article written by Jack Ebling in which he quoted McPherson as saying he was looking for an athletics director who could serve five to 10 years. When McPherson originally told me he wanted a 10-year A.D., he suggested I should serve on an interim basis and not apply for the permanent post and I agreed.

Subsequently, there was a story in the *Lansing State Journal* that McPherson was courting Tom Osborne, the former Nebraska football coach (who was around my age) for the A.D. job on a five-year basis. I discussed that change with my wife and we agreed that I had to become a candidate because the criteria had been modified. We felt if Osborne could serve five years, so could I, so I followed procedures and wrote a letter to vice president Fred Poston, my immediate superior and the central administrator in charge of the athletics department, informing him of my candidacy. I hand delivered the letter to his office because I believed there was a deadline date for applicants. It so happened that Poston was out of town when I delivered it.

Three days later, I got a phone call from Larry Lage, a sports reporter from the *Lansing State Journal* (who now is the *Michigan Associated Press* sports editor) asking if I was going to throw my hat in the ring for the athletics director position. I said I was and he wrote an article in the paper the next day, May 12, about our conversation. Later that morning after the newspaper article appeared, McPherson called me from the office of Poston, who was back in town. The president was very angry with me, screaming and cussing, wanting to know why I changed my mind about applying for the position. I told them both that I made the decision after seeing the information about Osborne being wooed for the position on a five-year basis, half the term McPherson had told me earlier. I mentioned that my wife and I agreed, after reading the article, I should become a candidate. McPherson scolded me harshly, saying he believed I was obeying the wishes of trustee Ferguson, who he figured was calling the shots for me.

I tried to walk McPherson and Poston through the sequence of what had transpired, reiterating the conversation I had with my wife, the letter I had taken to Poston's office, the call from Lage, etc. I tried to make it clear that Ferguson, though a trustee and long-time friend, didn't control my life and no one does but me and the Lord. McPherson said he should have been told, in advance of the newspaper article, that I had changed my mind. I mentioned that I tried to follow protocol. (I remembered the first time I gave the president a confidential letter and things went crazy. I was accused of circumventing my boss. I wasn't about to repeat that process).

Poston agreed that if he had been in town or had read his mail first thing that morning he would have apprised McPherson of my intention. I offered to surrender my interim role, but that offer was rejected and McPherson and Poston encouraged me to continue to do good work in the department. The president never explained his reasons why he didn't want me to apply for the position and I never asked him. Noreese and I reasoned that I would become a candidate on a good-faith effort and let the administrators make the decision. I would accept whatever decision was made.

When I was the interim A.D., Poston and I often used to walk and exercise at 6 a.m. at the Duffy Daugherty Football Building. He supported me for the interim position and then again for the permanent post. So did trustee Ferguson. One trustee told me that if Ferguson had not been a strong advocate for me I never would have been appointed to the A.D. position.

Poston and I spent an hour together each morning discussing athletics department issues and intercollegiate athletics in general. I found Fred to be a tremendous man, a smart man, and a leader with compassion. He has integrity and knows how to work through the bureaucracy successfully and get things accomplished.

Poston internalizes information quickly and is an outstanding asset to the athletics department and to the university. I found him, in many respects, to be a people person comparable to former Executive Vice President Jack Breslin. I like him personally and was comfortable working with him.

Our athletics administrative staff and coaches worked together diligently to accomplish some remarkable goals, working hard to get our house in order. Expectations were met in the areas of compliance, staff unity, and respect for each other. We put a greater focus on the welfare of student-athletes. We cleaned up our image. We balanced the budget. Our football team won 9 and lost 2 in the 1999 season, success we hadn't experienced since 1987. We beat Florida in the Citrus Bowl, 37-34. Our men's basketball team had a 32-7 record, winning the 1999-2000 NCAA national championship game, 89-76, over Florida, after having won both the Big Ten regular season title and conference tournament championship. Our hockey team won the Central Collegiate Hockey Association tourney championship.

In December 1999, upon recommendation from McPherson, the MSU Board of Trustees appointed me director of athletics until Aug. 31, 2001, at which time I would be required to retire from the athletics department. The contract was later extended until June 30, 2002. I thank McPherson, Poston, Simon, and the board of trustees for giving me the opportunity to provide leadership to the athletics department, the university, our alumni, boosters, and friends.

I have never been one to boast about my accomplishments and I don't care for flattery. I would prefer to let those I serve decide whether I have met expectations. I'm not a politician and believe in letting my record speak for itself. But when Lage called me on May 11 to inquire whether I would become a candidate for the athletics director position, I concluded my interview with him by saying, "If the university appointed me to the position they would never have any regrets under my leadership."

Throughout all the interviews for all the jobs I learned that you should always maintain a positive attitude, do your homework well, practice interviewing with a tape recorder if necessary, make up a list of questions to answer, work hard and smart. Also, you should volunteer, take on additional responsibilities, and be ethical in all things; attend meetings and conferences; network with all kinds of people; make a contribution in your present job; maintain and pursue your goals; and keep applying for appropriate openings, if that's one of your goals. Get yourself a mentor to help guide you through the maze and barriers you will encounter along the way and never give up on your dreams.

Search for a successor

The president appointed an advisory search committee in the early spring of 2002 to find an athletics director to administer the department following my retirement on June 30. I served on the committee, along with McPherson, Poston, Simon, faculty athletics representative Michael Kasavana, plus trustees Colleen McNamara and Dave

Porteous. McPherson also hired Jed Hughes from the search firm of Spencer Stuart to identify potential candidates. Hughes identified a pool of candidates and there were two internal ones, Ianni and Hollis.

As the committee began to review credentials, the name of Ron Mason, the legendary MSU ice hockey coach, was discussed. I learned during the discussion that McPherson tried to recruit Mason for the position in 1999 when I was the interim A.D., but Ron showed no interest. He was approached again in May 2002 and that time he agreed to leave his coaching job and become the 16th athletics director at Michigan State. He will do a great job and I wish him the very best.

Ron Mason, right, succeeded me as athletics director and Rick Comley, center, took over his job as hockey coach.

Growing my faith

I would be remiss if I didn't give much of the credit for my successes to my faith. I have always been a churchgoer, but I didn't get baptized until I was an adult. When I joined the Sixteenth Street Baptist Church in Gadsden at the age of 16, being baptized meant being submerged under water in a creek. I was mystified by the process and did not want to find out about it. My brothers and sisters told me it was non-threatening, but I wasn't convinced.

Going to church was a tradition for me, but I didn't understand many of the messages delivered by the ministers. Most of the preaching was about Biblical affairs that had happened centuries ago. I could not relate to the stories. Going to church and sitting for two hours or more was a good way for me to catch up on my sleep after working 60 hours or more during the week. My wife would often poke me in the side with her elbow each Sunday asking me to wake up. What I believed I needed then was a preacher who talked about today's problems, how to help the poor reduce crime and unemployment, improve the economy, etc.

Most everything else they preached seemed irrelevant. I did not understand the books of the Bible and its characters, language, and historical settings. I understood that Jesus died for my sins and that God was my real father, although I had never seen him and often wondered what he looked like and who made him. Through the years, I kept asking myself, where did God come from? And why wasn't he addressing all of the problems we faced here on earth? Yet I believed that God existed and that his love for me was greater than the love I had for myself.

My first baptism was in 1964 when I was 31. It was at a private ceremony on a Saturday evening in Edgewood United Church in East Lansing with Rev. Truman Morris presiding and my family in attendance.

It seemed the right thing to do, and this baptism was by sprinkling, not the dreaded immersion.

In the summer of 1982 at the age of 49, I earned my doctoral degree in higher education and administration from Michigan State. That August, I drove my family to Alabama to visit Noreese's and my parents, relatives, and friends. Our ultimate goal was to take our younger son, David, to enroll at Morehouse College. I was sitting on the warm, sunny porch Sunday morning at my parents' house, watching the colorful lizards play their games in the grass, then crawl on the porch. Laura Mae, the second-born child in our family, was visiting with my mother inside the house. She, Eva Lou, Loveless, and Earnest Lee are devout Christians. I was aware of their daily walk with Christ. They are consistent churchgoers, participating in church activities and ministering to prison inmates and others.

Laura came out to where I was sitting. Calling me by my nickname, she said, "Baby Clarence, although you have a Ph.D., have a good job at Michigan State, and drive a new car, in the sight of God all those things are filthy rags, unless you know the Lord." I didn't say anything because I honestly did not know what she was talking about. I asked myself, "Is she jealous of her own brother? Why is she saying those things to me?" We had always been close to each other and I had done nothing to disrespect her. Why was she attacking me?

During the remainder of that weekend, after dropping David off at Morehouse and driving back to Michigan from Atlanta, I kept thinking to myself, what was my sister saying to me and why?

Two weeks later on campus, I ran into Jerry Barker, who worked in the development office. He invited me to come to a Bible study class taught by Dr. Lanny Johnson, an orthopedic surgeon, in his Okemos office on Wednesday. At first I said no because I was just too busy at work. I saw Jerry a couple of days later and he extended the same invitation for the following week. I was reluctant, but something urged me to go and give it a try. I did attend the next session. Lanny was gracious and hospitable. There were at least 20 to 25 people in attendance. Lanny read from the Bible. He read the scripture and explained what it meant. Most of the people had their own Bibles with them and read along with Lanny.

The next session, I brought my Bible, and my wife. For the first time in my life I was beginning to understand what those ancient stories meant in the Bible. I even learned to understand what my sister, Laura Mae, was trying to tell me. I enjoyed several months of study before I moved to Chicago in November to join the Big Ten Conference office staff.

I was fired up to learn more about the Bible. Once in Chicago, I began visiting churches. At one church I heard a powerful sermon that made me want to be baptized by immersion right then and there. I wanted to confirm my faith by taking the step I had avoided for so long. So I went ahead, without friends or family to lend support. Some time after that I began attending Bible study class at Gammon Methodist Church in Chicago and sang in the choir. I was hungry for the words of God and tried to make Him a greater part of my life. I felt a whole new revelation that I had not experienced before.

I started to make Bible study and prayer a regular part of my personal life. I now read the Bible and pray each morning prior to breakfast. I have noticed a difference in my attitude toward my family, friends, co-workers, and persons I come in contact with. I still encounter many problems, but believe I have a Savior I can lean on while I solve them.

Several years ago I joined a Bible study and prayer group consisting of MSU professors and others. Paul Vogel, Mark Whalon, and Ken Reeder are three of the most studious and devout Christians I have ever encountered. We meet each Wednesday at 7 a.m. to discuss the scriptures and to pray. We help and encourage each other in our faith by telling the truth and sharing our thoughts. As brothers in Christ, we try to keep each other focused on the Lord and what he expects us to do each day in worshiping him and helping our brothers. Those meetings have blessed me in so many different ways. I feel fortunate to be a part of such a group and through our work together my faith has been strengthened.

Since the early 1970s, my wife and I have been members of the Trinity AME Church in Lansing. I'm often asked to speak to inmates in Michigan prisons and to other young people who are leaning in the wrong direction. I am thankful to be able to pass on to others the hope and faith that now guide my steps. I know I'm a better person today than I was yesterday.

'Status of Minorities in Sports' symposium

On May 21, 2002, I planned, organized, and sponsored a seminar at Michigan State University to address the "Status of Minorities in Sports: Current Issues, Problems and Recommendations." It was one of my last major chores before leaving the athletics department. I felt compelled to address the problems collegiate athletics has in hiring head football coaches from the minority ranks. Going into the 2002 season there were 117 NCAA Division I head football coach positions — with minorities hired for only four of them. I believed it was a football issue and it was needed to open discussion in a forum with other athletics administrators, about 60 who were in attendance.

There were four purposes for the symposium: to examine the concept of diversity in sports; to review the role of minority coaches in sports; to encourage the development of career paths for aspiring minority coaches; and to continue to identify the obstacles to the appointment of minority coaches to head football positions. To achieve those objectives, a dynamic group of professionals were selected to lead specific topics:

- McPherson welcomed speakers and guests to the university.
- Provost Simon introduced professor James Duderstadt as a speaker.
- Dr. Duderstadt, president emeritus of the University of Michigan, gave an outstanding keynote address on "Affirmative Action/Equal Opportunity and the Sports System: The Need for Change."
- Dr. Richard Lapchick expertly highlighted the subject, "Black Student Athletes: White Perceptions."
- Panelist Earl Robinson of MSU's WKAR radio, moderated a lively and enlightened discussion on "The Media and Race in Sports," with Terry Foster of *The Detroit News*, Bill Rhoden of the *New York Times*, and Leo Willingham of the *Atlanta Journal Constitution*.
- Attorney Ted Shaw of the National Association for the Advancement of Colored People's Legal Defense Fund, addressed some "Legal Issues in Sports."
- Dr. Fitzgerald Hill, head football coach at San Jose State University, shared his thorough research findings on "Contrasting Perceptions of Employment Opportunities Among Collegiate Football Coaches — the Truth and the Consequences."
- Wendy Lewis from Major League baseball, provided "A Review of an Affirmative Action Plan."
- Floyd Keith, executive director of the Black Coaches Association, gave insights into "Networking Strategies and Referral System."
- George Perles, executive director of the Motor City Bowl football game and former MSU head football coach, spoke on "Managing a Diverse Staff."
- Dr. Dan Kruger, professor emeritus at Michigan

State and co-planner of the symposium, concluded by speaking on "Where Do We Go From Here?"

I believe virtually everyone in attendance agreed the symposium successfully identified and addressed the issues and while solutions to the problems were suggested, it was the consensus that a follow-up session was needed. I'm pleased to say that the Black Coaches Association followed up the symposium by sponsoring a forum in August 2002 in Lincoln, Neb., on the issues. I was invited to be a participant but was unable to attend.

Retirement receptions

I am honored and grateful to have been given commendable recognition upon my retirement announcement by some prestigious organizations and individuals. The honors, commendations, gifts, and words of gratitude were overwhelming and much more than I expected. Here are those who formally recognized my retirement with various functions in 2002:

- The Big Ten Conference Joint Group, consisting of faculty athletics representatives, directors of athletics, senior women administrators and conference office executive staff, along with the other retiring joint group representatives, at a dinner in the Hyatt Regency Coconut Resort in Bonita Springs, Fla., at its May 19 spring meetings. Speaking on my behalf were faculty athletics representatives Kasavana of Michigan State and Bonnie Slatton of the University of Iowa; plus Mark Rudner, director of the conference bureau. It was a festive celebration and my wife, Noreese, was there to enjoy it with me.
- The MSU athletics department sponsored a dynamic university-wide farewell reception for my family and I on May 29 at the Kellogg Center

on campus. It was highlighted by speeches in my behalf by McPherson, Simon, Poston, Kasavana, Ferguson, Big Ten Commissioner James Delany, and University of Michigan Athletics Director Bill Martin. The affair was well organized and many people were there, including my wife, plus daughter, Jacqueline; son, David, and his wife, Cheryl and their children, Morgan, 8, Parker, 5, and Blake, 2.

- The Trinity AME Church Sons of Allen, of which I am a member, honored me with a recognition banquet on June 1, with Noreese also in attendance.
- Sparrow Hospital Foundation sponsored a salute in my honor on June 20 with a sumptuous dinner at Kellogg Center. The proceeds from it were to benefit the Coaches for Kids and Athletes for Kids funds to build a new pediatric emergency room at Sparrow. It was an outstanding tribute that featured commentary by university administrators, community leaders, and former MSU student-athletes. My family was there. Former Big Ten Commissioner Wayne Duke and his wife, Martha, were in attendance from Barrington, Ill. The master of ceremonies was Tim Staudt, sports director for WILX-TV Channel 10 in Lansing. Proclamations were given by: East Lansing Councilman Bill Sharp; Robert Johnson, chief of staff of the office of the Lansing mayor; Michigan House Rep. Paul DeWeese of District 67; and State Sen. Dianne Byrum of District 25.

Other speakers were Joe Damore, president and chief executive officer of Sparrow Health Systems of Lansing; Mary P. Sharp M.D., a former elementary student of mine; James C. Epolito, former MSU student and current president of The Accident Fund, a private company owned by Blue Cross/Blue Shield of Michigan that manages workmen's compensation; Dr. John Shinksy, former university student-athlete and current administrator at Grand Valley State University; Dr. William Lazer, professor emeritus at MSU who was a Distinguished Scholar at Florida Atlantic University and professor who was the chairman of that institution's Sensormatic endowment fund; former MSU basketball coach Gus Ganakas; MSU football coach Bobby Williams; Braverman; MSU basketball coach Tom Izzo; Willingham; Poston; my son, David, the human resources director then at Home Depot in Lansing; and incoming A.D. Mason.

- The East Lansing Educational Foundation honored me and some other East Lansing dignitaries at its annual dinner on April 25. George Brookover, a former East Lansing junior high student and now a successful lawyer in the city, provided the tribute on my behalf. It was a fun evening for friends and family.
- Poston sponsored a special dinner at his home on June 15 to honor the impending retiring directors from his MSU division for the 2002 academic year. Honored with me were Dr. Bruce Benson, chief of campus police; and John Lewis, director of university services. I wasn't able to participate due to another commitment. I thank Fred, his wife Charlotte and his staff for their generosity.
- The Grand Rapids MSU Alumni Club coupled with the Steve Smith Golf Outing to honor Braverman and I on July 15 as retiring members. It was an outstanding afternoon, with some long-time true friends and Spartans. Chip Emery of the club was master of ceremonies. Also participating were Peter Secchia, the former U.S. ambassador to Italy and resident of Grand Rapids; MSU trustee Dee Cook and her husband, Byron; Smith, the former MSU basketball star who went

457

on to a successful NBA career; Dr. Charles Tucker, Smith's agent; MSU trustee Randall Pittman; and many others.

- Members of the fraternity to which I belong, Alpha Chi Boule of Sigma Pi Phi, plus their spouses and guests, bestowed honors on Noreese and I by sponsoring an elegant retirement party July 19 at the Walnut Hills Country Club in East Lansing. The ambiance was great and the food delicious on what was a fun evening.
- Izzo and his wife, Lupe, invited me and a few friends to his beautiful summer home July 11 in the Grand Rapids area to help celebrate my retirement. It was another lovely and fun-filled afternoon.
- Also, the University of Michigan sent me a beautifully framed tribute signed by its interim president, B. Joseph White, and the U-M A.D, Martin, gave me a rocking chair from his department — naturally, trimmed in maize and blue, not green and white. Pat Richter, the A.D. at the University of Wisconsin, sent me a red and white Wisconsin varsity blanket. I appreciate those fine gifts and won't ever forget my association with Martin and Richter and all the other very fine folks.

Other special honors

In April 1999 the National Consortium for Academics and Sports (NCAC) selected me to receive a National Student-Athlete Day Giant Steps Award. It was while I was senior associate athletics director. There were several categories in the selection process. I was chosen in the administration category. There were seven recipients in all, representing various categories.

We met at a reception April 7 at the White House in Washington, D.C., with President Bill Clinton. I felt like it was make-believe to be in the Oval Office speaking with and shaking the hand of the president, who greeted each of us with a warm welcome. I hadn't realized how tall he was until I shook his hand. He is over 6-feet tall and he looked down on me and my 5-8 frame.

Clinton spent some time with us in a picture-taking session, using his photographer. We also were permitted to take pictures with his dog, Buddy. The president appeared to be a great sports fan and was intrigued with a prospective student-athlete who was one of the recipients and who had signed a grant-in-aid to attend Duke University. The actual awards were handed out at a great affair, the NCAC annual Giant Steps Award Banquet and Hall of Fame induction ceremony in Orlando, Fla., in February 2000.

On Dec. 17, 2002, I was fortunate to be honored by the Michigan chapter of the National Football Foundation and College Hall of Fame,

I got to meet President Bill Clinton in the White House – and also his dog "Buddy".

receiving its Distinguished American Award, given in conjunction with the *Detroit Free Press* annual All-State Football Awards Banquet. The award is given to the individual who has set standards for excellence in a life of service to the community. That award means a lot to me because it embodies the qualities I have tried to promote throughout my life. I'm indeed grateful to Tom Versaci, president of the Michigan chapter, and his committee for endorsing me for the award.

In May 2003 I was the recipient of the Michigan State University Distinguished Alumni Award, which is the crowning jewel of my service awards.

In retrospect

I was blessed to have experienced a wonderful and satisfying life as an educator and athletics administrator. The few bumps I experienced on the road along the way were meant to be and made me a better person. Each bump prepared me for handling future adversities, which reinforced my philosophy of remaining humble irrespective of the good and bad things that happened to me. I have enjoyed working with some wonderful people and maintain friendship with many of them today.

I'm grateful of having a lovely wife, Noreese, who has been most supportive of me throughout my entire employment career. Even when we relocated several times due to job changes she never complained or found fault with my decisions to move. She continues to demonstrate patience and understanding in the endeavors I choose to pursue.

Noreese worked 20 years with the state of Michigan in the departments of Secretary of State, Public Services Commission, and Michigan Employment Security Commission. Today she is retired but stays busy as a housewife and volunteer in civic and community service organizations, including: the women's board of Sparrow Hospital; the Lansing/East Lansing chapter of Links; and as a member of Trinity AME Church.

We are happy to have been blessed with three children and three grandchildren. Our daughter, Jacqueline, was a baby when we arrived in East Lansing in 1955. She graduated from East Lansing High School and earned her bachelor's degree from MSU's College of Communications. She lives in Lansing and works for the Meijer's Corp. Alvin, our son, also graduated from East Lansing High, as did his brother, David. Alvin attended Lansing Community College and lives in Lansing. David is a graduate of Michigan State's College of Communications and Cooley Law School and works in the human resources department of the American Red Cross in Lansing.

Now that I'm in a working retirement arrangement, I plan to spend more time with my family, particularly my wife and grandchildren. I continue to work part-time for the university in the office of admissions, as an outreach consultant responsible for meeting with school personnel and church groups to help educate young folks on the need for a college education. I speak to many student groups. It is a great opportunity for me to promote the university and encourage students to perform well in school and attend a college of their choice. I also meet with church and community groups to promote education for our youth.

Noreese and I